Technology for Facility Managers

The Impact of Cutting-Edge Technology on Facility Management

IFMA
IFMA Foundation

Eric Teicholz, IFMA Fellow, Editor

JOHN WILEY & SONS, INC.
WILEY

International Facility Management Association | Learn. Connect. Advance.™
Empowering Facility Professionals Worldwide

IFMA FOUNDATION
WWW.IFMAFOUNDATION.ORG
EDUCATION • RESEARCH • SCHOLARSHIPS

Library of Congress Cataloging-in-Publication Data:

FM technology update.
    Technology for facility managers : the impact of cutting-edge technology on facility management / IFMA, IFMA Foundation ; Eric Teicholz, IFMA fellow, editor.
        pages   cm
    Includes bibliographical references and index.
    ISBN 978-1-118-38283-7 (hardback); 978-1-118-41728-7 (ebk.); 978-1-118-42077-5 (ebk.);
    978-1-118-43434-5 (ebk.); 978-1-118-44172-5 (ebk.); 978-1-118-44173-2 (ebk.)
        1. Facility management—Technological innovations. 2. Intelligent buildings. 3. Electronic apparatus and appliances. I. Teicholz, Eric. II. IFMA Foundation. III. Title. IV. Title: Impact of cutting-edge technology on facility management.
    TH6012.F63   2012
    658.200285—dc23
                                                                                    2012032667

Printed in the United States of America

10 9 8 7 6 5 4 3 2 1

Contents

PART 1: Technology

CHAPTER 5

Radio Frequency Identification / 75

Geoff Williams

PART 2: Applications

CHAPTER 10
Computer Modeling / 171
Eric Teicholz

CHAPTER 11
Technology and the Workplace / 191
Erik Jaspers and Eric Teicholz

Acknowledgments

The editor wishes first to thank all of the authors who contributed to this publication. Their knowledge, energy, and dedication greatly facilitated my job as book editor.

Special thanks go to the subject matter experts (SMEs) who not only authored their own chapters but also reviewed the work of other contributors. Chief among the SMEs was Jim Clayton, author of Chapter 9, who also provided edits and commentary on chapters from several other authors. Also contributing beyond authoring their own chapters were Angela Lewis (Chapter 12) and Paul Head (Chapter 7), both of whom additionally participated in the quality assurance/quality control process. Heather McLean Wiederhoeft edited several of the chapters before they were sent to Wiley. And Wiley's Kathryn Bourgoine, Amy Odum, and Danielle Giordano presided over the final book production on an extremely tight deadline. All of these authors, SMEs, and editors brought to bear high standards of excellence in support of this project.

Finally, I wish to thank Bentley Corp. (www.bentley.com) for sponsoring this publication. Bentley is dedicated to providing architects, engineers, constructors, and facility managers with comprehensive software solutions for sustaining infrastructure.

ERIC TEICHOLZ

IFMA FOUNDATION
WWW.IFMAFOUNDATION.ORG
EDUCATION • RESEARCH • SCHOLARSHIPS

Established in 1990 as a nonprofit 501(c)(3) corporation, the IFMA Foundation works for the public good to promote research and educational opportunities for the advancement of facility management. The IFMA Foundation is supported by the generosity of the facility management community, including IFMA members, chapters, councils, corporate sponsors, and private contributors who are united by the belief that education and research improve the facility management profession. To learn more about the good works of the IFMA Foundation, visit www.ifmafoundation.org. For more information about IFMA, visit www.ifma.org.

Contributions to the IFMA Foundation are used to:

■ Advance FM education—increase the number of colleges and universities offering accredited FM degree programs worldwide and to keep facility managers up-to-date on the latest techniques and technology
■ Underwrite research—to generate knowledge that directly benefits the profession
■ Provide scholarships—to support education and the future of the facility management profession by encouraging FM as a career of choice.

Without the support of workplace professionals, the IFMA Foundation would be unable to contribute to the future development and direction of facility management. If you care about improving the profession and your career potential, we encourage you to make a donation or get involved in a fund-raising event. Donations can be made at www.ifmafoundation.org.

IFMA FOUNDATION SPONSORS AT PUBLICATION

Platinum Sponsors

Atlanta Chapter of IFMA

Bentley Prince Street

Bentley Systems

Corporate Facilities Council of IFMA

East Bay Chapter of IFMA

FM:Systems

Gensler

ISS World Services

Milliken & Co.

Los Angeles Chapter of IFMA

Planon Corporation

Gold and Silver Sponsors

A&A Maintenance

ActiuBerbegal Y Formas S.A.

ARAMARK

Autodesk

Boston Chapter of IFMA

Capital Chapter of IFMA

EMCOR

Eurest Services

Forbes Charitable Foundation

Graphic Systems

Greater New York Chapter of IFMA

Haworth

HC Olsen Construction

Houston Chapter of IFMA

InterfaceFLOR

JCI

Kayhan International

Kimball International

Manhattan Software

Orange County Chapter of IFMA

Panduit

Polsky Family Supporting Foundation

Rentokil Initial

San Diego Chapter of IFMA

San Francisco Chapter of IFMA

Steelcase

Wolcott Architecture Interiors

Additional copies of this book and other IFMA Foundation and IFMA publications can be ordered through the IFMA bookstore online at www.ifma.org/bookstore.

Foreword

Facility managers are tasked with ensuring that the built environment effectively supports people and activities by providing the appropriate functionality and quality of experience. To accomplish this they must understand and address social, business, and process issues that impact infrastructure needs. Increasingly, technology empowers problem solving and enables new opportunities and approaches that expand the role and capabilities of facilities management.

In recent years much attention has been given to the utilization of new technologies in the design and delivery of buildings and other infrastructure facility projects. It is clear that the use of *information modeling* to simulate a facility during the design and construction phases of a project provides substantial benefits to both the design teams and construction teams. Information modeling supports rigorous simulation of an infrastructure asset's performance so that the project teams can explore the implications of options as they work to maximize design objectives. Working in the context of a unifying 3D modeling environment enables highly immersive interaction within the design process, and ensures the production of trusted design and construction documents that reflect the latest decisions and changes throughout the project timeline.

From design through delivery, the use of collaboration servers and services for *integrated projects* enables well-managed collaboration and work sharing across distributed teams, and best equips them to harness the contributions of all project participants by appropriately bringing to bear the right people and expertise. This benefits design, construction, and delivery teams by reducing and managing risk, while enhancing project efficiency and quality, and accelerating project delivery.

Facility managers benefit from these trends, and can similarly gain advantage through the operational phase of the facility by effectively using the latest technology for facilities management. Utilizing the resultant digital asset with the operational information platform for ongoing maintenance, operations, and compliance activities empowers *intelligent infrastructure*. Facility managers also can provide business advantages that extend beyond the conventional operations and maintenance functions. Moreover, safety, security, health, productivity, maintenance, business planning, and operational management can be better understood and optimized, and disaster and incident response and corrective actions can be addressed with assured information integrity. In addition, proactive lifecycle planning can be applied for operational changes such as remodeling, expansion, or repurposing. Ultimately, all of this results in higher-quality and better-performing infrastructure assets with improved operational efficiency and safety, reduced waste, increased resilience, and a greater return on infrastructure investments.

Eric Teicholz—a widely recognized authority on all aspects of facilities management—and a dedicated group of co-authors, share their in-depth knowledge and wealth of experience with the readers of this book, imparting valuable insight into a topic of growing importance to the entire community of building and other infrastructure professionals.

HUW W. ROBERTS, AIA
VICE PRESIDENT, MARKETING
BENTLEY SYSTEMS

Introduction

HISTORY AND OVERVIEW

This book is an expanded and revised version of the 2008 "FM Technology Update" published by the IFMA Foundation. Chapter topics for the 2008 publication were determined by analyzing the results of a comprehensive survey of facility managers. In the years since that survey, the technology employed by facility managers has changed dramatically. For instance, applications such as sustainability, and technology such as building information modeling (BIM), were included in the earlier publication but were of minor importance to most professional facility managers at that time. Other technologies and applications such as mobile communications, social networking, cloud computing, and various types of sensors and control systems also existed in 2008 but since then have dramatically increased in their use by facility managers.

The primary purpose of this book is to present an overview of the current and near-term future state of FM technologies and their near term impact on facility management practices. All of the topics included in the 2008 publication are included in the current publication as well, but are presented here in ways that highlight their evolution since that time.

Additionally, the organization of the current book is different from that of the original publication. The current book is divided into two primary sections: Technology and Applications. Nevertheless, all technology sections contain information about how the specific technology is being used by facility managers, while all applications chapters include a discussion of how one or more facility management functions have been affected by changes in technology. For instance, the Technology section has chapters on computer-aided facility management (CAFM), BIM and geographic information system (GIS) with suggestions concerning how each of these are being used, while the Applications section includes chapters on workplace, space management, and condition assessment, with discussions of the role that technology plays in each.

CONTENT

Chapters that appear in Part 1: Technology include:

1. CAFM/IWMS: Balancing Technology, Processes, and Objectives
2. Building Information Modeling
3. Building Automation and Control Systems
4. Roles of GIS in Facility Management
5. Radio Frequency Identification
6. Information and Communications Technology
7. Workflow Technology: Knowledge in Motion

Chapters that appear in Part 2: Applications include:

8. Sustainability
9. Condition Assessment in Facility Asset Management
10. Computer Modeling
11. Technology and the Workplace
12. The Role of People and Process in Technology
13. Social Media

Besides the content contained in the chapters themselves, *Technology for Facility Managers* contains chapter abstracts, author bios, and an extensive glossary of relevant terms.

CROSSWALK

A *crosswalk* is a tool that compares all of the chapters according to desired entities and attributes associated with each of the chapters Several of the chapters discuss multiple technologies and applications which are the attributes compared in the crosswalk. The tables below relate each of the chapters to the technologies and applications discussed therein. The goal of the crosswalk is to assist readers in identifying which technology chapters discuss what applications (Table I.1) and what applications are discussed in each of the chapters (Table I.2 and I.3). The applications listed in Table I.2 and I.3 are those that comprise IFMA's Core Competencies (i.e., those skills required for earning IFMA's Certified Facility Manager certification).[1] These competencies are defined as follows:

[1] See www.ifmacredentials.org/.

TABLE I.1 Technologies discussed (rows) in the application chapters (columns).

Tech. Chapters \ App. Chapters	8. Sustainability	9. Condition Assessment	10. Modeling	11. Workplace Technology	12. People and Process	13. Social Media
1. CAFM/IWMS	X	X	X	X	X	X
2. BIM	X		X	X	X	
3. BAS	X	X	X		X	
4. GIS			X	X	X	
5. RFID	X	X		X		X
6. ICT				X		X
7. Workflow		X				

Communication. Communication plans and processes for both internal and external stakeholders.

Emergency Preparedness and Business Continuity. Emergency and risk management plans and procedures.

Environmental Stewardship and Sustainability. Sustainable management of built and natural environments.

Finance. Strategic plans, budgets, financial analyses, and procurement.

Human and Environmental Factors. Healthful and safe environment, security, FM employee development.

Leadership and Management. Strategic planning, organize staff and lead organization.

Operations and Maintenance. Building operations and maintenance, and occupant services.

Planning and Project Management. Oversight and management of all projects and related contracts.

Quality Assessment and Innovation. Best practices, process improvements, audits, and measurements.

Real Estate. Real estate planning, acquisition, and disposition.

Technology. Facility management technology and workplace management systems.

TABLE I.2 Technology chapters (columns) that discuss facility management functions.

	1. CAFM/IWMS	2. BIM	3. BAS	4. GIS	5. RFID	6. ICT	7. Workflow
1. Communication	X			X		X	
2. Emergency Preparedness and Business Continuity		X					
3. Stewardship and Sustainability	X	X	X		X		
4. Finance	X						
5. Human and Environmental Factors	X						
6. Leadership and Management	X						X
7. Operations and Maintenance	X	X	X	X	X		X
8. Planning and Project Management	X						X
9. Quality Assessment and Innovation	X		X			X	
10. Real Estate					X		X
11. Technology	X	X	X	X	X	X	X

TABLE I.3 Application chapters (columns) versus facility management functions.

	8. Sustainability	9. Condition Assessment	10. Computer Modeling	11. Workplace Technology	12. Role of People and Process	13. Social Media
1. Communication		X	X	X	X	X
2. Emergency Preparedness and Business Continuity						
3. Stewardship and Sustainability	X	X	X	X	X	
4. Finance		X		X		
5. Human and Environmental Factors					X	
6. Leadership and Management		X				X
7. Operations and Maintenance	X	X	X	X	X	X
8. Planning and Project Management	X					
9. Quality Assessment and Innovation			X	X	X	
10. Real Estate			X	X		
11. Technology	X	X	X	X	X	X

Part 1: Technology

Table I.1 lists the application chapters as column headings and the technologies as row headings. If an application chapter contains an "X" in a particular row, it means that the technology associated with that row is discussed in the chapter. Similarly, an "X" in an application chapter indicates that a specific technology is discussed in that chapter.

Part 2: Applications

Tables I.2 and I.3 relate applications (IFMA's 11 core competencies) discussed (rows) to the chapters. Table I.2A relates the technology chapters (columns) to applications (rows), and Table I.3 relates the application chapters (columns) to facility applications discussed within the chapter (rows).

Chapter Abstracts

CHAPTER 1: CAFM/IWMS: BALANCING TECHNOLOGY, PROCESSES, AND OBJECTIVES

Chris Keller

FM automation (CAFM/IWMS) primarily is viewed as an FM department tool that supports FM operations. The facility can be a key tool for the leadership of an organization to use to achieve its goals. Proper selection and implementation of these tools is critical in determining the current and future value these tools and the FM department have to the organization as a whole.

Most IT projects fail—primarily through a misalignment of the project objectives and the project solution. FM automation tools facilitate processes that deliver FM departmental objectives in support of an organization's mission. Integrating organizational objectives with the selection and implementation process can ensure the FM department's successful support of these objectives.

Facility managers need to adjust technology tools and processes well in advance of a problem's visibility in order to successfully address the new requirements for their customers. Proactively preparing the facility to address its inhabitants, future needs requires analyzing trends in facility management, business, and technology.

New and future technology will facilitate the daunting task of achieving organizational objectives and more easily convey to leadership the value of FM to the organization. The advancing technology relevant to FM is in transition from providing feature enhancements to facilitating process and culture transformations.

CHAPTER 2: BUILDING INFORMATION MODELING

Louise Sabol

Building information modeling (BIM) is a software technology gaining rapid acceptance throughout the architecture, engineering, and construction (AEC) industries. BIM incorporates the accurate 3D real-life geometry of a building, along with a structured information base of nongraphic data, providing detailed information about the building components. BIM has the potential to enable fundamental changes in project delivery by supporting the information needs of all stakeholders in the process from conceptual design through facility management.

To date, BIM has been used most extensively in design and construction. Its adoption for facility management is less straightforward. BIM has the potential to offer a new level of functionality for managing buildings and the physical assets within them by offering an integrated information base rich in detail, and powerful by virtue of its capabilities to realistically visualize building environments.

Capabilities to track space and assets in BIM, along with their quantities, locations, and attributes are important for facility management. The technology's potential for estimating and quantifying building performance is also increasingly important. Aspects that can be tracked within a building information model can include space allocations, asset management, energy efficiency, security operations, sustainability, compliance issues, and many other activities.

Standards for data exchange in the building and FM industry are undergoing development in order to support new information workflows and enabling technologies such as BIM. The National Building Information Model Standard, under the direction of the buildingSMART alliance (bSa), is developing open standards to guide adoption and use of the technology. Several core components are being developed, including industry foundation classes (IFCs) that are an open data format intended to facilitate the transfer and integrity of information between intelligent building models and the information systems that play a role in building management. One notable bSa initiative is the Construction Operations Building Information Exchange (COBie), which improves project data delivery to owner/operators.

The next few years will see facility professionals and solutions vendors work in multiple arenas to leverage BIM's promise in order to deliver better information management to facility management. BIM is a robust information technology, offering a lot of potential for facility management; however, there are many challenges ahead in making the technology truly useful to FM.

Facility owners are looking to utilize BIM to bring added efficiencies to their processes. The Military Health System (U.S. Department of Defense) are investigating automated tools to export data from their facilities planning programs into BIM models, demonstrating health care uses for sustainability and BIM.

CHAPTER 3: BUILDING AUTOMATION AND CONTROL SYSTEMS

Terry Hoffmann

Facility managers rely on automated systems for monitoring and control of buildings they manage. In this chapter, the author describes the evolution of building automation systems (BASs) as energy management and control systems, their current use in FM, and how they are evolving, and presents a case study of a Florida university.

The author summarizes BAS today as follows: "Building automation systems use current technology to provide safety for both occupants and assets. They contribute to the productivity of the enterprise by conserving energy and optimizing the efficiency of equipment throughout facilities and the people who are responsible for operating and maintaining them. They provide a foundation for sustainable programs and projects by providing the accurate and secure data required for decision making and verification." However, although this represents the current state of BAS, most buildings still maintain older stand-alone systems from multiple vendors. In turn, this results in extreme energy inefficiencies. Hoffmann explores what he believes are the technologies that have the greatest impact on these factors:

- Harmonized standards
- Wireless technology
- Internet protocol (IP)-based control

The author maintains that installed BAS systems will receive the greatest benefit from enterprise applications associated with energy optimization, asset allocation, resource planning, sustainability application, and dashboards. These applications will require new network infrastructures that can take advantage of state-of-the-art software and hardware technologies including semantic technologies, augmented reality, context aware control, and ubiquitous access. What is the BAS system of the future going to look like? The author responds that it "is likely to be comprised of very intelligent nodes that are capable of making informed decisions on their own. But they will also know when it is necessary to ask for help from other devices on the local network—or escalate the search to the enterprise or Web level as the situation requires."

CHAPTER 4: ROLES OF GEOGRAPHIC INFORMATION SYSTEMS IN FACILITY MANAGEMENT

William P. Witts Jr.

Geographic information systems (GISs) is software for analyzing geospatial information (i.e., point, line, areas) tied to a global coordinate system. Because of this, GIS can perform certain types of analysis that cannot be done with traditional CAFM systems. Traditionally, GIS has not been used for FM applications. Rather, it has been used for applications such as land analysis, utility distributions, and asset management.

Witts uses GIS technology for analyzing spatial components of a building such as floor plans, building information, and utility structures. GIS can analyze vector, raster, and tabular data, and each has a role for FM applications. For example, vector data can perform traditional computer-aided design (CAD) analysis; raster data can analyze a building in the context of the other buildings using a vast array of existing geospatial databases; and tabular data can store attributes associated with vector or raster data or exist outside of a spatial reference.

This chapter describes and illustrates both traditional FM applications as well as applications that traditionally fall outside the scope of CAFM or IWMS software. For example, location maps can depict the closest exit of a fire hydrant to a building; density maps might display population densities on a campus at different times of the day; and change detection maps can show how a facility has changed over several years. Finally, Witts presents a case study of how GIS is deployed at MIT for facility management applications—both inside and outside of a building.

CHAPTER 5: RADIO FREQUENCY IDENTIFICATION

Geoff Williams

Radio frequency identification (RFID) is a new technology that is just beginning to be adopted by facility managers. RFID uses radio waves to automate the identification of objects (e.g., assets, people). This is accomplished by storing data about the object within a microchip (an RFID tag) that is attached to an antenna. The tag is able to transmit the data using radio frequencies back to a reader which converts the radio waves back into digital information. These tags are very inexpensive and offer a host of potential applications for the facility manager.

The chapter explores barcoding and RFP technology. Barcoding currently is used extensively for the tracking of furniture and equipment. In the past, the asset management of a facility relied heavily on barcoding systems for tracking a site's furniture and equipment. RFID differs from barcoding in a number of ways that are explored in the chapter.

Finally, the chapter focuses on how this new technology is being used for facility management. Given the technology and characteristics of RFID technology, Williams discusses a number of FM applications that lend themselves to this technology. These include:

- **Asset tagging for antitheft**. Organizations can embed tags in assets above a certain dollar threshold that can trigger an alarm if the asset changes location.
- **Asset tagging for asset management**. Tracking assets (FF+E, for example) can be done automatically and update asset management software systems such as those found in CAFM and IWMS.
- **RFID tags for personal management**. This application has privacy implications, but RFID tags on people will locate them automatically in terms of emergency.
- **RFID tags for security management**. Tags can be used as a key to access a building or certain spaces within a building.
- **BAS applications**. When deployed with a sensor, RFID tags can record, for example, temperature, movement, and radiation. Such data can be used to control real-time systems or trigger work orders for a computerized maintenance management systems (CMMS).

CHAPTER 6: INFORMATION AND COMMUNICATIONS TECHNOLOGY

Richard Hodges

This chapter describes how the accelerating rate of innovation in information and communications technology (ICT) is shaping life in the twenty-first century, and the effect those changes will have on the design and use of commercial buildings. He identifies five major technology trends:

- Ubiquity
- Mobility
- Personalization
- Virtualization
- Visual Communication

For each of these trends, the author analyzes the behavioral effects of those trends and argues that FM professionals must understand and plan for operating in a world of technology-driven change. As an example, the chapter includes a review of wired and wireless communications infrastructure technologies and presents ideas for new "future-proofed" designs that reduce both cost and eco-footprint of ICT infrastructure. The chapter concludes with case studies that provide real-world examples of the new design approaches in various types of buildings.

CHAPTER 7: WORKFLOW TECHNOLOGY

Paul Head

Workflow technology moves business forward by supporting enterprise requirements for transactional and human-centric processes. The facility management organization can leverage the extended enterprise to propel knowledge into motion. Evolving from imaging and transactional processes, workflow technologies have come a long way to support the more human-centric business requirements to positively affect every employee, manager, supplier, and customer. Standards developed by the Workflow Management Coalition (WfMC) have helped establish an effective framework to support a common software development and communication method between diverse technologies that require workflow to drive their requirements. Documentation standards such as business process modeling notation (BPMN) benefit the organizations leveraging workflow and ensure a common way for business process consultants to document the business requirements and technology consultants to implement the requirements.

As a facility management professional, it is important to understand the basics of workflow and the significance of how it can influence daily life. Through a better understanding of the types of workflow and areas that can be effectively controlled by workflow solutions, you can leverage your expertise and current facility management technologies into a series of repeatable best practices. In a period of uncertainty and an ever-changing workforce, workflow technology can ensure a faster ramp-up for new employees, reinforce standard operating procedures for existing employees, and support regulatory reporting for compliance. As with any benefit, to maximize your investment requires the necessary time to capture effective processes and correct broken processes to provide the highest yield. Whether interacting with multiple organizations to complete a task, monitoring systems to ensure maximum up time, or interacting with internal groups to communicate change, workflow technologies support facility managers to execute their strategic mission through the leveraged use of the extended enterprise.

CHAPTER 8: SUSTAINABILITY

Louise A. Sabol

Buildings consume significant natural resources and have a vast impact on the environment. Building operation alone accounts for approximately 40 percent of U.S. primary energy use. A well-crafted plan to improve the environmental performance of facilities often will result in significant benefits to both the organizational bottom line and to our overall energy efficiency and independence.

Achieving sustainability certification is one approach facility owners can take to benchmark progress and achievement for their facilities. To facilitate these endeavors, there is a growing number of software applications available commercially to handle a range of data requirements throughout the building life cycle—from initial assessments, to project planning, implementation, and into sustainable operations and maintenance.

Although design and construction of facilities is a critical area for achieving sustainability, organizations spend most of their infrastructure dollars operating and maintaining facilities over their life cycle. A life-cycle cost analysis (LCCA) is a method for assessing the total cost of ownership (TCO) for a facility. LCCA especially is useful to evaluate project alternatives that fulfill the same performance requirements, differing with respect to initial costs and operating costs, to determine the option that maximizes net savings.

Measuring and improving a building's carbon footprint (greenhouse gas emissions or GHG) is becoming an important metric for building owners and facility management. Carbon management software and services is a rapidly growing area fueled by unpredictable energy costs, greenhouse gas compliance requirements, and more robust sustainability strategies within organizations.

Owners increasingly will need to make informed decisions to control and reduce their facility's energy use in sync with the costs and efficiencies of their building systems. Software technologies are being rapidly developed and enhanced to support decision making on sustainability initiatives and energy analysis. One of these, building information modeling (BIM), offers a means of analyzing building designs for sustainability requirements and energy efficiency, and increasingly can interact with a range of external software applications for advanced analysis.

Support for the operational management of sustainable and energy-efficient buildings (high-performance green buildings) is another rapidly expanding area of technology development. In a case study for the use of sustainable operational management (building monitoring, commissioning, and data management), the state of Missouri was facing many rapidly escalating facilities issues during the period 2000 to 2005, including increased energy expenditures, escalating real estate costs, and a growing backlog of deferred maintenance items. The state's energy reduction initiative returned annual savings from the combined projects of more than US$35 million per year, US$20 million from energy savings alone. Efficiencies were achieved through reduced energy usage, process improvements in facility automation, monitoring and management, and more efficiently real estate portfolio management.

CHAPTER 9: CONDITION ASSESSMENT IN FACILITY ASSET MANAGEMENT

James B. Clayton

Facility asset management is an emerging, strategic approach to capital budgeting and optimal allocation of scarce funds for the repair, renewal, and modernization of aging facilities. The promise of facility asset management is that practitioners will reap budget success, reliable mission performance, and grateful stakeholders. Advocates also claim the approach can control operational risk, reduce cost of ownership, prolong component life, eliminate unforeseen dollar demands and, thus, help optimize return on investment in facility performance.

The facility asset management process entails systematically collecting key data and delivering the data to computer models and analytic tools to create business intelligence. Facility managers use business intelligence to conduct organized, logical, and complementary decision making at strategic, operational, and tactical levels.

The author sets the stage for the chapter's main topic of condition assessment by discussing the origins of facility asset management, describing each phase of the process in detail, and explaining the role that condition assessment plays in one of the phases.

Clayton then drills down into the four techniques of building condition assessment, describing in detail and with cited references the origins, characteristics, strengths, and weaknesses of each. The chapter concludes with guidance on how to decide which technique is best for an organization.

CHAPTER 10: COMPUTER MODELING

Eric Teicholz

This chapter presents an overview of computer modeling and simulation related to facility management applications. Following a brief review of computer models and simulation, the chapter describes four areas in which models have been successfully used: visualization, space allocation, facility asset management, and energy.

Every model represents some simplification of a more complex reality to allow for the calculation of relevant variables (heat flow, stress, cost, etc.). A computer model consists of two components: the computer-based mathematical representation of a physical process and the definition of conditions for testing that representation against desired criteria. Such models attempt to calculate solutions that predict how systems behave based on various parameters and the model's initial conditions.

Simulation models require external data input into the model because the universe of possible solutions for the model cannot be computed without such input. For example, an energy model designed to calculate an ENERGY STAR score for a building might have initial input from a variety of sources: from the user (e.g., building type, address, age), from prestored tables (weather conditions, energy costs for that location), or from building automation sensors (BAS) that automatically track and control energy usage for various assets.

Visualization models discussed in this chapter include CAFM and BIM. The BIM discussion is meant to complement the discussion included in Chapter 2 of this book. The space allocation discussion breaks down space management into its discrete inputs: space inventory, requirements, allocation, and planning/forecasting. Asset management modeling (authored by James Clayton) is likewise written to complement Chapter 9, which deals in detail with this subject. Finally, the energy management modeling component of the chapter describes some of the newly emerging parametric models and how they are used to calculate cost-effective energy retrofits.

CHAPTER 11: TECHNOLOGY AND THE WORKPLACE

Erik Jaspers and Eric Teicholz

A key challenge for today's facility manager is to effectively adapt to change. Change caused by globalization, economics, changing work styles, and technology innovation directly impact the world of facility management, the services performed by facility managers, how they communicate, and the physical workplace itself.

Traditional IT technologies such as computer-aided facility management (CAFM), integrated workplace management systems (IWMSs), computerized maintenance management system (CMMSs), and geographic information systems (GISs) as well as new mobile, collaborative, workflow, and sensor-based technologies are valuable tools for facility managers that increasingly will impact the workplace. The scope of new and emerging tools is vast and the FM needs to understand not only the technologies but when and how to apply them so as to realize the greatest benefit for the organization. The facility manager needs to establish priorities regarding what to automate and be able to understand the potential impact of that technology on the workplace. Factors such as the type of organization, available resources, culture, and IT competency level must all be taken into account.

This chapter is designed to assist the facility manager in understanding these traditional and emerging technologies, their impact on the workplace, and when and how to apply them. Numerous examples of how these technologies are being used are likewise presented. In this manner, facility managers not only are assisted in acquiring an understanding of relevant technologies available, but how and when to apply them.

CHAPTER 12: THE ROLE OF PEOPLE AND PROCESS IN TECHNOLOGY

Angela Lewis

Technology is a foundational part of the daily responsibilities of facility managers. In fact, IFMA defines facility management as "a profession that encompasses multiple disciplines to ensure functionality of the built environment by integrating people, process and technology" (www.ifma.org/resources/what-is-fm/fm-definitions.htm). The focus of this chapter is to discuss the importance and interactions between people, process, and technology. Although the concepts discussed within the chapter can apply to many facility management technologies, the chapter uses energy and maintenance management software to frame the discussion.

The chapter first discusses some fundamental concepts and definitions. The chapter then provides an overview of the challenges that result when technology, people, and process are not balanced during a technology planning and implementation project. The chapter acknowledges current needs using examples from energy and maintenance software planning and implementation projects. The discussion of current needs is followed by a discussion of what is needed to support emerging technologies. The chapter closes with two case studies. The first case study provides an overview of how to use a building automation system (BAS) to benchmark and improve energy efficiency within a lab building. The second case study summarizes the importance of people and organizational roles within a software enterprise system integration project, with an emphasis on lessons learned.

CHAPTER 13: SOCIAL MEDIA

Dean Stanberry

Social media has infiltrated most everyone's professional and personal life. Whether you herald its arrival or curse its existence, you can't escape its impact on the world around you. In step with the swell of technological advancement, social media is evolving at a pace seemingly beyond our capacity to absorb.

The objective of this chapter is to strip away the irrelevant and focus on the elements of social media that matter to you professionally. We start by providing a historical perspective on the evolution of social media. While it may seem revolutionary, it has, in fact, evolved over the past 30-plus years, beginning with the introduction of the personal computer in 1982. Next, we explore facility management–focused social media, pointing you toward a wealth of FM knowledge.

Finally, pointers are offered on making social media work for you. In this age of shifting priorities and tenuous employment, everyone needs to maintain a professional edge. Social media is one of the many vehicles at your disposal to maintain that edge—but it does not happen without some effort on your part. Ultimately, engaging in social media is a matter of personal choice.

Author Bios

JAMES B. CLAYTON, PE, MSEE, RIS
Director of the Institute for Responsible Infrastructure Stewardship

Jim Clayton is a senior fellow and director of the Institute for Responsible Infrastructure Stewardship (IRIS), an independent, not-for-profit "think tank" that researches and promotes the use of business analytics and multicriteria decision making for obtaining best and highest use of scarce capital repair/renewal funds.

Clayton is a registered professional engineer, holds an MSEE from the University of Michigan, and has served 45 years as a facility manager, business executive, and private consultant to building owners, commercial firms, and public agencies. In 1984, following a distinguished career in the Navy Civil Engineer Corps, he joined Kaiser Engineers Inc. as a principal engineer. Later, he advanced to vice president of two other companies, and subsequently founded UNITY Inc., where he was president from 1996 to 2007.

In addition to speaking at technical conferences and writing for the IFMA Foundation, Clayton conducts peer reviews of papers submitted to the *ASCE Journal of Infrastructure Systems*. He also recently assisted the Federal Accounting Standards Advisory Board in amending SFFAS 6, a facility-related, generally accepted accounting principle (GAAP) for the federal government and used by many state and local governments.

PAUL HEAD
Manager, Ernst & Young Advisory Services

Paul Head is a manager in Ernst & Young's Construction and Real Estate Advisory Services Practice. With more than 20 years in the strategic and operational management of facilities and real estate spanning the full spectrum of the real estate life cycle from design, construction, to operations and technology implementation.

As a Lean Six Sigma Greenbelt, Head has helped organizations streamline operations, reduce risk, and eliminate waste. His experience is concentrated in business transformation, strategic alignment with organizational mission, operational efficiency, knowledge management, and enterprise technologies.

He has provided these services to a broad array of clientele in the following industries: government, oil and gas, manufacturing, utilities, architectural/engineering/construction, finance, health care, and education.

Head holds an undergraduate degree in architecture and environmental design from Ball State University.

RICHARD HODGES
Founder and Principal, GreenIT

Richard Hodges is the founder and a principal of GreenIT. He has 25 years of experience in the technology industry and as a consultant. Hodges established GreenIT as the first consultancy to develop a systemic and strategic approach to sustainability for information and communications technology (ICT) systems.

Hodges has a unique breadth and depth of experience in the technology, energy, and real estate industries. He has consulted to utilities, real estate developers, and a broad variety of public- and private-sector clients, and has established himself as a leading expert in the integration of ICT systems and buildings to enable sustainable development.

TERRY W. HOFFMANN
Adjunct Professor, Milwaukee School of Engineering

Terry Hoffmann has been an active participant in the building controls industry for more than 37 years. He recently retired from Johnson Controls after serving there in various positions related to product development, sales, and marketing. He is the writer of numerous articles on subjects related to building intelligence and building systems integration published in trade and technical journals and has spoken at conferences on these topics around the world. Hoffmann has served as a committee member for both LonMark International and BACnet International.

He holds a bachelor of science degree in electrical engineering from Marquette University and a master's degree in engineering management from the Milwaukee School of Engineering.

ERIK JASPERS
CTO, Planon

Erik Jaspers has more than 27 years of experience in IT and has held various positions, primarily in IT project management and information management for multinational companies like ATOS (Origin) and Philips.

For the past 12 years he has been working for Planon, a European-based CAFM/IWMS software vendor. Over these years, he has held leadership positions concerning the development of CAFM/IWMS software solutions. He led the introduction of agile project management for software product development (SCRUM), at the forefront of the adoption of these methodologies.

Currently, Jaspers is primarily concerned with innovation policy and the management of the Products and Solutions Roadmap for Planon, translating market developments (technical as well as nontechnical) into solutions for facility management.

Planon is committed to developing leading solutions for companies in managing their real estate, space, maintenance, and service management operations. Planon products are well suited for worldwide deployment.

CHRIS KELLER
Managing Director, Facilities Solutions Group, LLC

After earning a bachelor of arts degree from Wesleyan University and a master's degree in architecture from the Graduate School of Architecture and Urban Planning at UCLA, Chris Keller began his professional career as an architect. Keller's passion for architecture and computers led him into the world of FM automation.

Keller has been implementing FM automation systems since 1988 across many industries, including education; finance; insurance; pharmaceutical; local, state, and federal government; health care; utilities; manufacturing; intelligence community; aerospace; and defense. In 1993, Keller formed Integrated Data Solutions (IDS). IDS was an FM automation services company that generated value to its customers by improving FM processes through technology. Keller merged his company with Facilities Solutions Group in 2006. As managing director of FSG, he continues to provide FM process and automation services to commercial, institutional, and federal government organizations.

Since 1996 Keller has been an active member of IFMA and has served as an officer of the Information Technology Council from 2000 to the present. He was president of the Council from 2005 to 2007 and currently stays active as a past president. Keller's architectural work was published in *Southern Homes* magazine. Keller has written a host of articles relative to FM automation appearing in *Maintenance Solutions*, *Building Operations Management*, and *Total Maintenance Solutions* magazines. He was a contributing author for the *RS Means Guide* and has been published in the *Facility Management Journal*. Additionally, Keller has given more than 100 seminars and webinars on FM automation and has been invited to speak at conferences sponsored by: American Institute of Architects (AIA); Architecture, Engineering and Construction (AEC); Business Products Industry Association (BPIA) Neocon; International Facility Management Association (IFMA) World Work Place; Realcomm; FAECOM World Technology Conference; FIATECH; Autodesk University (AU); and APPA.

ANGELA LEWIS, PE, PhD, LEED AP
Project Manager, Facility Engineering Associates

Angela Lewis, P.E., PhD, LEED AP, is a Project Manager at Facility Engineering Associates in Fairfax, VA. Lewis is an engineer and facility management consultant with a background in heating, ventilating, and air-conditioning (HVAC) systems, building controls, and energy and maintenance management. Lewis has a PhD from the University of Reading and has served as an editor and technical writer for several publications, including the IFMA Foundation 2009 North American Facility Management Degree Program Guide, the IFMA Foundation Sustainability How-To Guide Sustainability in the Food Service Environment and has authored multiple articles in research journals and trade magazines. Lewis served as the 2009–2011 managing editor for the IFMA Foundation Sustainability How-To Sustainability Guide series.

LOUISE A. SABOL, AIA, LEED AP
Director of Technology Solutions, Design + Construction Strategies, LLC

Louise Sabol, director of technology solutions with Design + Construction Strategies, is an architect and technologist with more than 20 years of experience in leveraging technology to improve project delivery and life-cycle management of the built environment. Sabol's experience in the AEC, IT, and facility management consulting arenas provide her with unique capabilities for developing complex and versatile information-enabled solutions. She brings particular expertise in sustain-ability, real property data systems, and technology-enabled workflow analysis. For D+C Strategies, she directs the development of solutions that combine data and visualization technologies to meet rapidly changing business needs affecting the built environment.

Clients have included Autodesk, Smithsonian Institution, Veterans Administration, and GSA, among many others. Her degrees include a bachelor of science degree in architecture from The Ohio State University and a master of architecture from Catholic University. She is a registered architect and a LEED AP certified professional. Guest speaking engagements have included George Mason University, SAME, Autodesk University, and the Federal Facilities Council.

DEAN STANBERRY
National Engineering Operations Manager, Jones Lang LaSalle

Dean Stanberry is a facility management and corporate real estate professional with a diverse background in facilities organizational development and operations, quality and process management, facility design and construction, FM outsourcing, procurement, and data center operations. His current role is national engineering operations manager for Jones Lang LaSalle supporting Charles Schwab.

Stanberry is a past president of the Denver Chapter of IFMA. He currently serves as a trustee for the IFMA Foundation, member of the IFMA Sustainability Committee, and member of the U.S. Green Building Council (USGBC) Colorado Chapter board of directors.

ERIC TEICHOLZ, IFMA FELLOW
President, Graphic Systems, Inc.

Eric Teicholz is president of Graphic Systems, Inc., a Cambridge, Massachusetts firm specializing in facility management and real estate automation consulting. He is an IFMA fellow, a member of IFMA's Board of Directors, past chair of the IFMA Sustainability Committee, member of the IFMA Foundation board of trustees, and a member of the National Academies National Research Council committee. His current work with IFMA includes his position as co-chair of Knowledge Management for the IFMA Sustainability Committee, executive editor of IFMA's "How-To" sustainability guides, and member of IFMA's Strategic Planning Oversight Team. Teicholz is also co-editor of the peer-reviewed *International Journal of Facility Management* and a member of the Commonwealth of Massachusetts's Facility Advisory Committee.

Teicholz is the author/editor of 12 books related to computer-aided design and architecture, computer-aided facility management, and geographic information system technology. Teicholz was educated as an architect at Harvard University. Before Graphic Systems, he spent 12 years at Harvard's Graduate School of Design as an associate professor of architecture and associate director of Harvard's largest research and development facility, the Laboratory for Computer Graphics and Spatial Analysis.

GEOFF D. WILLIAMS
Facilities Director, The Centre for Health & Safety Innovation

Geoff Williams is the Manager of SeawoodFM and an associate at Seawood Solutions and Services Inc. Seawood is a wholly owned subsidiary of MMM Group Limited, which is headquartered in Toronto, Ontario, Canada. In his capacity at Seawood, he has overseen the development, implementation, and marketing of SeawoodFM, Seawood's own Web-based FM solution. SeawoodFM is currently assisting the day-to-day operations of a wide variety of health care facilities in managing more than 10 million square feet of property.

Williams is also the past president (and current secretary) of the IT Council of IFMA and the past president of the Toronto Chapter of IFMA. In all of these roles, he supports the FM industry at large. Williams is a graduate of the University of Waterloo's School of Architecture, holding degrees in both architecture and environmental studies.

Williams resides northeast of Toronto, Ontario, where he lives with his wife, Laurie, and their two children, Claire and Lauren.

WILLIAM P. WITTS JR.
GIS/CAD Specialist, MIT Department of Facilities

William Witts is the GIS/CAD specialist for the Massachusetts Institute of Technology Department of Facilities. He has nine years' experience in the GIS field working in municipal government and as a consultant in the AEC industry. Earlier in Witts's career, he worked as the GIS coordinator for the town of Bedford, Massachusetts. There, Witts oversaw all aspects of GIS management within the town. Just prior to joining MIT, Witts worked on GIS integration with asset management products for a large AEC firm.

In his current position, Witts is working on several GIS mapping projects, support of GIS/CAD-based applications, and administration of enterprise wide databases and servers for the department. Witts has a bachelor's degree in regional planning and a master's degree in geographic information science.

Technology

CAFM/IWMS—Balancing Technology, Processes, and Objectives

1

Chris Keller

EXECUTIVE SUMMARY

Facility management automation (computer-aided facility management or **CAFM** and integrated workplace management system or **IWMS**) primarily is viewed as a facility management departmental tool that supports facility management **(FM)** operations. Proper selection and implementation of technology tools are critical in determining the current and future value of the FM department to the organization. Optimization of the organizational value of the FM department occurs when the tools facilitate processes that deliver facility departmental objectives in support of an organization's mission.

Facility managers need to adjust the technology tools and processes well in advance of a problem's visibility in order to successfully address the new requirements for their customers. Proactively preparing the facility for inhabitants' future needs requires analyzing trends in facility management, business, and technology. New and future technology will facilitate the considerable task of achieving organizational objectives and more easily convey to leadership the value of FM to the organization.

INTRODUCTION

Most papers about CAFM/IWMS are written from either a market perspective or a system perspective. This book is written from an FM perspective with the primary focus on CAFM/IWMS as a facility management automation tool that facilitates the processes that deliver FM departmental objectives in support of an organization's mission.

Facility managers have three masters: the organization, the FM department, and the facility itself (see Figure 1.1). The success of any FM project is contingent upon appropriately balancing the project objectives with the requirements of these three masters.

Facility management automation projects also have three masters: the objectives, the technology, and the project.

There have been many studies over the past 25 years regarding the success of information technology **(IT)** projects. The general consensus is that 7 of 10 IT projects fail in some way. This "success" rate has remained consistent over the past 25 years. The cited causes of those projects that fail range from technology issues and poor project management to collaboration issues and inadequate interoperability. The bottom line is that most standard identified issues are symptoms rather than causes. The majority of IT projects fail primarily because the project objectives and the project solution are not aligned. A NASA study of hundreds of IT projects in the late 1990s supports this conclusion.

Many facility management stakeholders focus only on technology when they think about **FM automation**. This is evident in the myriad of cryptic industry acronyms such as IWMS, CAFM, **CMMS** (computerized maintenance and management systems) and BIM (building information modeling). While selecting the most appropriate technology is critical for optimizing value, it is not sufficient for success. Balancing technology and the organizational objectives is the key to optimizing the value and ensuring a successful FM automation implementation.

This chapter explores the interrelationship between the objectives and the technology for a successful FM automation project. In addition, the chapter addresses the history of CAFM/IWMS, the current technology, and a look into

FIGURE 1.1 Input sources for the facility manager.

Organizational Input

Facility Department Input   } Facility Manager

Facility Input

the near-term future. It focuses on the business objectives of selecting and implementing technology for FM rather than on an analysis of the technical tools. Since both the tools and an organization's objectives change continually, the need for aligning the two remains constant and therefore is the focus of this chapter.

OVERVIEW AND OBJECTIVES

Facility management automation has made significant progress over the past 20 years as technology has progressed at a rapid pace as defined by Moore's Law. Although Moore's Law was originally an observation regarding the number of transistors in an integrated circuit, it seems to apply to many forms of technology. The basic law states that the number of transistors on a circuit board will double every two years—an exponential rate of growth. Loosely translated to the technology used in the workplace, this means technology increases by an order of magnitude every 24 months. Measuring exponential increases in FM automation technology may not be as visible as it is in the commercial world. Compare the changes in consumer electronics from decade to decade, starting with the 1970s. For example, audio technology has progressed from reel-to-reel to 8-track to cassette to CD to DVD to MP3 in the past 40 years. The time between these first few advancements was much greater than the last few. Facility management automation tools have made similar advances and will be discussed in the technology section of this chapter.

Advances in technology can be evaluated best by the value provided, not by evaluating the technology itself. It often is difficult to separate the sales hyperbole from the true advances and equally difficult to distinguish the value added by the technology from the value added by process change. In order to fully understand the value added, we need to analyze the value of facility management to an organization and the value that process improvement adds to the use and implementation of technology.

Consider the aforementioned audio technology example. The initial improvements were to the quality of the product, the durability of the media, the price, the capacity, and finally the size. Combining the price, capacity, and mobility allowed the technology to enable a lifestyle change for the consumer. This is an example of the value provided by the advances in the technology following an exponential trajectory. In the author's opinion, FM technology is at the lower end of the exponential value curve, and technology advances will cease impressing us and the business landscape suddenly will be different. Reference the music recording and distribution industry to see this type of transformation in real time. For the

FM industry collaboration, social media and nano technologies[1] are starting to affect industry shifts.

Technology, without the context of process and objectives, cannot be evaluated. Before reviewing FM automation, FM objectives and the value of FM automation need to be defined.

As mentioned earlier, facility managers have three masters: the organization, the facility, and the FM department. The organization can be divided further into two customer categories: leadership and departments. Leadership is focused on an organization's market position, branding, strategic direction, and organizational culture, while, at least in traditional hierarchical organizations, departments are tasked with achieving the objectives defined by senior management.

Facility managers have to understand and reconcile the often conflicting objectives generated by the organization, the facility, and the FM department. These juxtaposed objectives require a myriad of tasks to achieve them. The facility manager needs to design and implement a strategic plan that balances budget, facility functionality, and occupant productivity in order to optimize the reconciled objectives.

VALUE OF FACILITY MANAGEMENT AUTOMATION TO THE ORGANIZATION

The value of FM to the organization normally can be evaluated by a variety of metrics such as employee attraction and retention, improved productivity, risk mitigation, sustainable initiatives, and strategic business planning support. All of these can be supported and enhanced by processes facilitated by FM automation tools. These tools provide value to the organization in three ways: interoperability, reorganization, and culture.

Interoperability

CAFM/IWMS systems generate far greater value than FM efficacy by providing information to other departments (see Figure 1.2). Improving efficiency for production departments could add more value than saving costs in managing a facility. Information interoperability generated by integrating strategic space planning with strategic organization planning can shorten the time to bring products and services to market and reduce the disruption time for space churn (see Figure 1.3).

---

[1] Nanoscience has to do with studying and manipulating processes and materials at their molecular or atomic level (see http://free.ed.gov/resource.cfm?resource_id=1945).

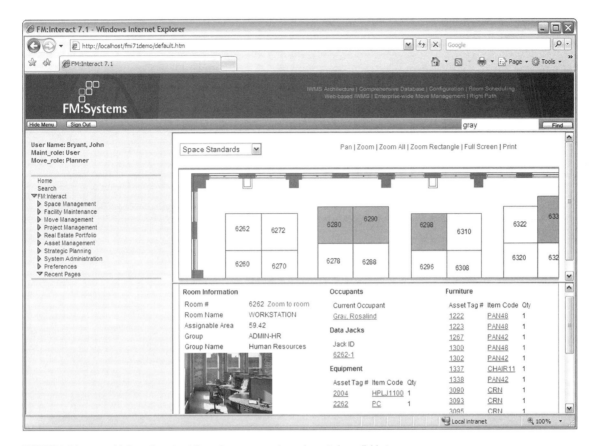

FIGURE 1.2 Integrated information about floor plans, occupants, and assets is available to everyone in the organization in a Web browser.

Reproduced by permission of FM Systems

Since CAFM/IWMS systems are a primary organizational information source that relates assets, people, and space, this information can be invaluable to departments for planning and executing processes to achieve their objectives.

Opportunity for Reorganization

A significant value of technology advances to an organization is its ability to flatten the organizational structure and eliminate silos. The computer greatly enhances communication, accountability, and delegation. This allows the elimination of data, process, and organizational silos that exist based on the past need for the organization to be the communication system between the field staff and senior management. The author believes there is a strong argument that real estate **(RE)**, FM, and most parts of IT should be merged into one organizational department.

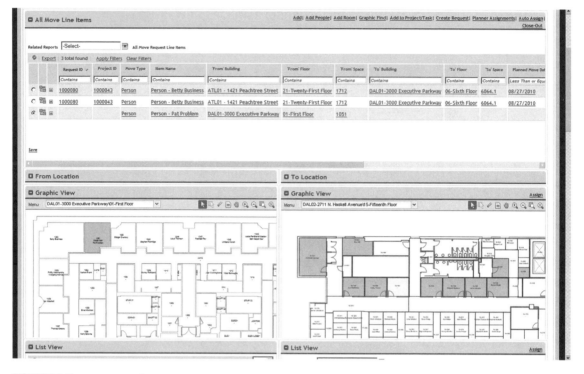

FIGURE 1.3 Move management.

Reprint courtesy of International Business Machines Corporation, © 2012 International Business Machines Corporation

Conveying Culture

While it is obvious that everyone in an organization has more direct daily contact with the facility and technology than anything else, most organizations do not leverage the facility and FM as tools to convey and promote culture. Facility management automation tools can be used to convey the culture, promote employee retention, and facilitate productivity. Facility management departments can use a web site for conveying information, enforcing processes, and marketing the organizational value of facility management to the organization.

FACILITY MANAGEMENT TECHNOLOGY

In the 1980s, FM automation needs and desires far exceeded available technology. FM business processes were far more advanced than the technology could address. In 1980, the platform for FM automation was based on the mainframe computer. For most organizations, technology was limited to financial information only. During the 1980s, personal computers **(PCs)** had less power than the calculators used by college students 10 years ago. The applications were a combination of general office tools such as word processors, spreadsheets, and a few single application tools like computer-aided design **(CAD)** or CMMS. CAFM systems were created that combined a few single applications into one system and, most importantly, integrated CAD and data. During the late 1980s and early 1990s, PCs were networked with local area networks **(LANs)**. The PCs became powerful enough to make CAFM systems viable for larger organizations. In the late 1990s and early 2000s, the conditions were reversed and technology advances outpaced an organization's ability to assimilate it. The 1990s saw the proliferation of the Internet, Web-based applications, and personal digital assistants **(PDAs)** (see Figure 1.4 to see the evolution of FM automation tools). Since 2000, significant advances have occurred with wireless communication, **radio**

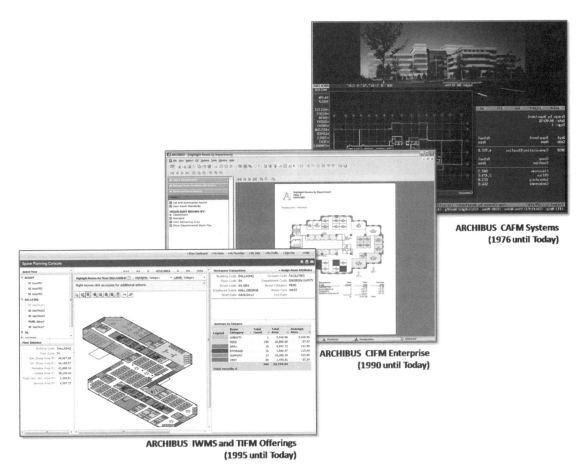

ARCHIBUS CAFM Systems
(1976 until Today)

ARCHIBUS CIFM Enterprise
(1990 until Today)

ARCHIBUS IWMS and TIFM Offerings
(1995 until Today)

FIGURE 1.4 Thirty-five-plus-year history of CAFM/IWMS showing DOS, Windows, and Web formats.
Reproduced by permission of ARCHIBUS

frequency identification (RFID), motes,[2] building information modeling (BIM), Google Earth, and interoperability. CAFM/IWMS applications have become more sophisticated, integrating many FM, RE, and IT applications.

Today, technology is advancing far faster than an organization's ability to evolve its work processes and organizational structure to take advantage of the new tools. This trend will continue far into the future. For hardware, Moore's time frame of 24 months per hardware generation is shrinking and it is currently closer to 12 months. For software, the time frame also is shrinking (but at a slower rate) and is currently 24 to 36 months. Regardless of the pace of advances, the technology already has outpaced an organization's ability to assimilate it into its processes, management approach, culture, and objectives.

The convergence of FM, RE, and IT is an example of how technology is more advanced than the industry's ability to integrate its tools into best practice processes. In the late 1990s, there was technology to integrate all functions of these three typically separate departments. Only a handful of companies actually tried to merge these departments. Most convergence experiments focused on the move process in organizations that had high churn rates and high-technology requirements for staff, with most being in the financial industry. The current industry emphasis seems to be the integration of human resources (HR) with FM. All of these integration trends point to the need for interoperable FM information for enterprise analytics.

Given the rapid pace of technological advancement, many organizations seem to implement technology using a "leap frog" approach: that is, they implement a technology, integrate the processes and the technology over a few years, and then repeat the process. During the time between technology implementations, technology often advances significantly. The author believes that many organizations do not realize that the value life cycle of hardware, software, and processes is two to four years. Most change management initiatives take longer than the technology life cycle. By the time the new technology and processes are rolled out, the objectives and technology have shifted.

Balancing Act

The balancing act consists of selecting and implementing tools that support the processes that achieve clearly defined objectives. Misalignment typically begins by starting with the wrong part of the equation. Most FM automation projects start

---

[2] A mote is a node within a wireless network containing sensors. It is capable of reading the sensor data, performing data processing, and then communicating with other connected network nodes (see http://en.wikipedia.org/wiki/Sensor_node, May 2011).

with either a broken process as the focal point or by trying to find a tool to facilitate accomplishing a task more efficiently (better, faster, cheaper). The primary focus and starting point should be the organization's objectives.

Processes may break for a variety of reasons, with a common reason being that initial objectives have shifted. Trying to fix a broken process without validating the objectives will have limited success. Similarly, making a task that achieves the wrong objective more efficient only accomplishes getting to the wrong objective faster.

Once the objectives have been identified, the processes that will accomplish the objectives should be defined or refined. Only after the objectives and processes have been established can the requirements for the tools be defined.

The system selection process should be based on:

- Organizational objectives
- FM department objectives
- The value provided to the organization
- The value provided to the FM department

Each function or feature should be mapped directly to the objective supported and the value provided. Table 1.1 is an example of this mapping for a move management process. This matrix can be used as a reference to ensure that the technical solution and the project objectives stay in alignment throughout the life of the project.

TABLE 1.1 Mapping objectives to values and features.

Objective	Organization		FM Department	
	Value	Feature	Value	Feature
Shorten planning time	Reduce effort of the organization Faster to market	Share, move documents (including drawings)	Reduce risk, reduce cost, and improve services	Integrate with strategic space planning
Improve information sharing between all move project team members	Reduce effort of the organization, reduce redundant work, reduce risk of failure, reduce the rumors	Facilitate team communication via a Web portal	Increase service, reduce effort, lower cost, and reduce risk	Facilitate interdepartmental communication via a shared Web-based application
Improve quality of services by reducing failed move projects	Reduce effort of the organization	Mandatory move request form with key information required	Reduce risk, reduce cost, and improve services	Implement Six Sigma and use the system to provide metrics

TECHNOLOGY OF THE (NEAR) FUTURE

A well-respected facility manager made the analogy that managing real estate was like steering an ocean liner: you have to start turning miles (or years for facility managers) in advance of the actual turn. Anticipating changes in both technology and an organization's objectives is not much different, except that instead of navigating the ocean, FM navigates the rapids. Reacting to changes in either technology or the organization's objectives is not sufficient for success. Facility managers need to proactively anticipate their customer's requirements before the customer is even aware of the problems that generate the new requirements. Facility managers need to adjust the technology tools and processes well in advance of a problem's visibility in order to successfully address the new requirements.

Proactively preparing the facility to address its inhabitants' future needs requires analyzing trends in FM, business, and technology.

Trends in Facility Management

The International Facility Management Association **(IFMA)**, **APPA**,[3] and the U.S. General Services Administration **(GSA)** all have their own view of current trends in facility management for their primary focus. Not surprising to facility managers, the trends have a high degree of correlation. The common trends are:

- Energy, sustainability, and Leadership in Energy and Environmental Design **(LEED)** certification (see Figure 1.5).
- Aligning FM planning with institutional goals; linking facility management to strategy.
- IT, building automation systems, and emerging technologies impacting enterprise production.
- Performance measurement and accountability; instituting metrics for performance measurement and transparency.
- Implementing total cost of ownership **(TCO)** strategies, managing aging building, and facilitating change management.
- Globalization; hiring the best candidates for the future.
- Security and institutional safety.
- Dynamic and dramatic shifts in the way people need the facility and the FM services to support a global and increasingly virtual collaborative work methodology (e.g., alternative workplace, virtual classrooms, and telework).

---

[3] Originally established as the Association of Physical Plant Administrators of Universities and Colleges, the organization changed its name to the Association of Higher Education Facilities Officers (see www.appa.org).

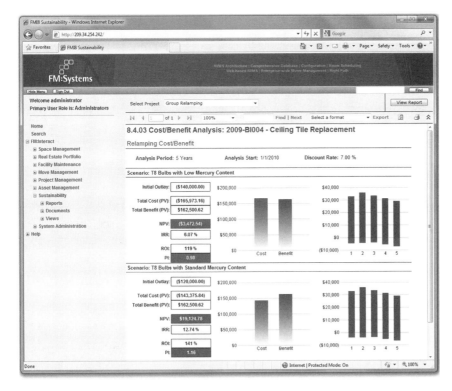

FIGURE 1.5 Sustainability module showing costs and benefits of planned initiatives.
Reproduced by permission of FM:Systems

Trends in Business

Business drivers are typically focused on supporting the organizational mission and improving the bottom line. Technology advancements have added several new tools, and a few difficulties, to this objective by creating the ability to cost effectively collect accurate, timely, and relevant metrics, reducing the requirement of people to filter and process information, and increasing the speed of change.

■ **Business by the numbers: Numerati.**[4] There are many groups using numeric analysis for managing businesses. While this always has been true for financial analysis (e.g., economic value added [**EVA**] and market value added [**MVA**]), it is becoming more commonplace to use numeric analysis for process improvement (e.g., Six Sigma).[5] The newest trends include analyzing how an organization

[4] *Numerati* relates to a nonfiction book written by Stephen L. Baker. Baker maintains that, because of the data explosion caused by the Internet, smartphones, social networking, and so on, the people who can manage this data explosion will change the world.

[5] A business strategy (see http://en.wikipedia.org/wiki/Six_Sigma, May 2011).

interacts much the way a web site monitor program analyzes how people navigate a web site. The analysis can be on communication patterns, information flow patterns, and talent usage and location patterns. There is also a growing trend to use value analytics to determine the value and optimization of technology implementation.

■ **Permanent elimination of middle management**. Each of the last four recessions has resulted in the permanent loss of middle management positions. Technology has eliminated the need for most of middle management.

■ **Continuous improvement and reorganizations**. Technology has removed most of the reasons that justified and guided the design of organizational structures. New business processes are created to respond to the changes in the business environment. Some of those changes include globalization, global recession, Internet commerce, demographic shift to Asia, analytics, security, and government change in the Middle East.

Trends in Technology

While most manufacturers of facility management automation technology are wrestling with the maturation of Web technology as it progresses from childhood into adolescence, the advances in technology that will have the greatest impact on facility management will be in fields other than FM automation software.

FM automation software will be driving more and more toward interoperability by integrating existing technologies like geographic information systems **(GIS)** with CAFM/IWMS, RFID with CAFM/IWMS, building control systems with CAFM/IWMS, security with CAFM/IWMS, and so on (see Figure 1.6). There are two limiting factors holding back these integrations: (1) manufacturers strive to own their market via proprietary technology, and (2) an organization's departments striving to own the silo via organizational boundaries and information hoarding. Assuming these hurdles are overcome, the next great obstacle for advancement is the organization's ability to rapidly alter its structure and culture to take advantage of the new processes and tools.

The advances that will impact facility management will be in the following areas:

■ Gestural interfaces like iPad, Wii, Kinect, and Google's Gmail Motion will transform the way people interact with the computer/telephone and workspaces.

■ Web-based CAD **(cloud computing)**.

■ Open source digital camera. Frankencamera is a "hackable" camera. This allows innovators to integrate state-of-the-art digital camera technology with any other open technology. Both the hardware and software are open source,

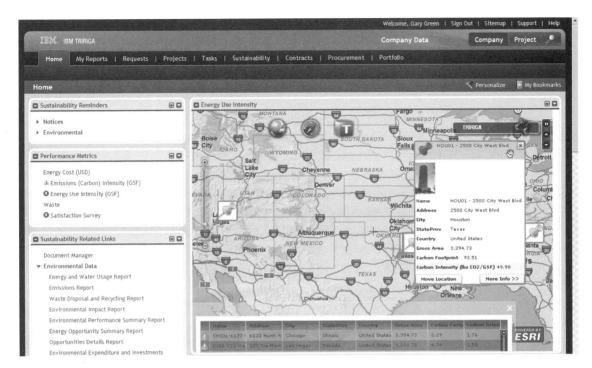

FIGURE 1.6 Sustainability portal with GIS interface.
Reprint courtesy of International Business Machines Corporation, © 2012 International Business Machines Corporation

so an innovator can hook it up to other technology or extend its capability. Potential FM applications are security, automated visual maintenance inspections, interactive way finding, visual mobile communication, and virtual visual design sessions.

■ RFID will provide the ability to effortlessly track any asset dynamically. This means facility management can manage more types of assets and a greater number of assets with far more accuracy in real time.

■ The greatest impact BIM will bring to the FM industry will be changes to the design and construction processes and to the relationships between the owner, architect, engineer, contractor, and manufacturer. Another significant potential area of impact will be real-time energy management optimization.

■ **Nanotechnology** probably will have the greatest impact on the facility management profession than any other. It will profoundly change everything from the materials buildings are made of, the products used for services, the generation and consumption of energy, communication, asset management, types of required facility management service, and risk management.

- Motes will allow facility managers to easily and cost effectively collect a variety of information by remote sensors. This will allow real-time monitoring and adjustments for all building systems and will greatly reduce energy consumption while increasing the level of comfort and service.

- **Electronic paper** will be able to quickly change from a contract to a newspaper, to a blueprint, to an Internet search, to an interactive 3D model, to a series of images, to a presentation, to a teleconference, with a simple command, therefore greatly reducing paper consumption.

- 5D has many definitions in the FM industry. Essentially, 5D expands a 3D model by integrating the detail of information and time. The value of information is well established through CAFM/IWMS and BIM tools. Adding a time component enhances the value of the information considerably. The time component allows continuous real-time modeling, predictive analytics, preventative action, and real-time interaction and communication between the FM department, the occupants, and the facility. In short, 5D enables optimal facility management. Combining real-time information enables productivity optimization for the facility occupants by facilitating communication, providing just-in-time FM services, enhancing predictive FM services for long lead items, and real-time resource management for space, equipment, energy, utilities, and professional services. 5D can not only increase productivity but can also reduce risk by improving facility operations, faster emergency response, and real-time risk analysis and alerts. Scream!point is an example of 5D technology. Scream!point provides several time components on a cloud-based, technology mashup platform of gaming, GIS, and BIM (Figure 1.7). It integrates time, information, and the 3D model in several ways. It integrates 3D models with various time-based technologies, including project scheduling tools, mobile communication devices, the cloud, animation tools, and gaming tools. Moreover, 5D supports and promotes interoperability.

- Interoperability of data and communications. Most CAFM/IWMS systems are becoming interoperable. There are several new software applications that are facilitating interoperability, including:

  Google. Google is expanding its services to include data and application sharing on a worldwide basis. One pertinent example for the architecture, engineering, and construction **(AEC)**/FM industries is how BIMStorm[6] uses Google as a key component.

---

[6] BIMStorm, developed by Onuma Inc., an architectural firm and software development company, is a dynamic collaborative process whereby professions collaborate in real time on the Internet. It has implications for the convergence of GIS, FM, and BIM.

FIGURE 1.7 5D cloud-based, technology mashup platform of gaming, GIS, and BIM.
Reproduced by permission of scream!point

BIMStorm™ (Figure 1.8). One critical lesson that BIMStorm teaches is that many team members utilizing a vast array of technologies can collaborate on very large projects without explicit communication, direction, delegation, or technology integration. The BIMStorm accelerates design and analysis by engaging architects, engineers, contractors, developers, building owners, urban planners, code officials, lawyers, insurers, and other building industry professionals. The strength of the BIMStorm is mobilizing a team to utilize a wide range of tools that directly address the specific needs of the project. BIMStorm allows all the experts to collaborate in real-time decision making. This collaboration allows the team to spot problems and identify patterns and trends as the project progresses and make real-time corrections. External experts can view the project data while the design evolves without knowing the technology tool sets used by the designers. BIMStorm extends both interoperable data and technology to include interoperable design and communication processes.

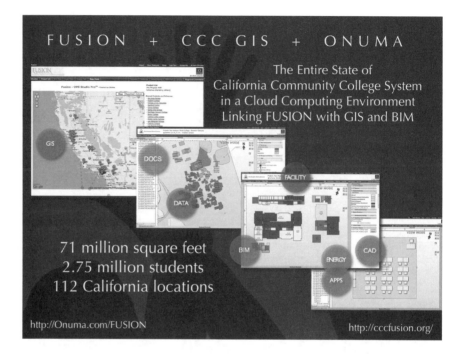

FIGURE 1.8 BIMStorm real-time interoperable collaboration throughout the design process.

Reproduced by permission of FUSION+CCC GIS+ONUMA. Linking facility data to BIM and GIS. Onuma, Inc. and the Foundation for California Community Colleges

MS SharePoint. This collaboration application is the PowerPoint equivalent to document management. While it is useful as a document-sharing device, its greatest value will be making collaborative document sharing as commonplace as PowerPoint presentations.

Newforma. The Newforma suite of products provides interoperability of information and processes across many FM activities throughout the life cycle of the facility. The Newforma Project Center application is the first step in integrating data and processes for AEC/FM projects. The current focus of the tool set is on project Information management for the AEC industry. The interoperability development track for most CAFM/IWMS systems is toward integrating data and processes via workflow tools. Newforma accomplishes both data and process interoperability through application and data integration. Some of the interoperability is achieved through effective project information management **(PIM)** (Figure 1.9). Newforma captures the information created throughout planning, design, procurement, construction, commissioning, and operation of a facility, as well as the relationships between the disparate pieces of information. Newforma provides tools for exchanging files and integrating project communication between all AEC/FM parties in real time. The introduction of real-time integration and mobility capability is another example of 5D (adding the time component to the facility information

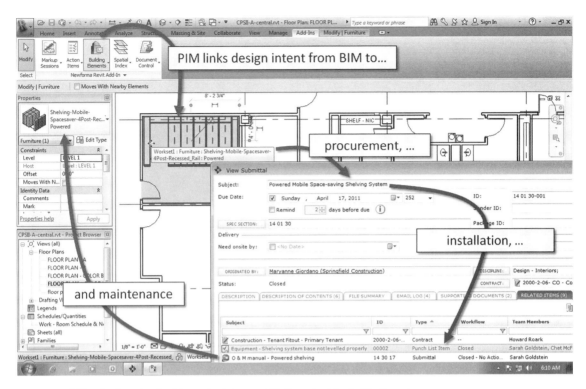

FIGURE 1.9 PIM technology showing information interoperability throughout the facility life cycle.
Reproduced by permission of Newforma

model). This kind of interoperability enables better decision making through-out the facility life cycle.

- Seamless collaboration using many technology tools, some of which will be integrated directly with the building infrastructure and the assets within the building (see Figure 1.10). Some examples are:
  - Convergence of phones, e-mail, IM, blogs, **wikis**, and searches.
  - MIT's Oxygen project.
  - Convergence of technology and furniture to create collaborative workspaces.
  - Tablet PCs and smartphones.
  - Integration of GPS, RFID, motes, nanotechnology, and artificial intelligence (AI) to interactively link assets into the collaboration process.
  - Social networks.
  - Cloud computing and cloud streaming.
  - Real-time translation—both aural and visual (Nuance, Google Goggles, Word Lens).
  - Web for the Illiterate—Web navigation that does not require the ability to read.

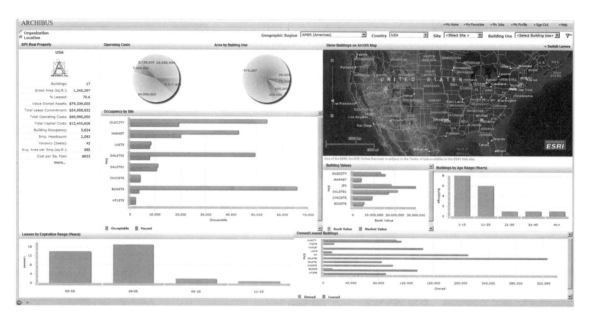

FIGURE 1.10 Strategic Master Planning showing the integration of multiple data sources, types, and technologies.
Reproduced by permission of ARCHIBUS

ADDITIONAL RESOURCES

APPA—Leadership in Educational Facilities, www.appa.org

GSA—General Services Administration, www.gsa.gov

IFMA—International Facility Management Association, www.ifma.org

BIMStorm—www.onuma.com/services/BimStorm.php

MIT Oxygen project—Bringing abundant computation and communication, as pervasive and free as air, naturally into people's lives, http://oxygen.lcs.mit.edu

MIT Technology Review, www.technologyreview.com

Stanford University CIFE—Center for Integrated Facility Engineering, http://cife.stanford.edu/

Building Information Modeling

2

Louise A. Sabol

INTRODUCTION

Building information modeling (BIM) is a software technology gaining rapid acceptance throughout the architecture, engineering, and construction (AEC) industry. BIM provides a visually and dimensionally accurate three-dimensional digital representation of a building (Figure 2.1). It also is a database, offering the capability to track data attributes for the components that comprise the building model.

Building information models describe the three-dimensional geometry, objects, and attributes of a physical facility. The core of BIM is the building geometry, but BIM also is a structured information base of nongraphic data that provides detailed information about the building components. In the building information model, a wall exists as a wall, a boiler is a boiler—all objects have accurate 3D geometry and attributes. They can be sorted, counted, and queried. BIM is a significant advancement in technology over CAD, the software for drawing and documentation that has been in use for over 20 years (Figure 2.2). Current development and use of BIM resides primarily in the design sector, and increasingly among contractors and builders.

Because BIM is a data application with the inherent capability to affiliate data fields with the objects that comprise the model, it facilitates a wide range of capabilities

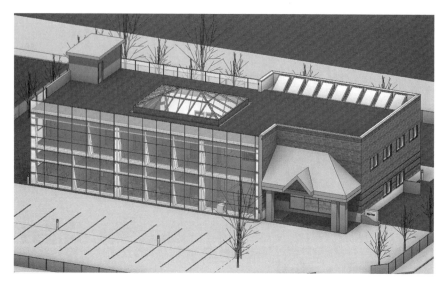

FIGURE 2.1 A building
information model.

*Reproduced by permission of
Design + Construction Strategies*

over the building life cycle, including quantity take-offs, cost estimating, construction simulation, space and asset management, and energy analyses, along with a plethora of other applications.

BIM can also incorporate parametric capabilities that allow components in a model to have attributes or parameters that define relationships with other components. For example, a door object will be dependent on, or relate to, a wall object. An effective BIM application manages the relationships of all components embedded in a model, along with their individual characteristics. This can be a very powerful tool for expediting change management.

Aside from being a powerful data application, BIM technology has the potential to enable fundamental changes in project delivery, promising to support a more integrated, efficient process. As a highly collaborative, data-rich environment, BIM has the inherent capability to reduce costs and promote efficiencies in the following manner:

- **Early decision making**. BIM allows earlier evaluation of building performance so that decisions and changes can be made with a reduced impact to time and costs.
- **Improved accuracy**. The accuracy of the model fosters more effective communication between the diverse parties involved in building projects and reinforces understanding. This reduces errors and changes throughout the

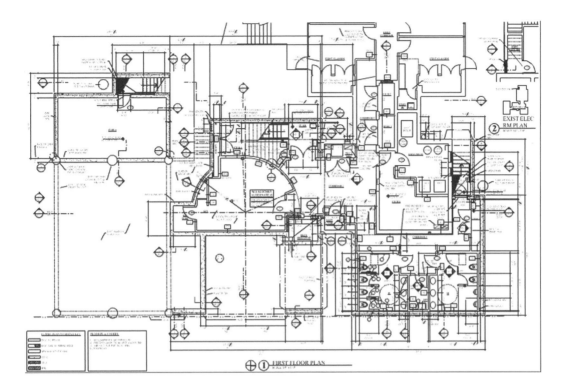

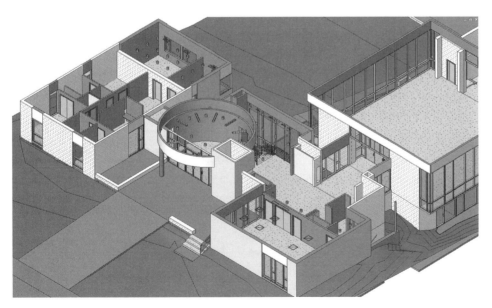

FIGURE 2.2 Traditional CAD documents (top) are difficult to interpret. A 3D BIM (bottom) provides an improved means of describing a building, leading to improved process efficiencies.

Reproduced by permission of Design + Construction Strategies

design and construction process. The parametric capabilities of BIM allow for the consistent, coordinated representation of the model in all views and drawing outputs.

■ **Rapid quantification**. The model can automatically generate quantities and report on data, producing estimates and workflows more efficiently and quickly than conventional processes.

■ **Robust analytics**. BIM executes complex analysis, including such tasks as clash detection, scheduling and sequencing (termed *4D modeling*), energy analysis, clarifying decision making, resolving issues, and producing less process delay.

■ **Improved project delivery**. BIM provides the capability to deliver a more coherent, structured, accurate, and complete body of data at project turnover.

BIM is a complex technology based on a collaborative approach to project production and facilities management. Organizations intent on deploying and leveraging BIM fully will need to evaluate and adopt new business processes in addition to the technology. Sharing, integrating, tracking, and maintaining a coherent building information model will affect all processes and participants that interact with that data.

BIM FOR FACILITIES MANAGEMENT

BIM has been used most extensively in design and construction. Its adoption for facilities management (FM) is still in its earliest stages, and software technologies to support BIM in FM have yet to emerge, whereas in AEC, BIM authoring applications such as Autodesk Revit and Bentley Microstation have established significant footholds in professional practice. There is no institutionalized "best practice" for using BIM in the FM sector, although facilities professionals are developing and instituting BIM guidelines and standards for their organizations.

The use of any software technology, including BIM, within facilities management varies depending on the organizational mission and the requirements of the facilities infrastructure supporting it. The informational needs of most FM organizations are also quite diverse. An alphabet soup of enterprise data systems—computer-aided facility management (CAFM), computer-aided design (CAD), integrated workplace management system (IWMS), computerized maintenance management systems (CMMS), enterprise resource planning (ERP), enterprise asset management (EAM)—along with stand-alone software applications like spreadsheets currently support a wide range of information requirements in the facilities management arena.

Facility managers are continually faced with the challenge of improving and stan-dardizing the quality of the information they have at their disposal, in order to meet day-to-day operational needs, as well as providing reliable data to building owners for life-cycle management and ongoing capital planning. An emerging technology, BIM is poised to offer a new level of functionality for managing buildings and the physical assets within them, in addition to similar benefits for FM, compelling firms in the building management industry to rapidly adopt BIM.

The business needs within a facilities management organization have very different requirements, workflows, and **users** than the AEC business needs for design and construction projects. As buildings become strategic assets in addition to financial assets, data retrieval to track spending and building performance is increas-ingly important. Aspects of building performance that can be monitored within a building information model may include work orders, space allocations, asset management, energy efficiency, security operations, and many other activities. Priorities for what is to be tracked in a BIM will vary with the organization. Although BIM authoring applications do not natively support facilities management, BIM can potentially be leveraged to facilitate many building life-cycle requirements, some of which include:

- **BIM templates for efficient project development**. Organizations that have well-developed project standards can foster significant efficiencies in proj-ect development and execution by providing smart BIM templates to project teams (Figure 2.3). These customized templates can automate the population of BIMs with project-specific program data that specify space and/or asset requirements. Hospitals, retail establishments, hotels, and corporate offices are some of the many organizations that can leverage standards with BIM, thereby reducing the many inefficiencies of manual cross-checking and verifi-cation that are prevalent during project development.
- **Regularized project delivery**. Project BIMs can be defined and developed to incorporate organizational data to support facilities management data needs after project turnover. COBie2[1] offers one framework for organizing building information delivery at turnover (Figure 2.4). Organizations might also choose to develop more specific mechanisms to meet their defined needs using vari-ous means, some of which include BIM software add-in applications.
- **Space management**. BIM incorporates 3D spaces and objects as well as attributes for these components. It can accommodate custom space manage-ment requirements and space measurement rules. BIM applications

---

[1] Construction Operations Building Information Exchange (COBie); see www.wbdg.org/tools/cobiex.php.

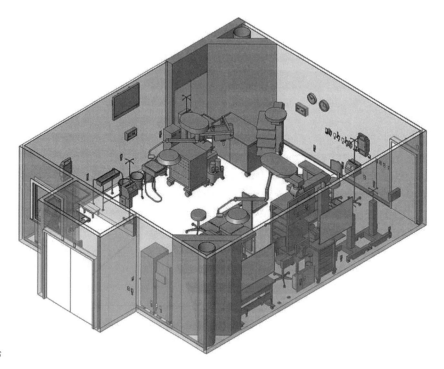

FIGURE 2.3 3D Template for an operating room (BIM data from Military Health Systems' project templates, www .wbdg.org).

Reproduced by permission of Design + Construction Strategies

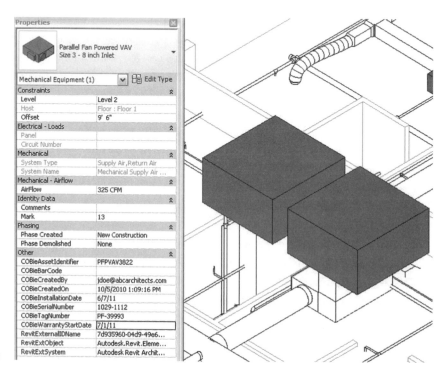

FIGURE 2.4 BIM mechanical component and COBie data.

Reproduced by permission of Design + Construction Strategies

can also be extended to offer additional capabilities such as automated rules checking. Also, BIM offers a more intuitive display of space layouts, supporting better management and communication of space assignments and change scenarios (Figure 2.5).

- **Visualization**. BIM's powerful capabilities for visualization, along with its extended capabilities to display potential changes over time (4D BIM), can effectively communicate critical building issues, especially in regard to scheduling and sequencing (Figure 2.6). Additional BIM decision support capabilities include clash detection, rules checking and validation, change tracking over time, and animated walkthroughs within the building model.
- **Energy and sustainability management**. Organizations are facing greater demand to increase the energy efficiency and sustainability of their facilities. BIM is well positioned to support a range of analytics, from conceptual energy analysis (Figure 2.7) to detailed engineering. It also can provide a means to track data and component information required for achieving a certification of sustainability for a building (LEED).
- **Emergency management/security**. Since BIM provides an accurate three-dimensional representation of a building, it can assist in analyzing and planning for emergency response requirements and security measures. Capabilities to include 3D human agents extend the potential for using BIM

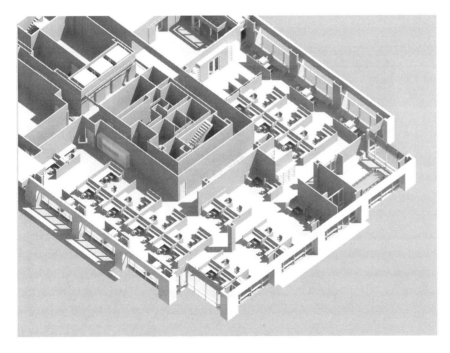

FIGURE 2.5 Spatial BIM model with furniture assets.

Reproduced by permission of Design + Construction Strategies

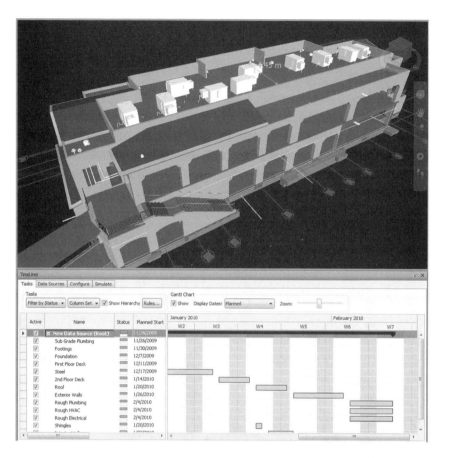

FIGURE 2.6 Autodesk Navisworks software 4D Timeline schedule feature linking BIM with project schedule.

Reproduced by permission of Design + Construction Strategies

FIGURE 2.7 Thermal analysis model created using Autodesk Ecotect.

Reproduced by permission of Design + Construction Strategies

to analyze how dynamic flow of people within a facility will change depending on an event and the configuration of the physical environment (Figure 2.8). This can assist with evaluating exit corridors and choke points, evaluating blast zones and setbacks, and establishing surveillance camera cones of vision, among other uses.

■ **Display of real-time data.** Some of the newest technologies being developed for BIM applications incorporate the capability to display real-time data analysis gathered from sensors, directly on the geometry of the building model (Figure 2.9). This powerful capability not only allows for more intuitive feedback from an analysis (such as displaying lighting levels, or temperature readings in a color range) but stands to position BIM as a 3D visual portal capable of accessing both static and dynamic data on building components.

FM BIM will, without a doubt, need to integrate with multiple enterprise data systems, including existing facilities systems, geographic information systems, and even ERP systems. BIM will need to coexist with current CAD systems for some time to come. Organizations will need to develop BIM deployment plans and organizational standards to set the groundwork for successful deployments of the technology. BIM applications will also need to be more versatile for FM use,

FIGURE 2.8 Simulation of human movement in a 3D model environment.
Reproduced by permission of Autodesk Labs, Project Geppetto

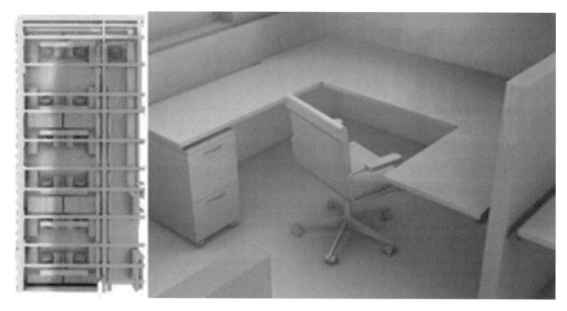

FIGURE 2.9 Temperature sensor data displayed on a BIM model of an office building.
Reproduced by permission of Azam Khan, Autodesk Research

incorporate different functionality and more data-centric facilities than the software employed by AEC practitioners. There is a critical need for a methodology and BIM definition that supports the rapid creation of BIM models for existing facilities. These are not design or construction models, but 3D visual data entities that support the information and workflow requirements of existing facilities with agility.

Laser scanning is an emerging technology that can serve to accurately capture the physical geometries of existing buildings into data files called *point clouds*. To support this data, many new and increasingly sophisticated software applications are also being developed that can interpret laser scanned point cloud data into surfaces and objects, thus helping to speed the workflow for developing accurate and realistic 3D building models. Laser scanning can accurately capture complex geometries, such as piping runs, mechanical equipment room layouts, and other as-built conditions that would take enormous and often prohibitive manual efforts to document.

New developments for FM BIM might include the development of rule sets to support improved information validation. These data sets would help automate BIM model checking, such as validating a delivered project model against the project program; or evaluating exiting in the model against code requirements, among other use cases.

Also on the development horizon are BIM server applications. These technologies would extend beyond the current BIM authoring applications, with functionality to support, distribute, and manage BIM on an enterprise basis; capabilities to manage multiple building models; and to provide support at an enterprise level for multiple users, administer secure access, manage updates and version control, distribute multiple potential locations, and provide capabilities to exchange data with external enterprise information systems. Commercial software applications and tools that support building information modeling for FM are rapidly evolving. Sources for more information on current offerings can be found on webzines, technical conferences, and blogs.[2]

STANDARDS AND DATA EXCHANGE

Standards for data exchange in the building and facilities industry are undergoing development in order to support new information workflows and enabling technologies such as BIM. The National Building Information Model Standard **(NBIMS)**, under the direction of the buildingSMART alliance (**bSa**; see Additional Resources), is developing open standards to guide adoption and use of the technology. This guidance aims to establish standard definitions for building information exchanges.

Within the NBIMS efforts, several core components are being developed. Among these developments are *industry foundation classes* or **IFCs**, which are an open data format intended to facilitate the transfer and integrity of information between intelligent building models and the information systems that play a role in building management. The bSa advocates the IFC format for BIM data exchange since it is a vendor-independent, open standard format that offers a framework to accommodate the many interdisciplinary information exchanges occurring during the building life cycle. Figure 2.10 provides an example of an IFC format BIM.

Building information models are the containers of data for a physical facility. The bSa standards initiatives are directed toward defining all of the information streams that will make the information model relevant to the facilities organizations for their business uses, from space planning to energy management and beyond. NBIMS is developing sets of data exchange requirements termed *IFC model view definitions* or MVDs. These are subsets of the IFC schema and detail specific sets of exchange requirements, such as a structural exchange.[3]

---

[2] AECbytes (www.aecbytes.com), an online webzine authored by Lachmi Khemlani, is one such source. Of note, this resource has reviewed BIM for FM software which provides a good comparison of current applications on the market with varying capabilities for FM. See www.aecbytes.com/feature/2011/BIMforFM.html.

[3] See the buildingSMART web site (http://buildingsmart.com/standards/ifc) for additional information on IFC standards, development, and use.

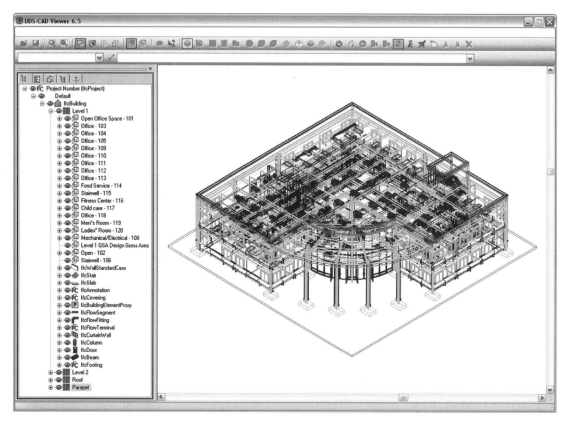

FIGURE 2.10 IFC-format building information model (displayed in an IFC viewing application).
Reproduced by permission of Model by Design + Construction Strategies

The Construction Operations Building Information Exchange (COBie) is one notable bSa initiative to improve project data delivery to owners/operators. COBie is a framework for organizing data developed and accumulated during the course of a building project for delivery to facilities owners and operators involved in life-cycle management. The COBie development project is evolving under the direction of the Engineer Research and Development Center (ERDC), U.S. Army Corps of Engineers, and is now in its second major version release: COBie2.

Although COBie may eventually provide a structure for the seamless transfer of data from BIM applications to FM data systems (IWMS, CAFM, or CMMS systems), in today's practice, COBie relies on organizing data in a series of structured and related spreadsheets (diagrammed in Figure 2.11). COBie information is compiled during different phases of a project by multiple participants—architects, engineers, constructors, specifiers, fabricators, and others. Only some of

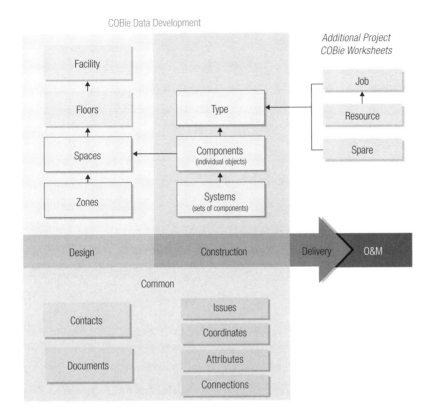

COBie Data Development

Additional Project
COBie Worksheets

FIGURE 2.11 COBie organizational framework. BIM authoring applications affiliate data with model geometry for certain COBie components (boxes with borders).
Reproduced by permission of Design + Construction Strategies

the data required in a typical COBie deliverable is, or can be, developed within a BIM authoring application.

Frameworks for organizing data for building projects have been around for years but have increased in importance as we progress with BIM and the need to regularize and structure building information we develop and manage with technology. UniFormat is emerging as a significant classification structure for specifying building information in a model.[4] BIM applications are including default capabilities to specify UniFormat codes for model components.

CHALLENGES OF BIM FOR FM

BIM is undergoing rapid adoption in the AEC industry but is still a young technology. As it has yet to be adopted to any great extent in facilities management, there

---

[4] See the Construction Specification Institute's web site (www.csinet.org/Home-Page-Category/Formats/UniFormat .aspx) for more information on UniFormat.

are many open issue for consideration with BIM, and more than a few technology and process issues to resolve.

Current BIM utilization reflects its primary focus—to design and construct a building project. Commercial BIM software tools are sophisticated applications, with functionality that is directed toward compiling or "authoring" a detailed information base from which a project can be understood, executed, and completed. BIM applications include many features to assist designers and constructors. Data entry, retrieval, and reporting—important tools for managing facilities—are generally ancillary in these authoring applications and not necessarily easy to set up or intuitive to execute.

Design and construction workflows are a small part of the facilities management practice. Indeed, the functionality of current BIM authoring software will not be useful to a broad portion of the facilities workforce. Software applications that fully leverage BIM information for facilities will most likely diverge in function from the authoring tools currently gaining acceptance in AEC practice.

BIMs delivered at project completion are a rich information source for FM, but not all of the information is valuable on a day-to-day basis within the broad range of an FM practice, where data retrieval, change management, and tracking costs and work activity are critical. Facility managers will need to detail and prioritize their information requirements—both to delineate the scope of project BIM deliverables and to define what to include in their FM BIMs, depending on what can reasonably be maintained over time based on available resources and workflows.

As-built drawings have often been required at project turnover, but this information has not necessarily been accurate at completion. BIM's effectiveness for supporting the full facilities life cycle for a building requires an accurate deliverable. The requirement for an accurate and complete BIM needs to be included in the contract for all project participants and vetted by the owner/operator throughout the project and at turnover.

Maintaining building information models will require organizations to develop organizational BIM guidelines that detail project BIM delivery requirements as well as define their usage within the facility practice. Deploying BIM within organizations that have many existing buildings in their portfolios will require a coherent road map and strategy as well. Many organizations maintain inconsistent inventories of building information that may include CAD, scanned drawings, physical drawings, and point cloud files. Throwing BIM into the mix without a strategy would be wasting a valuable information source and technology.

There are many functional details and commercial software technologies that need further evolution to fully support BIM use in FM. Central among these are software applications to maintain and manage BIM for organizational access— providing features such as versioning, user access and privilege control, and security. BIM requirements for data interoperability with enterprise systems is a complex topic, since facilities information systems are widely divergent, and will be a key issue with deploying BIM within FM.

For facilities organizations that choose to maintain an active inventory of BIM files in the native format of BIM authoring applications, the cost of BIM software may be a factor to consider. Also note that BIM application vendors generally release new updates and revisions of their software packages on a fairly frequent cycle, often annually. These facts may not dovetail well with the more static needs and budget constraints of an FM practice. Maintaining the currency of BIM files over time will be an issue for consideration for FM. Organizations will have to periodically, if not regularly, upgrade their BIM files to more current versions (if using commercial BIM software) since many vendors do not support backward compatibility between software versions. Maintaining currency of software versions to sync with outside contractors can be another hurdle for organizations that have a lengthy procurement cycle or that choose to maintain older BIM authoring software.

Many facilities organizations find it challenging to keep their CAD plans up to date, if they indeed have a consistent and up-to-date inventory in CAD format. Maintenance of a BIM inventory will be no easier. BIM brings along the additional challenge of updating affiliated data and object relationships, along with any (3D) geometry modifications. BIM authoring software is very complex, more so than CAD, requiring advanced user skills to master and employ. Facilities organizations will need to develop staffing, training, and perhaps outsourcing requirements to support the technology use for their particular practices.

Current facilities organizations have many sources of data, often overlapping. The goal of integrating BIM will not be to add another information system but to help regularize data delivery, clarify data ownership, and ease access to validated data. Technologies and work processes to support and fully integrate BIM with the range of applications and data repositories within facilities organizations will be an ongoing challenge as the technology is adopted.

Many questions have yet to be resolved with BIM technology in FM practice. For example, should an organization maintain a discreet, live BIM and extract, translate, and load data from it to external enterprise data systems, or will BIM pull information from a relational database from an existing enterprise system?

How can those links be automated and easily managed? What software tools and systems can best leverage BIM for FM? Can BIM offer a new, intuitive means to unify disparate building information streams into a single, visual information portal?

BIM is a robust information technology, offering a lot of potential for facilities management. It remains to be seen if it will be the single, game-changing application for FM that it promises to be in the design and construction arena. The next few years will see facilities professionals and solutions vendors work in multiple arenas to leverage BIM's promise in order to deliver better information management to FM.

FM BIM IN PRACTICE: HEALTH CARE BUILDING CONSORTIUM'S BIM INITIATIVES

Some efforts to extend BIM into facilities management are focused toward improving building information delivery at project turnover and defining standards, workflows, and tools to accommodate those exchanges.

The Healthcare BIM Consortium (HBC) has been created by health care owners[5] with the goal of finding and developing solutions for interoperability in order to fully support the Facility Life Cycle Management (FLCM). A central focus of this effort will be to leverage BIM across the building life cycle and facilitating a seamless data transfer of relevant data across disciplines and among stakeholders in the process.

Health care facilities are some of the most complex building types to build and maintain. In the current project development process, there are significant choke points in the process, where data is not easily exchanged between project participants. BIM is viewed as an enabling technology that can support an efficient, consolidated data framework for developing and managing health care facilities information for the full life cycle (Figure 2.12). Extending BIM for facilities management will involve capabilities to seamlessly pass organizational requirements into the building information model; develop, analyze, and check the model during project development; and, at turnover, deliver a robust, integrated BIM from the project team to the owner/operator.

One of the most powerful capabilities of BIM is its potential to rapidly provide an accurate, detailed representation of the inventory of a building, its components,

---

[5] As of March 2011, owner participants include: Department of Defense's Military Health System, Kaiser Permanente, Department of Veterans Affairs, Sutter Health, and Mayo Clinic.

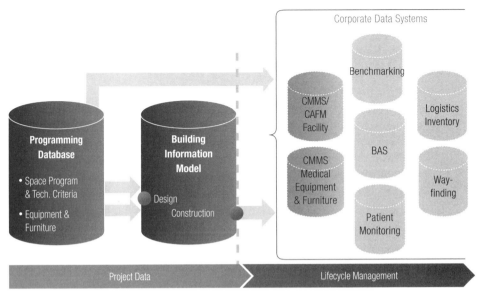

FIGURE 2.12 Data flow from health care planning systems to BIM and, at project turnover, to corporate systems. Choke points for data exchange currently exist during the project phase, where data is imported to BIM and at turnover, where information is delivered to the facility manager.
Reproduced by permission of Russ Manning/DoD MHS-PPMD

and affiliated data. Hospital construction projects typically consist of hundreds of rooms, each containing a substantial amount of equipment and furnishings. Automating the population of a building information model can save an enormous amount of project development time and also provide the capabilities to validate data, quantify project progress, and deliver complete and detailed project data to project participants and, ultimately, the client.

The Department of Veterans Affairs (VA) and the Department of Defense's Military Health System (MHS) are exploring automated tools to export data from their facilities planning programs into BIM models. These BIM add-in applications will also validate the model at any time during the design process against the project program. One BIM vendor[6] has developed a BIM add-on application that provides users with the capability to upload equipment and room data from the project program into the BIM authoring software. Each room specified in the program has a list of equipment that is required to be contained within it. The software

---

[6] Autodesk's SEPS tool is available from Autodesk Government as an add-in to Revit.

assists the BIM user in adding the required room to the project model, and then populates the room with equipment objects required by the program. The tool also provides the capability to run validation checks at any time to highlight rooms that might be out of compliance with the program and itemize missing equipment.

Figures 2.13 through 2.16 show a few snapshots of functions accomplished with the SEPS tool within Autodesk Revit. The VA and MHS use a medical facility planning data program called SEPS, which develops a detailed program for the new building. The SEPS tool reads this program's list of rooms and required equipment and specifications into Revit. Figure 2.13 shows a list of the program rooms that have been read into the workspace. The user selects rooms in the BIM and queues the SEPS tool to populate the space with the required equipment objects and specifications. Figure 2.14 shows how a compliance check, run with the tool, would highlight rooms that have the correct equipment objects. Figure 2.15 shows a 3D view of equipment objects (mass geometry) that have been placed in the BIM. In Figure 2.16, a rendered 3D view of an operating room in the BIM shows where, later in the project, initial mass objects have been replaced with more detailed versions.

A full life-cycle BIM will offer numerous benefits to facility owners. As BIM matures, additional workflows similar to those offered by the SEPS tool will be introduced into

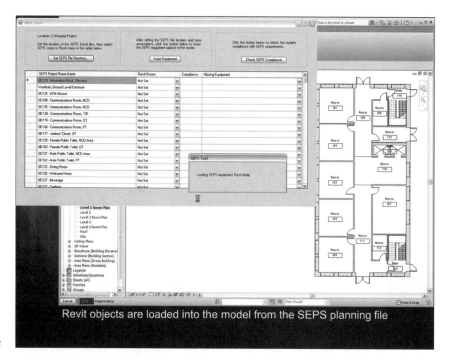

FIGURE 2.13 Room listings required by the project program and affiliated equipment. Displayed in the Revit SEPS tool interface.

Reproduced by permission of Design + Construction Strategies

Revit objects are loaded into the model from the SEPS planning file

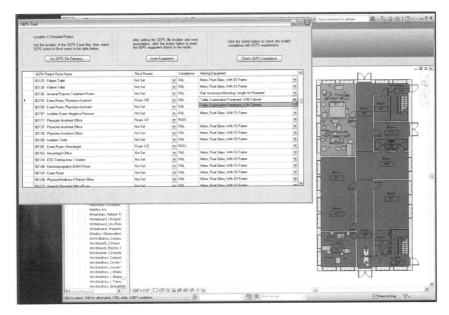

FIGURE 2.14 SEPS tool compliance check interface menu, with color-coded results displayed within the BIM application.

Reproduced by permission of Design + Construction Strategies

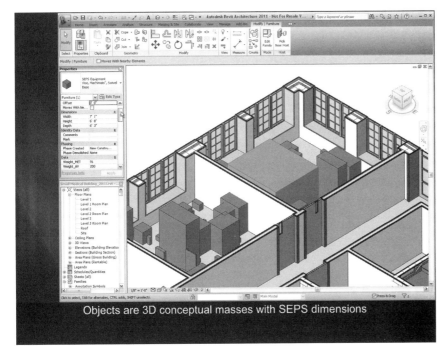

Objects are 3D conceptual masses with SEPS dimensions

FIGURE 2.15 3D view showing equipment placed in the project model's rooms as mass objects, with data attributes attached (from the project program).

Reproduced by permission of Design + Construction Strategies

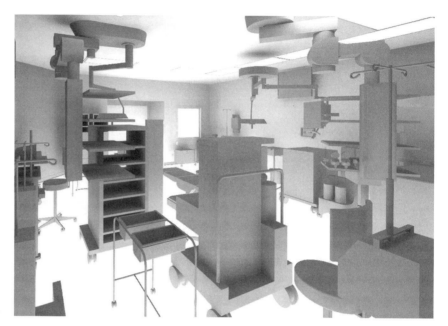

FIGURE 2.16 3D rendering of detailed equipment model, which can be refined as the project progresses.
Reproduced by permission of Design + Construction Strategies

practice. BIM's capability for automating workflows can reduce hundreds of hours of tedious data entry and cross-checking by the project team. It also provides quicker and more reliable validation of the project data model contributing greatly to improved project efficiencies.

ADDITIONAL RESOURCES

buildingSMART, http://buildingsmart.com/.

Construction Operations Building Information Exchange (COBie), Whole Building Design Guide, www.wbdg.org/resources/cobie.php.

International Alliance for Interoperability (www.iai-interoperability.org), including the IFC, Industry Foundation Classes specifications: www.iai-international.org/Model/IFC(ifcXML)Specs.html.

National 3D-4D Building Information Modeling Program, U.S. Government Services Administration, www.gsa.gov/portal/content/105075.

OmniClass, A Strategy for Classifying the Built Environment, www.omniclass.org.

Open BIM Standards for Communication Throughout the Facilities Industry. BuildingSMART alliance, a council of the National Institute of Building Sciences, www.buildingsmartalliance.org/.

Veterans Administration Building Information Lifecycle Vision, www.cfm.va.gov/til/bim/BIMGuide/lifecycle.htm.

Building Automation and Control Systems

3

Terry Hoffmann

Building automation and control systems are an important part of mechanical and electrical systems. In order to understand these systems, their functionality, and the benefits they deliver, it is necessary to investigate their evolution, their current state, and what the future may hold for building automation systems.

HISTORY OF BUILDING AUTOMATION SYSTEMS

The history of building automation and control systems begins in the early 1970s. It coincided with the first great energy crisis in North America, as well as the recognition that well-established electrical and electronic control systems could be improved with emerging digital technology. At that time, control systems typically involved a myriad of wires that snaked back to a central console and had either a selector switch that connected the correct thermocouple to an indicator dial or a relay to start or stop the systems connected to the control system. This presented little opportunity for energy management as it is known today.

The introduction of systems that utilized computer programming to start and stop equipment on command was a major step toward reducing commercial energy bills. These systems commonly were referred to as energy management and control systems (EMCSs) because that's what they were capable of doing. In the 1970s, the most common method for heating, ventilating, and air-conditioning

(HVAC) control was pneumatic, which was fundamentally incompatible with early computer-based control systems.

Throughout the 1970s, EMCSs were installed in large commercial spaces, such as office towers, airports, arenas, and hospitals. In addition to the benefits of reduced electrical consumption, less manual labor was required to check values and to start or stop equipment. This was especially welcome in high-rise facilities, where the distance between the facility manager's office and a mechanical system might not be measured in feet, but rather by floors. Most early systems used process control computers and special operating systems. In the late 1970s, EMCSs migrated toward the use of minicomputers (Figure 3.1).

The 1980s ushered in a major change in the method of monitoring and controlling mechanical and electrical systems within buildings. It marked the beginning of the direct digital control (DDC) revolution that replaced pneumatic control methods with the programmability and precision of digital control. The first-generation DDC systems were large and sometimes difficult to maintain, but, in general, the early adopters of this technology were rewarded with systems that required less maintenance and were easier to fine-tune than their pneumatic counterparts.

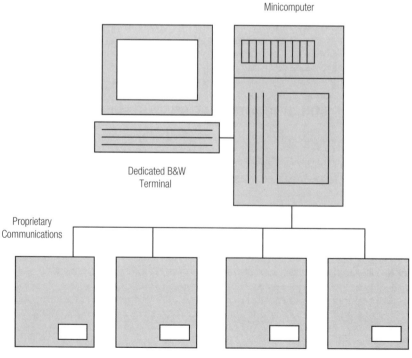

FIGURE 3.1 Energy management and control systems, circa 1978.

Although the actuation of these systems still was accomplished by pneumatic actuators, the advances in digital-to-analog conversion devices increased the precision of the control signals. The additional benefits of DDC included extra inputs and outputs that could be tied to the system for controlling lighting systems and electrical switchgear or monitoring fire and security devices. EMCSs were becoming building automation systems **(BASs)**.

By the end of the 1980s, there were major advances in the ability to integrate multiple systems into a central workstation, along with the refinement of color graphic terminals to display representations of floor plans and system schematics. Additionally, user programming languages emerged that allowed facility professionals to harness the power of automated systems without having to employ programmers from the manufacturer. The hardware platforms continued to be dependent on minicomputers for large systems and high-end workstations, while personal computers with special operating systems were the platform used for smaller systems. Very small properties were served by energy management systems that were small boxes providing local scheduling and energy optimization functions (Figure 3.2). The EMCSs were connected to a central location by telephone lines for alarm and monitoring purposes. Early adopters of BASs included

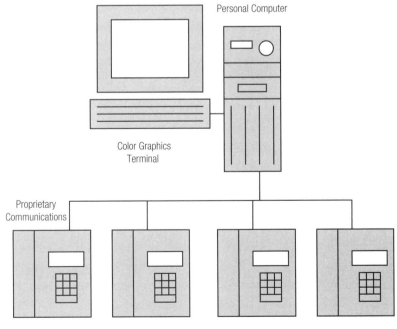

FIGURE 3.2 Small building automation system, circa 1986.

hospitals, commercial real estate customers, school districts, municipal buildings, airports, and universities.

The 1990s were notable for the introduction and refinement of two key BAS concepts:

1. *Connectivity*. Having systems and devices from one vendor accessible from a workstation provided by another vendor.
2. *Open protocols*. A method for systems and devices to be interoperable.

Connectivity first was conceived by major manufacturers as a product differentiator when they realized that BASs needed to handle more than lighting, HVAC, fire alarm, and intrusion detection, and that customers were interested in selecting systems from a variety of suppliers, instead of only one supplier. Connectivity enabled a facility with an emergency generator to transmit information from the generator to the BAS to monitor critical functions and also trigger alarms in the case of failure. A simple binary input indicating a fault was not enough. Savvy users wanted to trend temperatures and pressures, calculate runtimes and integrate the unit into their maintenance management system. In many cases, the connectivity was designed to replicate vendor error codes so the facility operator at a remote workstation could call the equipment manufacturer service department to request service to be dispatched based on the code.

By this time, minicomputers were completely abandoned as BAS platforms. As the cost of controls decreased, controls manufacturers began to build and distribute application-specific controllers. Thus, the need to apply a single controller to multiple pieces of equipment due to the high cost of digital control components was no longer a limiting factor. Individual system controllers added a layer to the control network because it was still desirable for many of the supervisory tasks the DDC controllers handled to be on an area-wide or building-wide basis.

With this architecture in place, there was opportunity for widespread system connectivity. Manufacturers developed special gateways that could be custom programmed and they recruited manufacturers of associated systems to develop software to support the interaction. Manufacturers tested the functionality of the integration and created lists of approved or certified devices.

These certification lists became unwieldy when the number of software solutions that had to be tested and maintained mushroomed from dozens to hundreds. The solution to the problem was for the BAS supplier to open its field protocols and make them available for other suppliers to develop communication protocols that could be used between vendors. For example, a boiler manufacturer might have one daughter card for its controller to be sold and shipped for Johnson Controls

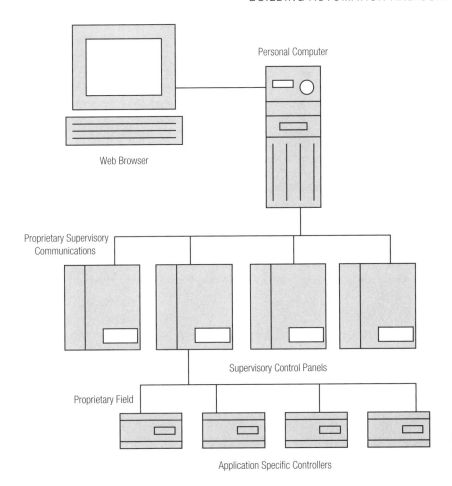

FIGURE 3.3 Building automation system circa 1995.

projects, another for Honeywell, and yet a third for Landis + Gyr. However, this had its drawbacks because resolving problems related to software and hardware updates simply were transferred to the device manufacturer.

In the end, it became obvious that the real opportunity for connectivity of all systems could best be achieved with industry developed standard protocols as the foundation for interoperability. This allowed devices from one manufacturer to connect to all automation systems. Interoperability became the goal of two organizations, with the BACnet and LonTalk protocols as the result.

BACnet was developed by the American Society for Heating, Refrigerating and Air-Conditioning Engineers (ASHRAE) and evolved into the de facto standard for connecting systems from multiple vendors into a common systems framework. It was issued in 1995 and immediately found popularity on university campus projects as well as multibuilding sites of large manufacturing concerns.

The LonTalk protocol and LonMark standards evolved from the hardware and software intellectual property of the Echelon Corp., based on its vision for a world where all devices would have access to an interoperable control network at a reasonable cost. Echelon recruited industry leaders from disciplines such as building automation, lighting control, industrial control, and food service into an international organization with the express purpose of creating device profiles and standard interoperability guidelines to ensure useful exchange of command, control and display information.

LonWorks devices designed following LonMark interoperability guidelines became the open systems standard for manufacturers seeking to control equipment from multiple vendors on the same field bus with a single building controller. The BACnet and LonTalk protocols have capabilities above and beyond those discussed here. The capabilities summarized in this chapter generally are accepted as their key strengths. These standards helped to drive building automation systems into smaller and more distributed properties like shopping malls, museums, and hotels. The 1990s also introduced Web browsers as an alternative method of accessing data, replacing many of the BAS workstations common in large applications.

As the twenty-first century arrived, BAS manufacturers started to use the open protocols developed in the 1990s and, more importantly, to use IP (Internet protocol) networks across business enterprises as the common vehicle for communication. This phenomenon generally is referred to as convergence. It transfers the burden of computer and network intelligence and understanding to the information technology (IT) department, and lets the facility manager concentrate on the task of operating the buildings. Convergence also leverages the standards from both domains to provide a better solution for the transfer of information from building systems to enterprise systems for use in operations planning and decision making. For example, real-time energy usage data could be integrated with information from the manufacturing and human resource systems through the enterprise accounting system to calculate the true cost of operating a company on a day-to-day basis.

Multiple changes in the way building automation systems are designed and built were required for this convergence to be realized. To make the user experience more like a Web browser, it was necessary for manufacturers to abandon the multiple workstation approach to the user interface and embrace a client/server methodology. This meant evaluating the functionality of supervisory controllers (the middle layer of the network architecture common in the 1990s) and adding capabilities for trending, scheduling, and other tasks formerly at the workstation level. To provide absolute compatibility with IP networks already in place, it was necessary for building automation systems to replace proprietary operating systems, proprietary communication protocols, and proprietary data storage methods with standards that the IT professionals were comfortable with and capable of maintaining. Finally, all major elements of the BAS network needed to be constructed and documented for use as an IT infrastructure component, not just a mechanical control device that mounted on a wall in the basement or penthouse equipment room.

More sophisticated controls are now available at lower costs because the cost of memory has decreased while the power of low-cost processors has increased. For example, high-tech, programmable, application-specific HVAC controllers now have the ability to provide advanced diagnostics to help facility managers identify key performance characteristics that impact both comfort and energy efficiency of zones being controlled. Another technological advancement is continuous adaptive tuning for control loops. Adaptive tuning takes key environmental values such as average outside air temperature and relative humidity into account when tuning the loop, thereby providing near-optimal tuning conditions regardless of the season. Continuous tuning means that tuning does not have to be commanded by an operator, but is implemented automatically by the controller as necessary. Some modern controllers have state-based algorithms that offer accuracy and reliability normally associated with high-end industrial control.

BUILDING AUTOMATION SYSTEMS TODAY

The past almost four decades of controls has greatly impacted the current state of controls. The original stated purpose of the BAS for saving energy and increasing productivity is greatly expanded, with the ability to integrate with many other systems across networks that literally span the globe. This ability to communicate vital systems information to the highest levels of the enterprise is the foundation for managing facilities. The latest BAS promise is best summarized as follows:

Building automation systems use current technology to provide safety for both occupants and assets. They contribute to the productivity of the enterprise by conserving energy and optimizing the efficiency of equipment throughout facilities and the people who are responsible for operating and maintaining them. They provide a foundation for sustainable programs and projects by providing the accurate and secure data required for decision making and verification.

These systems are likely to take the form as shown in Figure 3.4. Note that the networks illustrated here might be wired or wireless.

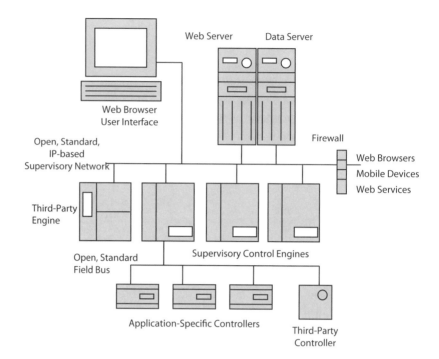

FIGURE 3.4 Building automation system.

BAS history reflects the current state of the market in terms of systems availability because there are a significant number of systems still used within buildings that were first installed in the 1980s and 1990s. As a result, most buildings have stand-alone systems from multiple vendors. They are under-instrumented and incapable of supporting the enterprise energy management and sustainability initiatives that are available and critical to today's operational models. In many cases, the systems were installed one piece at a time as the company grew over the years—much like a farmhouse that evolved from one room to a dozen rooms with no master plan. This means that global changes cannot easily be made to the control algorithms. For example, schedules must be maintained in multiple locations, demand-limiting programs do not include all significant shed-able loads, and multiple chilled water loops may be used.

As a result of these old and dysfunctional systems, many existing buildings are extremely inefficient. While most facility managers are capable of identifying waste and developing a plan to eliminate it, they do not have the tools or the capital to make much progress. Sometimes this is due to a lack of capital for system updates and improvements; other times, it is because the manufacturer of the original automation system provided no path for migration to the latest technologies they offer. Or it simply may be a case of not paying attention to every opportunity. For example, data centers and data closets consumed between 203.4 and 271.8 billion kilowatt-hours of electricity worldwide in 2010, which is equal to about 1.1 to 1.5 percent of total electricity usage.[1] However, only 30 percent of that energy ever touches a computer.

Within the United States, 75 percent of commercial building energy consumption is from lighting, space heating, cooling, and water heating. The remaining 25 percent of energy consumption is from ventilation, cooking, refrigeration, and operating office equipment.[2] In order to clearly understand sources of energy waste, buildings and systems need to be further instrumented as a first step to continuous improvement. Key performance indicators also need to be determined and closely measured. Key performance indicators serve as guidelines for decision makers to manage facilities in the most efficient manner and to benchmark for continuous improvement processes.

The answer to the energy waste and efficiency dilemma lies in the application of technology to attack specific needs unique to each facility, considering the construction, operation, and maintenance. To address the needs requires an evaluation of how important each need is, including the value it has to the organization. For example, a BAS should be purchased based on what the actual, quantified usefulness of the BAS will be to the organization.

It is certainly easy to pick one or two key issues that currently are receiving the greatest amount of attention in the trade and popular press and stop there. If that were the case, all systems decisions would be based on energy cost reduction and climate change reporting. However, modern technologies provide many more options. In addition to energy efficiency and sustainability, factors include:

- Reliability
- Compatibility
- Mobility
- Connectivity
- Scalability
- Security
- Interoperability

---

[1] J. Koomey, "Growth in Data Center Electricity Use 2005 to 2010." Oakland, CA: Analytics Press, August 1, 2011, www.analyticspress.com/datacenters.html.

[2] A. Swenson, "A Look at Commercial Buildings in 1995: Characteristics, Energy Consumption and Energy Expenditures." Department of Energy, Energy Information Administration, Office of Energy Markets and End Use, 1998.

- Flexibility
- Usability
- Maintainability

These factors actually may have more importance to the enterprise than the total dollars saved through energy efficiency improvements. Consider how vital a secure network is to the health of an organization. Mobile executives need to access information anywhere and at anytime from a wide variety of telephone and Web-based appliances. The rate of employee turnover in a particular geographic area may demand systems that are very easy to use and require minimal training. For many critical environments, there can be no substitute for the most reliable system available. Evaluating these issues is just as critical as calculating the simple payback on investments that promise reduced maintenance costs or energy consumption. Considering all these factors, appropriate technologies can be selected for systems implementation.

Four factors appear to be having the greatest impact on these issues:

- Harmonized standards
- Wireless technology
- Internet protocol (IP)-based control
- Fourth-generation mobile technology (4G)

As mentioned previously, harmonized standards for hardware, software, and communication, including standard protocols, provide the foundation for open, interoperable systems that allow facility managers to select best-of-breed hardware and software for use in their buildings. They enable future systems expansion with minimal additional outlays for network infrastructure, and provide a strategic foundation for future systems planning. Harmonized standards eliminate purchasing the second-best choice just because the best choice cannot communicate with the installed network.

Wireless technology provides a number of important benefits, including:

- Reduction of infrastructure cost.
- Reduction of maintenance cost.
- Reduction of move/change cost.
- Elimination of limitations (e.g., distance, location, mobility).

With the cost of copper wire increasing, it is easy to see how wireless connections to controllers from sensors, as well as wireless connections from controllers to supervisory engines, may provide reduced construction costs in many applications. However, the cost of wireless is not always more economical than wired solutions today. Additionally, the maintenance costs of systems can be lowered when the cost of troubleshooting poorly connected or severed wiring is taken into consideration. The use of wireless technology eliminates the tether between systems and operators that limits the use of mobile technologies for important user interface activities such as alarm notification and acknowledgment. Put simply, wireless networks provide the ultimate freedom to connect.

IP-based control enables so many technologies that it demands its own place on the list of important tools. Enterprise applications depend upon IP-connected Web services for the flow of critical information. Mobile workstations take advantage of the wireless IP infrastructure. Maintenance and operation of critical system elements such as electrical switchgear and chilled water systems are dependent on the IP knowledge of the IT staff. The reliability and availability of IP networks enable the interoperation of systems on a machine-to-machine basis. The standard IP-based Web-browsing capability on nearly every computing device provides ubiquitous access to the systems. The long-awaited adoption of Internet Protocol Version 6 (IPv6) promises to solve the problems associated with the current lack of IP addresses by expanding from 4 billion IP addresses available today with IPv4 to about 3.4×10^{38} IP addresses in the future.

4G wireless technology provides mobile users with advances in data rates and IP connectivity. Speeds from 100 Mbit/s (mobile) to 1 Gbit/s (stationary) are being specified. This facilitates the widespread use of advanced video and audio services as well as access to large amounts of cloud-based data by applications that reside on the mobile device. Recent advances in smartphone operating systems and the emergence of tablet computing devices have made these capabilities more important because end users are starting to rely on these applications instead of traditional desktop or laptop computers.

THE FUTURE OF BUILDING AUTOMATION SYSTEMS

Many technology leaders in the BAS industry suggest that the greatest benefits to users of automated building management and control systems will come through the extended use of new enterprise applications for functions such as:

- Enterprise energy optimization
  - Aggregation
  - Modeling
  - Demand limiting
  - Demand response

- Enterprise asset allocation and tracking
- Enterprise resource planning
- Enterprise sustainability validation
- Enterprise dashboards

In order to provide the greatest benefit to end users, these applications will require new network infrastructures that take advantage of concepts currently in development. It would take dozens of pages to describe these concepts, so perhaps it is better simply to provide a list of additional systems capabilities and applications that they could enable over the next several years.

Semantic technologies will allow systems to take commands from operators in their natural and spoken language, providing feedback to acknowledge the intended operation before proceeding. Context aware control allows the controller to judge the surroundings and conditions before proceeding with a particular action (aided by state-based control). Two examples of context aware controls for an air handling unit could be a Sunday April evening in Indianapolis, Indiana, and a Tuesday August afternoon in Phoenix, Arizona, during an ozone alert.

Ubiquitous access refers to the ability of any device, on virtually any global network, to authenticate and operate with an appropriate level of security and safety depending on the type of device being used by the requesting party. Some examples of devices include phones, laptops, servers, and home automation servers connected to digital televisions. User experience expands the concept of system usability beyond ease of use and the availability of context-sensitive help. Implemented correctly, it means that the interaction between system and BAS is truly user friendly.

The real value of systems interoperability and enterprise applications is greatly dependent on the ability of programmers to use mashups of information from different systems and devices to provide synergy. A mashup is a Web application that uses and combines data from multiple sources to create new services and applications. Thus, if a correlation is determined, the historical weather patterns in Lisbon, Portugal, for example, might be compared with data from the National Weather Service and information on the current atmospheric conditions to predict when to start a chiller in San Diego, California. Both cities have similar climates and represent significant opportunities for optimization.

The use of enterprise social software such as YouTube and Facebook actually might be of assistance to someone trying to locate an expert to quickly evaluate the degree of criticality for a mechanical equipment problem. User interest groups already exist on sites like LinkedIn, and many industry leaders follow their areas of interest on Twitter.

A natural question might be, "What is this going to look like?" The BAS of the future is likely to be comprised of very intelligent nodes, communicating wirelessly, that are capable of making informed decisions on their own (Figure 3.5). The BAS also will know when it is necessary to ask for information from other devices on the local network or escalate the search to the enterprise or Web level as the situation requires. Where higher levels of intelligence or data processing needs exist, these application and data servers may exist remotely in the cloud. Cloud-based computing promises greater economy of scale, better control over updates and maintenance, and the ability of users to pay for only what they use in a modular fashion.

CASE STUDY: AVE MARIA UNIVERSITY, NAPLES, FLORIDA

Ave Maria University, located in southwest Florida, is the first new Catholic university built in more than 40 years and is among the world's most technologically advanced educational institutions. By employing industry best practices, Ave Maria successfully converged 23 systems from IT to facility operations on a single IP network.

University officials, guided by the vice president of technology systems and engineering, had a unique vision for Ave Maria's technology division. The vice president sought to incorporate IT operations and facility operations into one group and to combine the university's IT infrastructure, fire, security, HVAC, and building

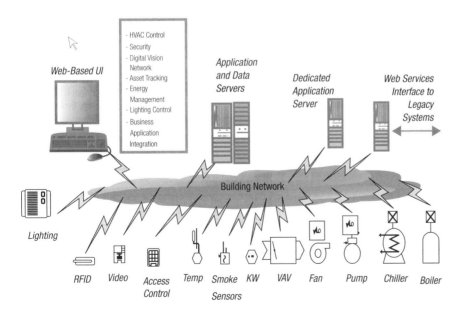

FIGURE 3.5 Integrated Enterprise Applications.

control systems on a common platform. To the vice president, convergence of these technologies made sense from both a construction and ongoing operations standpoint.

The convergence of the building automation system and the IT network, via IP-based control, has cost advantages in terms of installation and maintenance. A single cabling infrastructure is easier and cheaper to install than multiple proprietary networks for different building-related functions. Service costs for multiple networks would also be higher in order to maintain these different wiring systems, compared to a single network. In August 2007, it was estimated that the convergence already had avoided US$1.5 million in construction costs.

Management of campus operations, including facility systems and IT systems, was accomplished with just seven full-time employees. This compares to similar operations where as many as 24 employees are required to manage those same functions. According to the university's financial office, operating efficiencies free more resources for educating students.

At Ave Maria University, university leadership had the vision to combine the new university's IT and building systems groups to take full advantage of convergence. This resulted in reduced construction costs as well as reduced operational costs. The converged BAS-IT infrastructure allows Ave Maria University to be ready for future expansions and upgrades as new, emerging technologies enter the market to support even greater opportunities for efficiency.

ADDITIONAL RESOURCES
Books and Articles

B. Capehart, Handbook of Web-Based Energy Information and Control Systems (Lilburn, GA: Fairmont Press, 2011).

Computerworld Magazine, "The Computerworld Honors Program: Ave Maria University," 2008, www.cwhonors.org/viewCaseStudy2008.asp?NominationID=618.

T. Hoffmann, "Converging BAS with IT Architecture: Heating/Piping/Air Conditioning Engineering," March 1, 2008, http://hpac.com/bas-controls/converging_bas_architecture/.

Web Sites

ASHRAE—American Society of Heating, Refrigerating and Air-Conditioning Engineers, www.ashrae.org

BACnet International, www.bacnetinternational.org

CABA—Continental Automated Buildings Association, www.caba.org

LonMark International, www.LonMark.org

Roles of Geographic Information Systems in Facility Management

4

William P. Witts Jr.

ENHANCING FM CAPABILITIES WITH GIS

What is GIS? The term *GIS* is an acronym for **geographic information system**. As the term *information system* implies, a GIS is a software package that uses and/or stores various forms of data. Primarily, a GIS is used to store and analyze **geospatial** information.

GIS Technology

The use of GIS software has grown rapidly in recent decades because much of the information we use in computerized systems has a spatial component. Whether that spatial component is a parcel of land, a fire hydrant, or a road network, it can all be stored and analyzed through the use of a GIS. There are a variety of GIS software packages currently on the market. This chapter will not address any particular software package but rather focus on the use of GIS as a technology. Regardless of which software package is used, all GIS software packages rely on a common principle: to store/use/represent geospatial information so that it can be more easily utilized and analyzed by its user, especially when accompanied by various attributes.

GIS with Facilities Management

Historically, the common perception of a GIS is that it is a technology used primarily in the fields of urban planning, municipal government, and asset management. However, GIS technology can also be a powerful tool for facility management (FM). In recent years GIS technology has moved away from being primarily a tool for general analysis of a large environment toward being a primary tool for analysis of smaller and more localized areas, especially in terms of its use in FM. GIS technology can easily store and analyze spatial components of a facility such as floor plan space, building information, and utility structures. With GIS, a facility employee can easily create a variety of complex mapping outputs, visualize long-term planning scenarios, and access specific information about a particular building.

GIS DATA

Location

The core principle of all geospatial data in a GIS is the understanding of its own location on the Earth. What distinguishes GIS data from other data formats is that the GIS can understand where the data are. Therefore, the data do not simply model a feature; they represent the feature's true location on the Earth. This is what allows the GIS to perform many of its analytical and mapping functions. For this reason, all data that exists in a GIS must be tied to a known **projected coordinate system**. Data location is relevant with all three of the major GIS data formats: vector data, raster data, and tabular data.

Vector Data

Vector data is the primary data type that exists in a GIS. Vector data is the digital graphical data that are displayed on a map in the form of points, lines, and/or polygons. The vector data stores or links to a repository of attributes that are mapped and analyzed within the GIS. A popular vector format is computer-assisted design (CAD) drawings.

In Figure 4.1, the CAD plan shows the dimensions of a building and illustrates the use of each room. CAD data can be used within a GIS; however, the data would need to be projected to a known coordinate system or converted to a GIS format to harness the ability of the GIS's location awareness.

Figure 4.2 demonstrates the conversion of the CAD floor plan to a GIS. The GIS format stores information within each feature displayed on the map (or provides

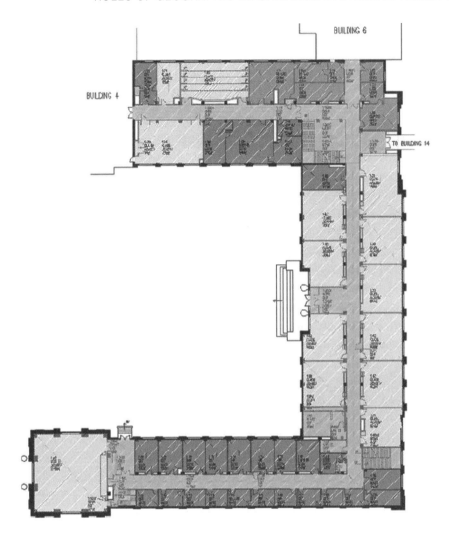

FIGURE 4.1 CAD building floor plan.

a link to an external attribute source). The GIS format is rotated from a horizontal axis because it is in its true location on the Earth.

Raster Data

Raster data is any type of imagery that contains location coordinates that can be added to the GIS. Raster data are often used to give GIS mapping context in the real world, such as viewing the actual image of a facility or the landscape it occupies.

Figure 4.3 shows a raster image of the MIT campus. Raster data can be in the form of several popular imaging formats such as .tif, .jpg, or .bmp. Raster data

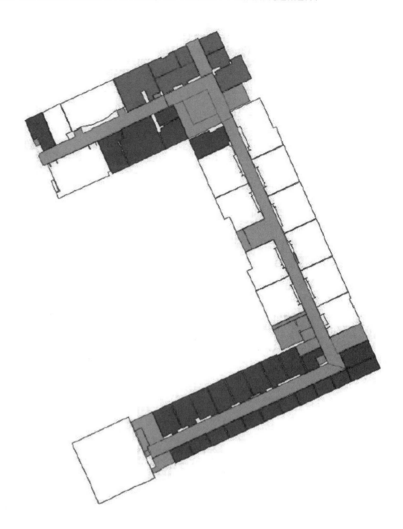

FIGURE 4.2 GIS building floor plan.

suitable for use in a GIS can be acquired from several sources such as a local municipality or a state agency. Many organizations also create their own raster data by conducting an aerial flyover.

Attribute Data

The final data format used in a GIS is **attribute data**. Attributes used in a GIS can be as simple as a basic **dBase** file or as complicated as a large-scale **Relational Database Managements System (RDBMS)** like **Oracle**. The GIS links vector data that has been created for the GIS to an attribute table through a unique

FIGURE 4.3 Raster image map of MIT campus.

identification number (ID) present in both data sets. Often, the ID must be manipulated to ensure compatibility between the two data sources so that the link functions properly. Figure 4.4 shows attribute data being linked to a feature in the GIS.

MAPPING FOR FM

Once a GIS has been developed, it can be used in a variety of mapping scenarios to enhance FM capabilities. In doing so, there are several common GIS mapping practices that can be employed.

Location Mapping

A GIS is an excellent resource for mapping location of objects and incidents.

Figure 4.5 shows a collection of trees that are maintained by a facilities department. With GIS, the location of these trees can be captured in a variety of ways.

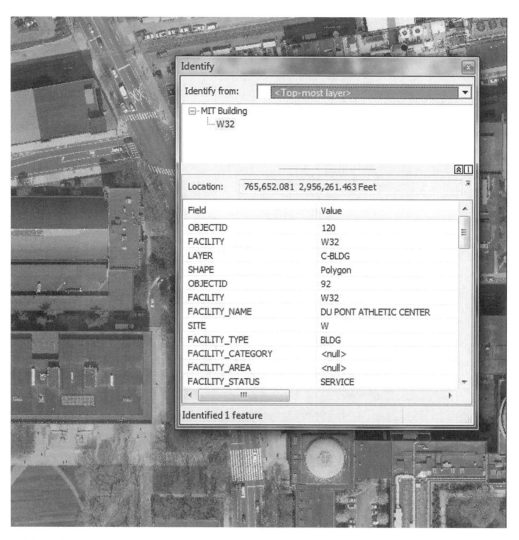

FIGURE 4.4 Vector, raster, and attribute data.

The location can be collected through traditional survey practices, mapped in CAD, and then converted to a GIS or collected through the use of a **global positioning system (GPS)**. Since a GIS displays information in a coordinate system, it is very simple to pinpoint locations on the map as long as **latitude-longitude** coordinates exist to locate the point. The GIS can then be used to store as much information about each feature as desired or needed. For trees, information such as address, species, condition, and diameter can be stored about each feature (Figure 4.5). The user can then, as one example, use the GIS to create a tree

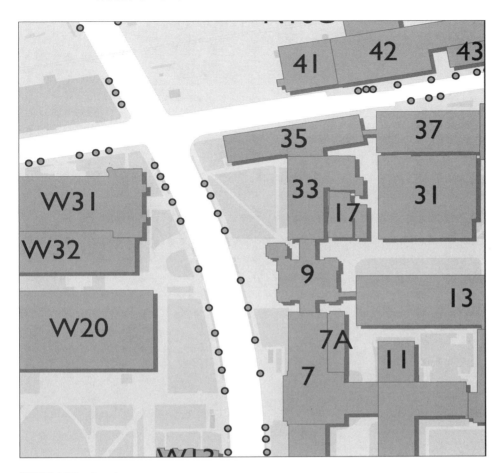

FIGURE 4.5 Tree inventory map.

maintenance plan by analyzing the information regarding each tree's condition to prioritize any and all maintenance. Although this example addresses trees, virtually any location can be mapped, such as bike racks, light posts, signs, and so on.

Thematic Mapping

The most visually obvious way that a GIS is used within FM is to display informa-tion for **thematic mapping**, such as determining the difference in building heights (see Figure 4.6). Buildings with a lower height are shown in light yellow, while buildings that have a higher height are shown in dark orange (shades of gray from light to dark in the illustration).

As Figure 4.6 illustrates, because building information is stored and linked into a GIS, displaying the information is done quickly and efficiently. The GIS links the building features to a database, which stores information about the building.

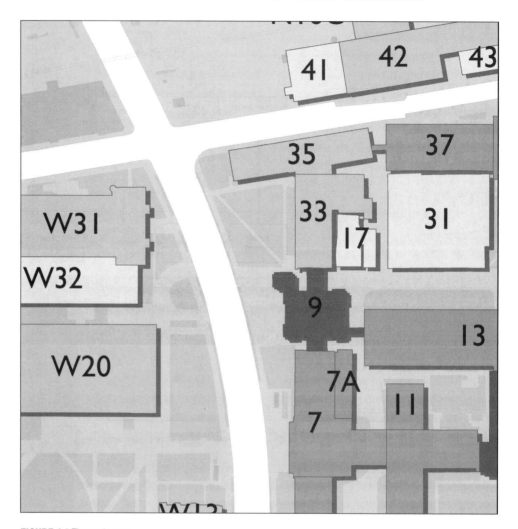

FIGURE 4.6 Thematic map.

When the GIS receives a request from the database, it retrieves the information from the building feature and displays the information directly on the map. There is no need to manually select any of the buildings or to color-code any of them individually because the GIS provides these indicators automatically as part of its technology. As a result, all of the information included in an FM database can be displayed on the map.

Mapping Density

Determining density is another important way of utilizing a GIS for FM purposes. Mapping density allows the user to see where the highest concentrations of certain features are located. Through density mapping, patterns can be seen within a certain geographic area or place.

Figure 4.7 illustrates population density around cafeteria locations. This is an excellent tool for future planning. Mapping density can also be used to detect patterns as they relate to certain times of the day.

In Figure 4.8, population density of a given facility during the day is mapped. By mapping population density to display patterns based on the time of the day, a GIS can be used to outline a plan for creating and using appropriate space in a facility over time.

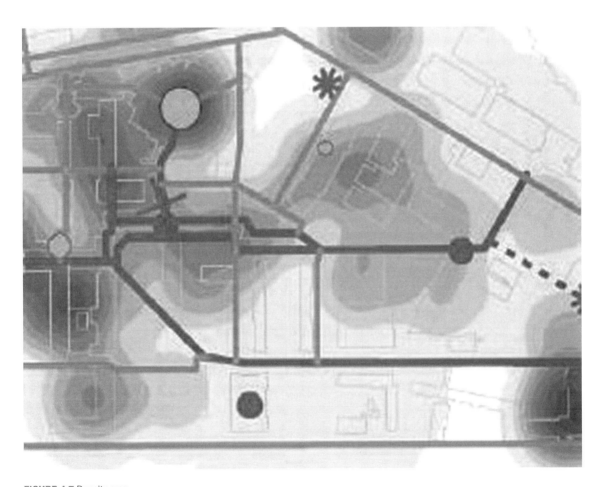

FIGURE 4.7 Density map.

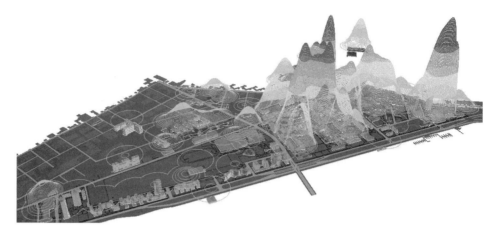

FIGURE 4.8 Daytime population map.

Mapping Change

Mapping change, or **change detection** as it is often referred to, is another great use of a GIS. Change is mapped to anticipate potential future conditions, to make strategic decisions for facilities planning, or to look at events that occurred at the facility in the past.

In Figure 4.9, a screenshot of a change detection **animation** within a facility is displayed. In the application, buildings in the design phase would be represented onscreen in blue, buildings in the construction phase in red, and buildings in yellow the completion phase. By creating an animation of this change, snapshots of the portfolio during periods of time can be evaluated side by side to give a better picture of the portfolio at large.

SPATIAL ANALYSIS FOR FM

Beyond just mapping, there is a series of **spatial analysis** tools that a GIS can provide in order to add value to an existing FM practice.

Attribute Selection

The GIS can perform analysis of features based upon any of the attributes linked to a feature from a database. The GIS can analyze very simple selections or extremely complex selections depending on the type of analysis needed.

In Figure 4.10, the GIS has been given a request to determine which buildings are less than 0.3 acres. The GIS highlights buildings fitting the selected criteria (in blue onscreen; outlined in white in the illustration). The number of attribute

FIGURE 4.9 Change detection map.

selections in a GIS is potentially limitless depending on how much information was gathered and entered into the linked database.

Nearest Selection

A GIS can do specific analysis of the proximity of one feature to another. This type of analysis can be very beneficial in FM strategies. For example, a GIS can determine which parking meters are closest to a certain building.

In Figure 4.11, the GIS has determined which parking meters are within 150 feet of a given building (Building 9). The parking meters and the building are highlighted to distinguish them on the map from the other features (distinguished by color in the application, by the larger gray dots in the illustration).

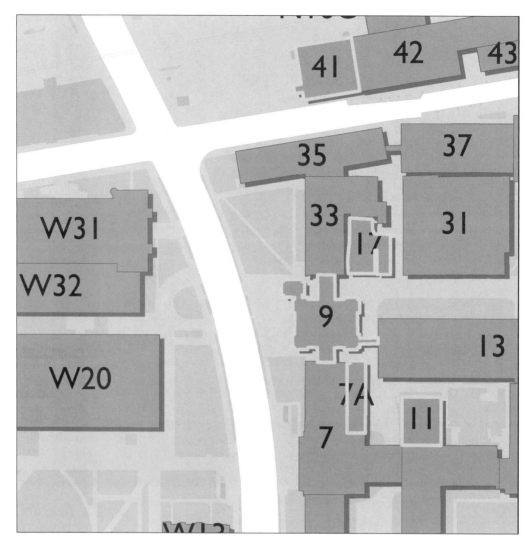

FIGURE 4.10 Attribute selection.

Inside Selection

Beyond just knowing what is near an object, it is also helpful to know what is contained directly inside an object. For example, a GIS can determine which bike racks are located directly within a building as opposed to just near the building.

Figure 4.12. illustrates bike racks that are located inside a building by highlighting them (in blue in the application; represented by gray dots in the illustration).

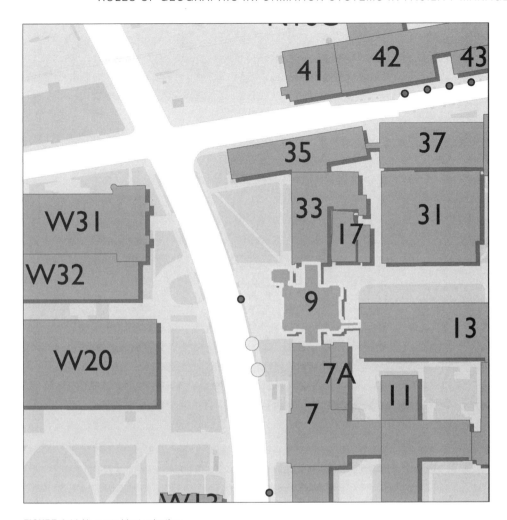

FIGURE 4.11 Nearest object selection.

Buffering Selection

A GIS is an excellent tool for buffering an object on the map. **Buffering** an object essentially means creating a specified radius around the object. By buffering an object, a GIS can determine which rooms, floors, or offices within a certain radius will or could be affected by an event.

In Figure 4.13, the circle illustrates a buffer zone of 150 feet from a given point where a specific incident occurred. In the GIS, the buffer zone and the buildings that were affected by the incident would be highlighted by color.

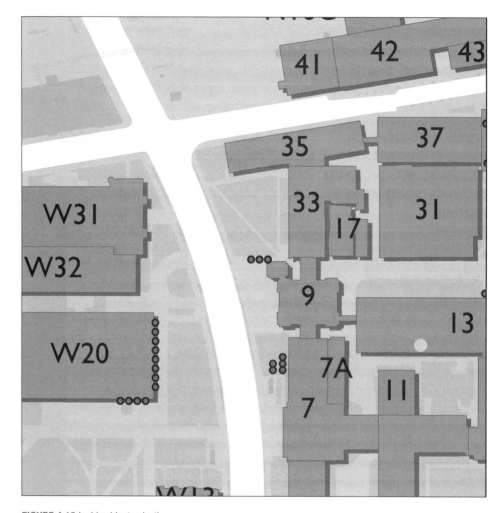

FIGURE 4.12 Inside object selection.

Geocoding

A GIS can display points on the map to represent physical locations or incidents that have occurred in a process called **geocoding**. These geocoded points can be in the form of addresses along a street, zip code locations within a region, or locations within a building.

CURRENT USE OF GIS AT MIT FACILITIES

MIT History

The **Massachusetts Institute of Technology** is a 159-acre college campus located in Kendall Square in Cambridge, Massachusetts. The campus is

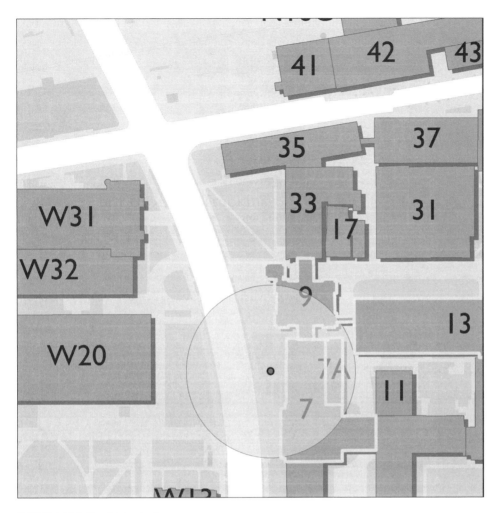

FIGURE 4.13 Buffer object selection.

comprised of 274 acres of floor space within 161 buildings and 14 different utilities within a very dense geographic area.[1] Early on, the MIT Facilities Department recognized the benefit of GIS in its FM practice.

Access to GIS through the Internet

MIT employs many of the GIS functions outlined in this chapter. However, there are a variety of other purposes for which MIT uses its GIS to enhance its current

---

[1] Michael Parkin, "Inside Out—Analyzing Your Facility in Its Geospatial Context." MIT Facility Information Systems, http://fis.mit.edu/resources/pub/misc/2011_03_24_IFMA.pdf.

FM practice. In the past few years MIT has released much of its GIS data onto the Internet. As a result, its GIS data are easily distributed to the campus community. For example, the **MIT campus map**, hosted by MIT and found at http://whereismit.edu, allows MIT community members, and the public at large, access to its GIS information (see Figure 4.14).

The MIT online campus map allows a user to find a particular building, find its occupants, and to find locations within the closest proximity of the building. Other GIS data have been added to the map such as emergency phones, public art locations, accessibility entrances, and bike rack locations. All of these data sets are from the department of facilities GIS database where they are updated on an as-needed basis. The online campus map also overlays directly with various public Web mapping services using an application programming interface **(API)**. As a result, GIS data from MIT servers can be mashed up with these public maps to make a comprehensive mapping product. The user has the ability to search numerous features on the campus map. By simply typing in the word *food*, all locations on campus offering food services will highlight.

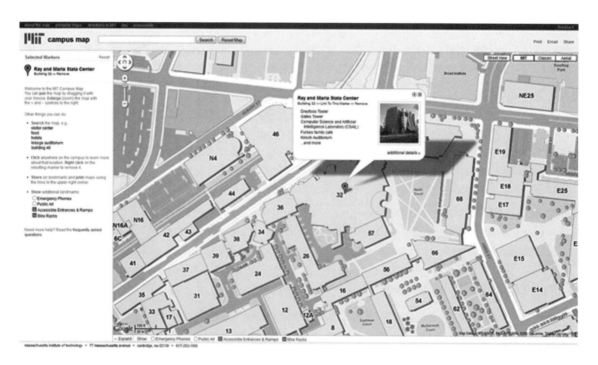

FIGURE 4.14 MIT online campus map.

GIS Analysis within the Building

At MIT you could say that GIS technology has moved from "outside of the building" to "inside of the building." MIT currently uses visualization in a three-dimensional (3D) environment. Much of the information present in a facilities department is far more understandable when seen and analyzed in 3D because it more closely represents what the data would look like in the context of the "real world." To enable 3D analysis in its GIS, MIT uses two-dimensional (2D) data viewed in a 3D environment. To clarify, the heights of buildings and facilities are based on a value from a database. The value is then applied to the corresponding building. Through the GIS software, this building height is displayed to represent its actual height. With the use of 3D, GIS techniques such as buffering have been applied to the MIT 3D environment (see Figure 4.15).

As Figure 4.15 demonstrates, by using buffering in a 3D environment, not only is the building highlighted, but also the affected room. In terms of 3D analysis, the integration with building information modeling (BIM) is also becoming a standard

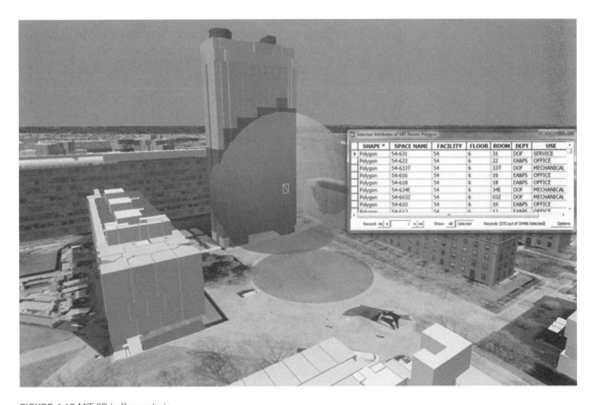

FIGURE 4.15 MIT 3D buffer analysis.

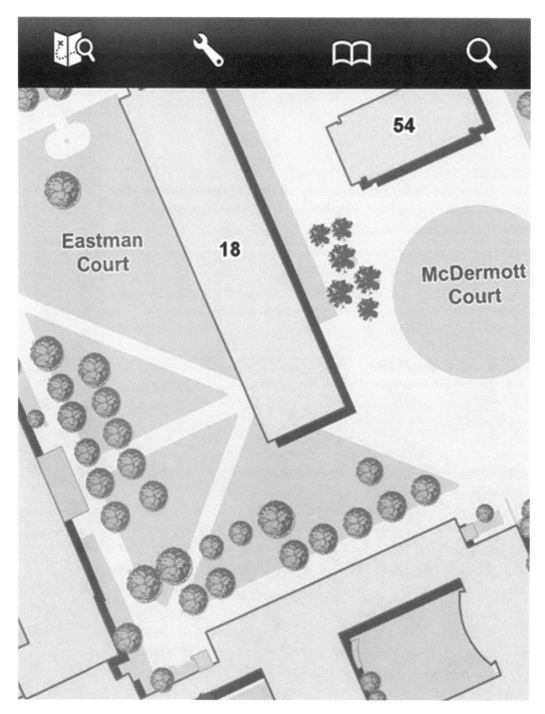

FIGURE 4.16 Tree inventory.

practice for GIS users within the FM industry. The ability to take relevant data from a BIM model and display it across a 3D campus to preform analysis over various buildings has the capability of providing insight into the location of assets, performance of building systems, and a host of other applications.

Mobile Technologies

Mobile GIS integration has become a standard practice over the past few years. With the growing use of smartphones, GIS-enabled services are now at the fingertips of many users. At MIT, a public-facing iPhone/Android application has been developed to assist visitors and students to navigate around campus. The iPhone app integrates with the department of facilities GIS to show locations of buildings and services such as shuttle stops and routes. MIT also has developed several internal iPhone/iPad applications for facility employees to conduct data collection and maintenance of various assets. Figure 4.16 shows a tree inventory application.

CONCLUSION

A fully operational GIS can leverage a great deal of information for the FM practitioner. A GIS can be used as a method for both mapping and data retrieval. As data needs expand within the FM community, a GIS may provide a well-rounded solution for common FM tasks.

ADDITIONAL RESOURCES

Books

Paul A. Longley, Michael F. Goodchild, David J. Maquire, and David W. Rhind, *Geographic Information Systems and Science* (New York: John Wiley & Sons, 2002).

Andy Mitchel, *The ESRI Guide to GIS Analysis Volume 1: Geographic Patterns and Relationships* (Redlands, CA: ESRI Press, 1999).

John O'Looney, *Beyond Maps: GIS and Decision Making in Local Government* (Redlands, CA: ESRI Press, 2000).

Robert Tomlinson, *Thinking About GIS: Geographic Information System Planning for Managers* (Redlands, CA: ESRI Press, 2003).

Web Sites

APPA, Leadership in Educational Facilities, www.appa.org/index.cfm.

AutoCAD 2008 Productivity Study, white paper to guide Autodesk customers in making an upgrade decision, http://images.autodesk.com/adsk/files/autocad_2008_productivity_study.pdf.

Building Education: From Fragmentation to Integration, www.bilkent.edu.tr/~pultar/Papers/EES99/Education.html.

Database glossary, http://databases.about.com/od/administration/a/glossary.htm.

ESRI Support Center, GIS Dictionary, http://support.esri.com/index.cfm?fa=knowledgebase.gisDictionary.gateway.

IFMA—International Facilities Management Association, www.ifma.org.

Massachusetts Geographic Information System, www.mass.gov/mgis/.

MIT—Massachusetts Institute of Technology, http://web.mit.edu/.

MIT campus map, http://whereis.mit.edu/map-jpg.

Understanding Coordinate Management in the Geodatabase, http://downloads2.esri.com/support/whitepapers/ao_/UnderstandingCoordinateManagement_June2007.pdf.

Radio Frequency Identification

5

Geoff Williams

INTRODUCTION

Radio frequency identification (RFID) technology uses radio waves to transmit data from a tag (information source) associated with an asset, to a reader (information collector) from several feet away. Some tags transmit static information such as an asset number, while others can transmit multiple dynamic pieces of data to provide the end user valuable information about the associated asset.

RFID technology was originally developed for military applications but has evolved beyond its military roots to support many commercial applications such as inventory control, toll collection, automated payment, and tracking species' migratory patterns to name a few. Major organizations are mandating the use of RFID technologies by their suppliers. The increased volume of business will help to fuel the continued technical development and drive down the cost per asset tag.

RFID technology supports traditional real estate and facility asset management requirements previously served by **barcode** technology, while providing new opportunities to optimize operational control through recent RFID tag innovations and enhanced capabilities.

ORIGINS AND EVOLUTION

RFID can be traced back to the Second World War. The German, Japanese, American, and British military were all using radar (discovered in 1935 by Scottish physicist Sir Robert Alexander Watson-Watt) to warn of approaching planes while they were still miles away, but there was no way to identify whose aircraft were approaching. To distinguish their planes, the German pilots would roll their planes when they returned to base to alter the radio signal reflected back to the radar receiver. This crude method (essentially, the first passive RFID system) alerted the radar crew on the ground that these were friendly planes and not Allied aircraft.

Under Watson-Watt's leadership, the British secretly developed the first active "identify friend or foe (IFF)" system. They put a transmitter on each British plane. When it received signals from radar stations on the ground, it began broadcasting a signal back that identified the aircraft as friendly. RFID works on this same basic concept. A signal is sent to a transponder, which wakes up and either reflects a signal (passive system) or broadcasts a signal (active system).[1]

The direct ancestors of current RFID technology were introduced in the 1970s. Since that time, many advancements have been incorporated into today's RFID technology. RFID frequency bandwidth has increased to include a full spectrum: from low frequency (LF) 120–150 kHz, high frequency (HF), ultra-high frequency, through microwave 3.1–10 GHz, allowing versatility to support multiple business requirements, constraints, and applications.[2] In addition, the accuracy and reliability of reading tags has dramatically increased to just under a 100 percent read rate. Similar to the evolution of other comparative hardware technologies, the form factor has decreased as well as the cost per tag, while the range of detection has increased to allow for versatility of application use. Some tags can withstand harsh conditions to support industrialized applications, while others have form factors small enough to be implanted under the skin, in book bindings, or sewn into clothing, creating endless possibilities for utilization.

STANDARDIZATION

The unifying foundation to this technology is the development and adoption of a common set of standards. A common misconception in the RFID world is that there are few standards other than those proprietary standards that are

---

[1] Mark Roberti, "The History of RFID," *RFID Journal*, 2009.

[2] Stephen Weis, RFID (Radio Frequency Identification): Principles and Applications, MIT CSAIL, 2007; http://citeseerx. ist.psu.edu/viewdoc/summary?doi=10.1.1.182.5224.

created by individual vendors. To the contrary, the International Organization for Standardization (ISO) is developing standards for use in supply chain management (ISO 18000 Series). The ISO 18000 series covers the air interface protocol for systems tracking goods within a supply chain. The standard is broken into seven parts and covers the frequencies used in RFID systems around the world.

In the retail sector, ultra-high frequency (UHF) and EPCGlobal (established standards for barcodes in the 1970s and 1980s) organizations are driving uniform platform standards. Market adoption of these platforms has been driven even further by retail giants that require all of their major vendors to ship products with tags conforming to these defined platforms. The continued maturation of RFID technologies will be paralleled by the maturation of standards.[3]

BEYOND BARCODE

Over the past 20 years barcode technology has helped facility managers effectively capture and manage asset inventories throughout their facilities. Like the RFID tag, a variety of barcode tags are available to support every environment and condition applicable. Barcode tags remain a very cost effective solution when compared tag for tag against RFID tags (the cost gap is narrowing); however, RFID tags offer many distinct advantages over barcode tags that should be considered when evaluating options for tagging assets:

- **Freedom from line of sight**. Barcode readers require a direct line of sight to the printed barcode; RFID readers do not require a direct line of sight to either active RFID tags or passive RFID tags. RFID tags can be read at much greater distances of up to 300 feet. In contrast, the range to read a barcode is typically within a few feet.
- **Faster read rates**. RFID readers can rapidly read up to 40 or more tags per second. Reading barcodes is much more time consuming, requiring a scan per individual tag, and usually takes a half-second or more to successfully complete a single read.
- **Less susceptible to damage**. Line-of-sight requirements also limit the ruggedness of barcodes as well as their reusability. Since line of sight is required, the printed barcode must be exposed on the outside of the asset, where it is subject to greater wear and tear. Ruggedized RFID tags' electronic components are protected in a plastic cover. A scratched shell does not affect RFID tag

[3] Ann De Vries and Paul Dietrich, "Standards Facilitate RFID Adoption," www.rfdesign.com, September 2007.

FIGURE 5.1 Ironside Slim and Ironside Micro are examples of ruggedized RFID tags that can be mounted to assets for outdoor and industrial environment applications.
Reproduced by permission of Confidex, LTD

information, since there are no visual elements to scan. RFID tags can also be secured within the product itself, guaranteeing greater ruggedness and reusability (Figure 5.1).

■ **Read/write capability**. Barcodes have no read/write capability; that is, you cannot add to the information written on a printed barcode. RFID tags, however, can be read/write devices. The RFID reader can communicate with the tag and alter as much of the information as the tag design will allow.

CORPORATE REAL ESTATE AND FACILITY MANAGEMENT LEVERAGE USE OF RFID

RFID technology can easily be applied to a variety of corporate real estate and facility management (FM) business requirements. While there are more traditional applications where RFID can be applied, a facility manager who understands the basics of RFID may also find opportunities to adapt this technology in new ways.

Theft Detection and Mitigation

Organizations often face thousands of dollars in theft of high-priced, yet portable items every year. Artwork, information technology (IT) equipment, and other valuable assets are carried right out through the front door in the middle of the day without anyone's knowledge. By utilizing RFID tags hidden on the asset and placing readers, paired with an audible alarm system, at all egress points, security personnel could be notified and instantly respond to the issue. A time-stamp record associated with the alarm and security video footage will provide additional support for effective prosecution.

Asset Management

As discussed above, there are many benefits over barcode tags for asset management. Common uses include assets that are mobile, have a higher asset value, and may be difficult to directly access, such as moveable carts, IT equipment, specialized tools, fleet vehicles, and so forth. An inventory of assets within a room is much easier and faster to record and requires only a single read, compared to multiple reads of a barcode scanner. Where there are aesthetic considerations, such as artwork, RFID tags can be placed out of sight.

Personnel and Guest Access and Tracking

Today, most companies use photo badging to keep unauthorized people from entering restricted areas. An RFID badge can limit or enable access to certain systems and locations. When tied with smart building systems, RFID badges can also control a user's lighting conditions, location-specific phone access, and temperature requirements. This information also helps facility managers understand building utilization trends occurring within their facilities so that they can plan more effective use of space.

Move Management

Many organizations have strategically developed facilities to accommodate churn by keeping furniture stationary and only moving boxes of personal effects (box moves) in order to maximize a changing work environment and team adjacencies.

Movers supply RFID-enabled crates (Figure 5.2) to accommodate personal items for each employee. The RFID tag affixed to a crate provides a way for the mover to know the employee being moved as well as the crate location at any point in the move (old location, on a truck, in the warehouse, or at the new site), to ensure that the contents arrive to the appropriate destination.

RFID with Sensors

Some companies have combined RFID tags with sensors that detect and record temperature, movement, and even radiation. This technology is currently used in health care at Belgium's University Hospital of Ghent, where they have implemented a system that detects when a patient is having cardiac distress and sends

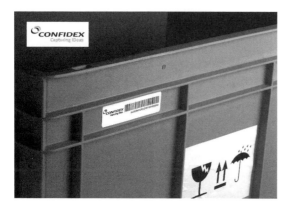 

FIGURE 5.2 Carrier pro RFID label also supports barcode scanner for maximum flexibility.
Reproduced by permission of Confidex, LTD

caregivers an alert indicating the patient's location.[4] Other sensors can support environmental and mechanical conditions.

To plan for FM-enabled RFID applications, it is necessary to understand the components, capabilities, and constraints of this technology.

COMPONENTS OF RFID

A system that utilizes RFID technology consists of many components. At the highest level are enterprise systems that transact and assess data feeds provided by RFID components. These are enterprise resource planning, inventory control, human resources, integrated workplace management, and enterprise asset management technologies that organizations have in place today. Most systems have protocols to accept information feeds from a variety of sources, and some may already have modules that can process information directly from RFID devices.

Applications (Middleware)

Other systems may require middleware applications (Figure 5.3) that interpret device information and retrieve it in a format that is easy to utilize. In some instances, these applications may even be used as a point solution to accomplish a very specific set of business functions.

---

[4] Beth Bacheldor, "Belgium Hospital Combines RFID, Sensors to Monitor Heart Patients," *RFID Journal*, March 6, 2007.

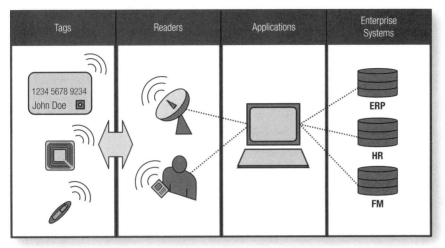

FIGURE 5.3 RFID and middleware applications.
Reproduced by permission of Paul Head II

RFID Interrogators or Readers

RFID tags cannot directly interface with an application. They require a device to send a signal to the tag and then read the response known as RFID interrogators or more typically RFID readers. There are two terms that are used loosely to describe RFID readers. An "intelligent" reader has the dual ability to run different protocols, and to filter data and run applications and communicates with the RFID tags. A "dumb" reader, by contrast, is a simple device that might read only one type of tag using one frequency and one protocol. This type typically has very little computing power, so it can't filter reads, store tag data, and the like.

Linked with the applications mentioned earlier, a series of readers transmit and receive signals from the RFID tags. For asset and inventory management, readers come in a variety of form factors and might be placed at significant locations on a property or within a building to track tags that fall within a specific zone. Egress points are common locations to track the incoming and outgoing tagged assets. Warehouses may have multiple short-range readers to process inventory within a tightly controlled area. Another way to read the tags is through the use of a handheld reader by a mobile worker for the collection of asset information.

For commercial sales application the readers are located at point of sale stations to gather credit card or asset data when placed within inches of the device.

RFID Tags

RFID tags are comprised of two key components. The first component is an integrated circuit that will store/process information about the asset, modulate/

demodulate the RF signal, and collect and process power and other specialized functions (temperature readings, etc.). The second component is an antenna to receive/transmit signals from the reader.

Similar to RFID readers, RFID tags are not equal. Tags may be read only (shipped to the customer with codes already assigned to the tag from the factory), or they can be read/write (programmable by the customer on site).

There are three types of RFID tags: active, passive, and semipassive:

1. **Active RFID tags** have a transmitter and their own power source. The power source is used to run the microchip's circuitry and to broadcast a signal to a reader (the way a cell phone transmits signals to a base station).
2. **Passive RFID tags** have no battery. Instead, they draw power from the reader's electromagnetic waves that induce a current in the tag's antenna.
3. **Semipassive RFID tags** use a battery to run the chip's circuitry but draw power from the reader's signal. Active and semipassive tags are useful for tracking high-value goods that need to be scanned over long ranges, such as railway cars on a track.

Retailers such as Walmart are focusing on passive tags because they are more cost effective and low cost by virtue of mass consumption. Their read range isn't as far, typically less than 20 feet versus 100 feet or more for active tags, but they are much less expensive than active tags and can be disposed of with the product packaging. Passive tags also have a longer life span since active tags rely on internal batteries.

EXTRA SENSORY IDENTIFICATION TO OPTIMIZE FM OPERATION

RFID is becoming increasingly popular and cost effective as a global standard. The real estate and FM communities are just starting to get a glimpse of how it can help them optimize operations. Under the right circumstances, RFID has numerous advantages over traditional barcoding and is already in use with many facility management applications. Such applications will multiply over time and eventually involve all aspects of FM—people, places, and things. RFID technology will lead to solutions, such as inventory management software applications, and will integrate with many enterprise systems and facilities technologies, including building automation, security applications, enterprise asset management, and integrated workplace management systems.

CONCLUSION

Radio frequency identification is an exciting new technology that is just beginning to be used for FM. It has numerous advantages over traditional barcoding and has many FM applications. Such applications will multiply over time and eventually involve all aspects of FM. RFID technology will serve as the basis for stand-alone applications as well as integrate with real-time (e.g., building automation) and passive (e.g., computer-aided facility management) systems.

ADDITIONAL RESOURCES

Articles

Erik Jasper and Eric Teicholz, "Work on the Move," IFMA Foundation, October 2011.
Prachi Patel, "Nanotube RFID: Better Barcodes?" March 24, 2010, www.technologyreview.com/computing/24852/.
Stephen A. Weis, "RFID (Radio Frequency Identification): Principles and Applications, MIT CSAIL, 2007, http://citeseerx.ist.psu.edu/viewdoc/summary?doi=10.1.1.182.5224.

Web Sites

Avid The Microchip Company, "Leaders in Pet Microchipping," www.microchipidsystems.com.
RFID Journal, "RFID (Radio Frequency Identification); The World's RFID Authority," www.rfidjournal.com.
RFID Lowdown, www.rfidlowdown.com; LibBest: Library RFID Management System, www.rfid-library.com.
RFIDNews, "Radio Frequency Identification Technology for Logistics, Tagging and EPC," http://www.rfidnews.org.

Information and Communications Technology

6

Richard Hodges

SUMMARY

The velocity of innovation for information and communications technology **(ICT)** will continue to accelerate in the twenty-first century. Facility management (FM) professionals must understand and plan for operating in a world of technology-driven change. Strategically, facility managers need to understand and adapt to major ICT trends that will affect buildings and workplaces. The first part of this chapter addresses five high-level trends—ubiquity, mobility, personalization, virtualization, and visual communications—that may cause facility managers to rethink established concepts and practices for building design and operation. Increasing requirements for material, energy, and financial efficiency create a demand for new ideas and approaches to designing and managing ICT networks within buildings. The second part of the chapter provides a summary of current connectivity technologies, an analysis of problems with current practices, and case studies for alternative approaches to ICT network design. Facility managers must be more educated about ICT trends and innovations to more actively participate in shaping ICT networks in workplaces of the future.

INTRODUCTION

In 1965, Gordon Moore suggested that the number of transistors on a **semi-conductor** would double about every two years. His prediction has been fulfilled for more than 40 years and is expected to carry on for another generation or more.[1] At this pace, innovation equates to an average performance improvement to close to 1 percent per week. Continued change at this rate supports the view of another well-known technologist: "Technological change is exponential, contrary to the common-sense intuitive linear view. So, in the twenty-first century, 100 years of progress will be more like 20,000 years of progress [at today's rate]."[2]

As consumers of products enabled by the ongoing fulfillment of Moore's prediction (Figure 6.1), examples of current real-world effects of Moore's Law in the workplace include smartphones, MP3 players, laptop computers, giant flat-screen video displays, and high-definition **telepresence** videoconferencing. The fundamental building block of these products is the geometrically increasing capacity of the semiconductor chips that are the brains of the devices.

In aggregate, these products can be seen as part of larger, long-term trends that have powerful implications for workplace design and the management of buildings. The five major trends are ubiquity, mobility, personalization, virtualization, and visual communication.

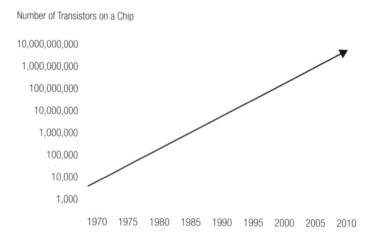

FIGURE 6.1 Illustration of Moore's Law.

[1] See www.intel.com/technology/mooreslaw/index.htm.

[2] www.kurzweilai.net/articles/art0134.html?printable=1.

- **Ubiquity**. The twenty-first century will be an era of pervasive connectivity, a world of the network of things rather than of just people. Virtually every device that is touched will be equipped to communicate over global, high-speed networks. In commercial buildings, almost every element of the building will be connected to and controlled using the communications network, including heating, ventilating, and air-conditioning (HVAC) systems, lighting systems, and security systems. Facility managers will be challenged to manage **smart buildings** that produce large amounts of data that must be monitored and acted on.

- **Mobility**. Within the past decade, a global wireless information society has emerged. Mobile communications devices are being produced at a rate of more than 1 billion units per year and commonly are used in every part of the world. High-speed wireless networks and powerful lightweight devices are enabling workers to be truly untethered. Information, in every conceivable form, is instantaneously available almost anywhere. Unlike earlier eras, information will come to people wherever they are. The role of the workplace as a store-house for information is over, and facility managers will be faced with managing a work environment where most people are constantly on the move.

- **Personalization**. IT is being used to personalize products and experiences for the individual consumer. Highly customizable products are readily available today; made-to-order individual electronics and clothing are not far off. Personalized advertising that adapts and is pushed to individuals is happening now and will be pervasive in only a few years. The experience of personalization will set the expectation level for the individual experience in the workplace, and facility managers will have to respond. Providing workplace services and comforts based on personal preferences, enabled by ICT, will be both possible and necessary.

- **Virtualization**. Virtualization has two meanings for ICT. One is technical: creating virtual machines by consolidating multiple functions. This means less building space will be required to store IT hardware, and ICT networks will be required for equivalent processing and storage capacity. The second meaning is the simulation of reality in electronically created environments. Simulators for training are fairly commonplace; electronically created three-dimensional (3D) worlds and multiplayer online role-playing games are emerging into widespread use. For some, high-definition videoconferencing may regularly replace physical travel. For others, cyberspace may become the workplace of the future.

- **Visual communication**. A significant trend that has emerged over the past few years is the increase in use of visual media for communications. Though person-to-person and workgroup video communication has been available for a generation, it is now easier and more effective. The use of visual displays in buildings, the displacement of text-based memos by visual slide-decks, and the rapid increase in use of recorded video to communicate are examples of a trend that has significant implications for how ICT services are architected and delivered, and also how space and the workplace environment will be laid out and managed.

In the twenty-first century, facility managers will need to anticipate how these trends will affect the behavior and expectations of the people who use buildings and the demand for space and services within buildings. Facility managers must understand the technologies and applications supporting these trends, particularly for ICT networks that have become an integral component of buildings.

TECHNOLOGY PRIMER: WIRED ICT NETWORKS IN BUILDINGS

Though mobility is one of the major trends for the future, this doesn't mean wires will disappear from buildings. Wired networks will continue to provide advantages over wireless networks in stability, performance, and security. Facility managers need to understand the basic design principles and components of communications networks to ensure their buildings have efficient and flexible wired ICT networks.

In most countries, communications cables within the building are the responsibility of the building owner or tenant, not a telecommunications common carrier. Buildings taller than one story require both **riser** cables that connect upper floors to the minimum point of entry **(MPOE)**, where cables from telecommunications carriers enter the building, and horizontal distribution cable. The MPOE, which is also sometimes called the **entrance facility** or **de-marc**, usually is located in the basement or first floor of the building. For separate voice and data infrastructure systems, typically copper cable is installed for voice systems and fiber-optic cables for data systems (Figure 6.2). Frequently, **coaxial cable** also is installed for audio/visual applications.

On each floor of a building, the current common design practice is to **home-run** copper voice (Category 3) and data cables (Category 5 or 6) from a main distribution frame or intermediate distribution frame (MDF/IDF),[3] also known

---

[3] Intermediate distribution frame consists of wiring closets on floors as opposed to main distribution frame (MDF), the wiring entrance facility to the building. IDFs frequently stack vertically above the MDF in the core of a high-rise building. In a low-rise campus, most buildings have an MDF and depending on size, no IDFs. See http://en.wikipedia .org/wiki/Intermediate_distribution_frame; http://en.wikipedia.org/wiki/Main_distribution_frame. For information on main distribution frames and intermediate distribution frames, see www.webopedia.com/TERM/M/MDF.html.

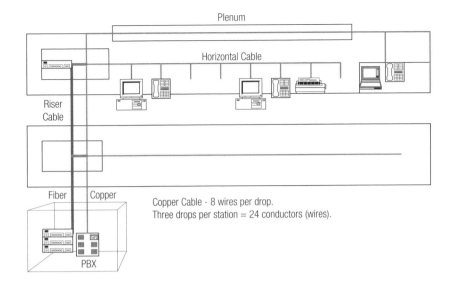

Copper Cable - 8 wires per drop.
Three drops per station = 24 conductors (wires).

FIGURE 6.2 Standard cable design.

as telecommunications or **telco closets**. The design of these systems is covered by **ANSI/TIA/EIA standard 569-A**, Commercial Building Standards for Telecommunication Pathways and Spaces, which specifies materials to be used, installation and testing procedures, and the amount and location of space to be provided. Normally, three or four horizontal cable **drops**, sometimes called *jacks*, are permanently installed to every location where connectivity might be needed.

Typically, commercial buildings are designed so riser cables are installed in 4-inch conduits through floor slabs connecting vertically stacked telco closets. Horizontal wires usually are routed through ceiling **plenums** and brought down to working level behind walls or from overhead drops integrated into **modular** furniture. Since installed cables are inaccessible after installation and at a fixed location, designers generally provision cable drops at about 6-foot intervals on longer walls, on each wall of an enclosed office, and other locations where there might be a requirement for connectivity.

WIRELESS NETWORKS: A QUICK REVIEW

Twenty-first-century workplaces will include wireless networks of various rapidly evolving types. The placement and management of the devices associated with these networks is an issue facility managers must cope with. They also must understand what technologies will enable building occupants to do.

Wi-fi, the IEEE 802.11 standard[4] for wireless local area networks (WLANs) introduced in 1997, has been widely adopted in both residential and commercial buildings. A very high percentage of homes and workplaces use wi-fi for connection to high-speed networks. Though a relatively short-range technology, 100 to 300 feet from a single radio, wi-fi nodes can be developed in mesh networks for covering broad areas. Urban scale wi-fi networks intended to provide ubiquitous availability are currently in development around the world, but financial viability and consistent coverage are problematic. While originally developed for wireless data local area networks (LANs), wi-fi systems now are being adapted for voice applications.

WiMax, the IEEE 802.16 standard[5] for broadband wireless metropolitan area networks (MANs), is a longer-range wireless technology that is in various stages of deployment in many countries around the world under various names. The technology originally was conceived as an alternative to high-speed wired connections provided by wireline telecommunications carriers for the "last mile" to buildings and homes, and it is being used in countries with sparsely populated areas or where adequate wired ICT networks don't exist. As mobile cellular carrier networks continue to increase their ability to deliver broadband services, WiMax is being used as a competing service for mobility applications.

Broadband cellular services for laptops and smartphones are now widely available and increasingly popular for both business and personal use. The industry commonly uses the terms 3G and 4G to brand current service offerings. Third-generation services (3G) are supposed to meet the International Telecommunications Union **(ITU)** IMT-2000 specification of a minimum 0.2 megabits per second (Mbps) peak data rate. In 2009, the ITU specified requirements for 4G performance, with peak speed of 100 Mbps for high-mobility communications, such as from trains and cars, and 1 gigabit per second (Gbps) for low-mobility communications, such as pedestrians and stationary users. These services are based on differing technology platforms in different carrier networks and parts of the world, but primarily Code Division Multiple Access (CDMA)[6] and Universal Mobile Telecommunications System/Global System for Mobile communications (UMTS/GSM).[7]

Adherence to the ITU standards and actual performance of 3G and 4G services varies considerably. However, at 1 Gbps for stationary users, 4G services can

---

[4] IEEE 802.11 is a set of standards for implementing wireless LANs communication in the 2.4, 3.6, and 5 GHz frequency bands (see http://ieee802.org/11/).

[5] A series of wireless broadband standards authored by the IEEE (see http://ieee802.org/16/).

[6] See www.cdg.org/.

[7] See http://electronics.howstuffworks.com/question537.htm or http://en.wikipedia.org/wiki/4G.

match or exceed the speeds currently available on many existing ethernet-wired building networks. It is still common to encounter problems in maintaining reliable cellular mobile connections in all parts of some buildings, so few organizations have adopted a connectivity strategy that depends solely on cellular wireless services in commercial workplaces.

ICT NETWORKS IN BUILDINGS—A CHANGING PARADIGM

The current state-of-the-art design and installation of communications cable networks in buildings has evolved over the past generation to a common standard of **structured cabling**. However, these practices have become inefficient and misaligned with larger trends. The main problems with current design practices for wired networks are overbuilding, inflexibility, and the lack of integrated planning, which results in unnecessarily high costs and waste.

Overbuilding

The unofficial design principle of in-building cabling systems is to put cable everywhere, since the budget for cabling is usually part of the construction package and available only once. Cabling is also usually a relatively small and specialized part of the overall budget that is not perceived as being susceptible to **value engineering**. Furthermore, it is frequently a profitable add-on item for electrical contractors. These factors create a strong incentive for installing more cable than is needed or will ever actually be used.

Inflexibility

Another incentive for overbuilding is that long after the construction budget is set, facility managers will have to address complaints about why some locations do not have network jacks where a building occupant wants one. Since cabling is installed permanently behind walls or in ceilings and is difficult to reconfigure, installing cable to every possible location is a practical response. Many furniture systems are chosen more for aesthetics or price, and not for easy reconfiguration of communications cables. Therefore, altering a space layout of a traditional design frequently requires removal and reinstallation of ICT cables.

Lack of Integrated Planning

Typically, the cabling designer is either part of the mechanical, electrical, and plumbing **(MEP)** design team or a specialized contractor. Only infrequently do cable system designers get involved in discussions about space design or programming. Instead, they provide a standard, packaged design based on the blueprints they have been given. These designs usually conform to the required ANSI/TIA/EIA standards and existing industry practice, but don't usually include consideration of future operational costs or environmental effects. There is also little incentive or time to investigate alternatives for lower first costs or future operating costs for the space.

Most workplaces now have some type of wireless network. Wireless nets usually are planned in isolation from wired ICT networks and implemented as an "**overlay**." In many cases, corporate wireless networks are the result of evolution rather than a master plan. However, as reliable, secure, and ubiquitous wireless access becomes a fundamental workplace requirement, many organizations are implementing centrally managed wireless LANs that can carry both voice and data. Only in rare instances, however, is an integrated design created that recognizes the reduced need for physical cabling in an environment where many, or most, devices use a wireless network connection.

ICT NETWORKS IN BUILDINGS—NEW DESIGN CONCEPTS

The first requirement for creating more cost-effective and flexible ICT connectivity solutions in buildings is to treat those systems as a critical and primary element of the workspace design rather than an invisible afterthought. For example, the first-cost and operating savings associated with cabling systems can make a major contribution toward justifying a raised access floor in a commercial building.

Figure 6.3 shows an active zone design for a converged voice, data, and video ICT network with integrated wired and wireless networks. All copper riser cable is replaced with fiber-optic cable that is smaller, higher capacity, and far more environmentally benign. The active network components, typically ethernet switches, uninterruptable power supplies (UPSs), and **wireless access points**, are placed in floor-mounted **zone boxes**, using space that would otherwise be empty and eliminating or reducing the size of telco closets. Copper cable only is used for short drops to connect the equipment in use. Because it is easy to reconfigure, overbuilding the horizontal cable isn't necessary in this type of design. Furthermore, in this design, it is also possible to use modular ICT cable systems that are easy and quick to assemble, take down, and redeploy.

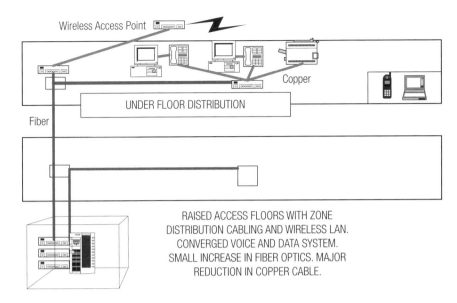

Wireless Access Point

Copper

UNDER FLOOR DISTRIBUTION

Fiber

RAISED ACCESS FLOORS WITH ZONE
DISTRIBUTION CABLING AND WIRELESS LAN.
CONVERGED VOICE AND DATA SYSTEM.
SMALL INCREASE IN FIBER OPTICS. MAJOR
REDUCTION IN COPPER CABLE.

FIGURE 6.3 Converged and integrated active zone design with underfloor distribution.

NEW DESIGN CONCEPTS IN PRACTICE: CASE STUDIES

Elementary School

For a private K–8 school, the ICT consultant was engaged early enough to significantly affect the design. The first step was the elimination of a large number of redundant and outmoded systems, including televisions with expensive earthquake mounting brackets, a traditional telephone system integrated with clocks and bells, the overhead paging system, all coaxial cable, and 75 percent of the copper cable.

The new system uses a converged, high-speed voice, data, and video backbone integrated with an advanced WLAN. However, neither underfloor nor overhead cable distribution strategies could be used. Therefore, in-wall metal conduit with pull-strings was retained from the original plan in case wired cables were required in the future. Only two copper cables actually were pulled into each classroom for an Internet protocol (IP) telephone and a network printer. All classroom computers, including the teachers' laptops, were connected via a centrally managed WLAN, which also can support wireless IP telephones. Wall-mounted IP telephones provide telephone service, voice paging, and listen-in capability. The net result of the design was an almost 60 percent reduction in cost and material for the school ICT network, including the cost of the advanced WLAN, for a system that is highly flexible and can be easily expanded.

Research Laboratory

The design for a wet lab space in a scientific research institute was based on the same principles as the aforementioned school. Earlier work at the facility used a traditional voice/data cable design shown in Figure 6.4. With this build-out of existing shell space, new design alternatives were considered from early stages of the project to ensure budget requirements were met while creating a forward-looking system.

The design (Figure 6.4) used a converged voice/data network, which required the addition of a new IP telephony system interfaced to the existing private branch exchange **(PBX)**,[8] preserving that legacy investment. A raised floor was not feasible, but space was available in the ceiling (see Figure 6.4) for installation of zone enclosures housing power over ethernet **(PoE)** network switches. Although an existing wireless network was available in the space, cable was provisioned permanently at workbenches and write-up spaces to support bandwidth-intensive scientific applications. The amount of copper cable required for the build-out was reduced by 50 percent compared to a standard design. A telco closet of approximately 25 square feet was recovered and reused as a vending machine area.

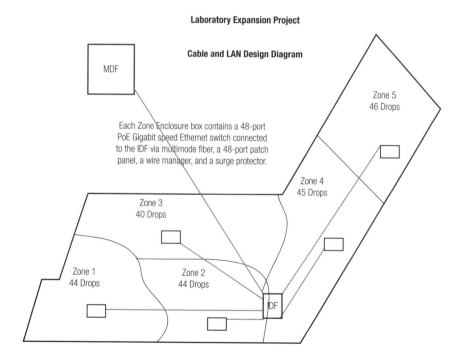

FIGURE 6.4 "Active zone" design with in-ceiling enclosures.

[8] A telephone exchange that serves a specific office or business (see www.webopedia.com/TERM/P/PBX.html).

This installation used a limited combustible **(LC)** copper cable that is 100 percent recyclable by the manufacturer at the end of life.

Commercial Office

This proof-of-concept project for a major technology company demonstrated that integrated technology planning and new office design concepts can both reduce the amount and cost of ICT systems in a workplace and increase occupancy by 40 percent or more while improving employee satisfaction and the overall environmental performance of the workspace.

This connected workspace was designed from the outset to be a new type of work environment built around mobility and the easy availability of network connectivity. Virtually all of the staff assigned to the space use laptop computers and carry cell phones. Wireless connectivity is available throughout the workspace. Wired connections and desktop IP telephones are also available. Conference rooms and meeting spaces are equipped with electronic whiteboards, displays, and projectors that easily can be connected to portable computers.

Even though the space uses a traditional homerun configuration for cabling, the amount of cable installed was reduced by 50 percent because voice, data, and video are converged onto a single network. The total amount of electronic equipment and furniture for the space was equivalently reduced. For example, a small number of high-quality and high-speed printers that are centrally managed and available to everyone were provided. Since the ICT network and office design creates an almost paperless environment, workers in the office actually see an improved service level for print services, while cost and environmental effects are significantly reduced.

The key to the successful design of this new and far more effective workspace was integrated planning. The design team partnered with IT from layout to move-in. They designed the workspace from both the physical construction and the ICT network perspective, with the specific intent of making the workspace efficient, flexible, convenient, and attractive to workers.

CONCLUSION

ICT networks in buildings are a particular concern for facility managers and provide a clear example of how technological innovation will drive change in building design and management. The trends for ubiquity, mobility, personalization, virtualization, and visual communications mean that technology is anywhere and everywhere.

Traditional cable system design can make it difficult to take advantage of these trends. New design concepts are needed to increase efficiency, reduce costs, and progress toward sustainable workplaces. Examples of new approaches to ICT network design illustrate how the major long-term trends will affect the design, use, and management of buildings. As new technologies, applications, and behaviors emerge, facility managers must learn and adapt to keep up with the accelerating pace of change.

ADDITIONAL RESOURCES

"Complete Guide to Flexible Working," www.flexibility.co.uk/Guide/index.htm.
"How Cisco Achieved Sustainability in the Connected Workplace," www.cisco.com/web/about/ciscoitatwork/downloads/ciscoitatwork/pdf/.
"IT Systems Cabling in Buildings: Environmental Issues," www.greenit.net/downloads/GreenIT-EnvIssues-ITCabling.pdf.
"The Whole Building Design Guide, The Changing Nature of Organizations, Work, and Workplace," www.wbdg.org/resources/chngorgwork.php.
"Working Beyond Walls: The Government Office as an Agent of Change," www.degw.com/publications/DEGW_WorkingBeyondWalls.pdf.

Workflow Technology— Knowledge in Motion

7

Paul Head

INTRODUCTION

Workflow technology automates the business **process**, in whole or part, during which documents, information, and tasks are passed on from one participant to another for action, according to a set of procedural rules.[1] Workflow technology is the facilitator, propelling knowledge in motion.

Workflow has historically played a fundamental role in image and document management, leveraging the nature of transactional processing inherent to those industries. These document-centric workflow solutions form the roots of workflow technology.

Today, workflow technology is a common service supporting enterprise-level platforms and human-centric processes. Workflow is an essential enabling technology used throughout and beyond the organization, to support various business functions. This is especially true for the facility management (FM) profession, where process often drives the majority of business decisions. Workflow in FM technologies today drives strategic decisions and operational activities through leveraged use of extended enterprise processes and knowledge.

---

[1] "What Is Workflow?," eWorkflow Portal, www.e-workflow.org.

TECHNOLOGY EVOLUTION

Workflow as a separate technology dates from the late 1980s, when a few pioneering organizations began using imaging to support basic business processes. It is not surprising that many of these early, large-scale, imaging efforts were applied to the insurance industry. Companies such as USAA, Prudential Insurance, and Empire Blue Cross and Blue Shield were enormous paper factories receiving thousands of paper documents per day for claims, customer service, and policy servicing.

Foundations

Imaging technology promised to reduce the significant effort involved in controlling, distributing, and managing daily intake of paper. The obvious issue for these imaging technology companies was how to allow their customers to redefine and change their business process on an ongoing basis once a transition was made to imaging technology. The introduction of automated workflow was the answer. A product called FileNet introduced the first script-based workflow product. Sigma Imaging Systems then introduced the first graphical workflow product at the 1989 AIIM[2] Expo. The workflow industry was thereby established (although no one called it that at the time).[3]

During the same period, many organizations were embracing the personal computing (PC) platform as a way to leverage the power of computing without the high costs associated with mainframe computing. Many FM departments utilized the technology platform advantageously, yet were limited by the capability of this new PC platform. Their information network consisted of multiple disparate technology silos, such as stand-alone computer-aided design (CAD) systems, work-order systems, and a host of spreadsheets. These FM technologies required special skill sets to maintain them, and were typically beyond the domain expertise of many information technology (IT) departments. Many FM departments had to internally source specialized IT resources or cross-train facility resources to maintain these systems.

Although not an optimum environment, these departments would finally automate many tedious and repetitive functions necessary to manage daily operations and planning tasks to work more efficiently. Similar to these emerging FM technologies, early workflow technologies were very code intensive, addressed only basic requirements, and were limited to individual systems. Some workflow

---

[2] AIIM, founded in 1943 as the National Microfilm Association, later changed its name to the Association for Information and Image Management.

[3] Mordechai Beizer, Chair, AIIM Accreditation Workflow Subcommittee, "Interesting Times for Workflow Technology," 1998.

technologies existed as part of larger solution offerings for document and image management, **enterprise resource planning** (ERP), electronic mail, and other data/database-driven software. Other software companies developed workflow products as core solutions, delivering functionality that supported other industry front and back office applications. Because no standards existed, each approach to workflow solutions was comprised of different development methods.

This singular approach provided robust functional capability for both FM and workflow applications as point solutions. As an organization's requirements expanded beyond their department, they realized the value of workflow, to integrate these complex requirements. FM developers incorporated complex requirements into consolidated platforms (e.g., computer-aided facility management [CAFM]). Workflow technology development also matured and support for workflow standards soon developed.

Formalization

Founded in 1993, the Workflow Management Coalition (WfMC), a global organization of adopters, developers, consultants, analysts, as well as university and research groups engaged in workflow and **business process management** (BPM) standards development.[4] They created a common model to address how multiple technologies can coexist and work together for a holistic enterprise workflow solution. This common "reference model" (Figure 7.1) identified characteristics, terminology, and components for the development of a workflow management system framework specification.

As these concepts gained acceptance, organizations leveraged advances in other business technologies to migrate siloed tasks to a single enterprise platform. Workflow is the binding element of the platform to support information flow and drive task completion. Organizations leveraged best practice and industry standards wherever possible to design workflows and mitigate risks associated with these complex enterprise deployments.

Since its origination almost two decades ago, the Workflow Management Coalition's reference model and business process modeling notation (BPMN) language provide a unified approach to leverage documented business process **flows** programmed into workflow technologies.

Originally, development of the BPMN standard was created and managed by the Business Process Management Institute (BPMI). BPMI merged with the Object

---

[4] "About the Workflow Management Coalition," www.wfmc.org/about/welcome.htm.

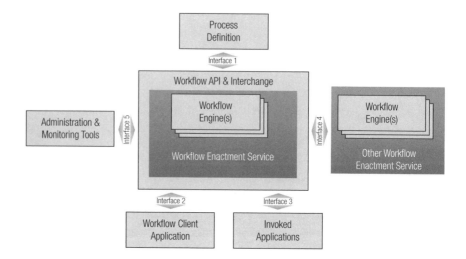

FIGURE 7.1 Workflow reference model diagram, Workflow Management Coalition.

Management Group (OMG) in 2005 and transitioned the BPMN standard under OMG's control. OMG, an international not-for-profit industry consortium with over 500 members, develops and maintains standards for a variety of information technologies. In 2006, OMG released BPMN standard version 1.0 to address workflow requirements drafted by WfMC. BPMN version 1.1, released in 2007, refined these main concepts, and provided a stable model for development by enterprise BPM vendors.

The BPMN 2.0 standard released in 2010 enhanced many aspects of the previous version, including integration of process diagrams automated functionality as well as process execution. Prior to the BPMN 2.0 standard, business analysts would diagram flowcharts in one tool and forward these diagrams to IT professionals as a blueprint to program technical workflows in a separate tool. This process duplicated effort and led to potential misinterpretation of the original mapped processes. The new standard promised a more user-friendly interface for business process own-ers and analysts to map processes easily. Some would argue that the 2.0 release is a step backward for the business user, citing that it is more difficult and has too many symbols for average business subject matter experts (SMEs) to use efficiently.

TRENDS DRIVING WORKFLOW AUTOMATION

According to Gartner's 2010 Magic Quadrant for Business Process Management Suite (BPMS)[5] review, there are over 60 vendors providing a range of workflow

[5] Jim Sinur, Janelle B. Hill, "2010 Magic Quadrant for Business Process Management Suites." Magic Quadrant for Business Process Management Suites, October 18, 2010, Gartner RAS Core Research Note G00205212, www.gartner.com/technology/media-products/reprints/oracle/article161/article161.html.

management functionality. These include leaders in the industry such as Adobe, Appian, Global 360, IBM, Metastorm, Oracle, Pegasystems, Savvion, Software AG, Cordys, Polymita, Singularity, AgilePoint, and SAP, to name a few. The reasons cited for customers adopting and implementing BPM technologies[6] primarily include continuous improvement of operations (over 50 percent), incremental gains (20 percent), and substantial benefits realized (19 percent) through automation of their business practices.

Business: Economy and Efficiency

A global survey for BPM enterprise workflow technology implementations (of approximately 500 organizations) was conducted in 2007 by the Transformation + Innovation and Workflow Management Coalition.[7] Industries investing today have a different focus from those traditionally investing in these technologies. Previously BPM efforts were transactional and focused on manual, paper-intensive events in the financial and insurance sectors. The current process focus is human-intensive and in the services sector, as illustrated in the results of the survey (Figure 7.2).

Defense, utilities, and manufacturing sectors are implementing workflow technology to support operational requirements. Nathaniel Palmer states, "Workflow and BPM today has evolved to a solution for personnel planning, for ensuring faster ramp-up of new staff, and for tackling the most difficult and dynamic processes that are impossible to completely automate, yet critical to manage."[8]

BPMS market sales estimates totaled just under $2 billion for 2009. A poor economy and slow recovery are cited factors attributed to an increased interest in business process improvement and waste reduction. These factors have contributed to a steady market growth in this software category. Since poor corporate sales and minimal profits have hampered top-line growth, many organizations have focused internally to reduce the bottom line by developing operational efficiencies and minimizing operating expenses. A recent report by Global Industry Analysts, Inc. estimates a continued growth of the business process market to exceed $5 billion in revenues by 2017.[9]

---

[6] Findings come from a September 2010 Gartner user adoption survey, which was completed by 593 respondents culled from a random sample.

[7] Nathaniel Palmer, "Workflow and BPM in 2008: A New Business Value Imperative," Transformation + Innovation and the Workflow Management Coalition, 2008 BPM and Workflow Handbook—Spotlight on Human-Centric BPM.

[8] Ibid.

[9] Global Industry Analysts, Inc., Global Strategic Business Report, Business Process Management (BPM) (MCP-6211)

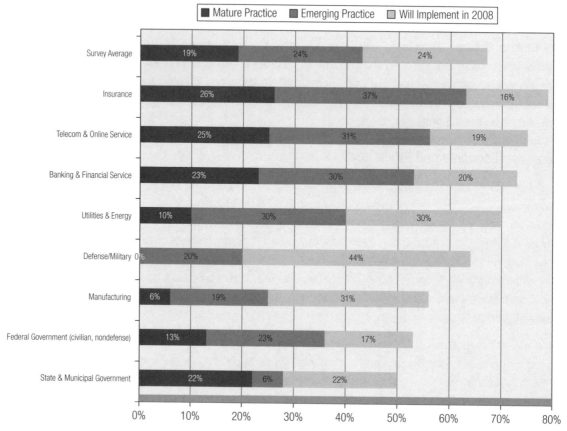

FIGURE 7.2 Level of maturity of BPM investments.
Source: Transformation + Innovation, 2008 Research

Facilities: Business Objectives and Environmental Awareness

In addition to the business economic drivers stated impacting facility budgets, facility managers have also been required to address environmental concerns such as carbon emissions and the resultant greenhouse gases **(GHGs)**. Sustainability and energy efficiency have become a significant challenge for facility managers. To certify buildings under "green" initiatives, every product is documented, relative to the total "carbon cost" surrounding its development, production, operation, and disposal. Facility managers are required to consider total life-cycle costs (total cost of ownership) for assets, as well as all products and materials used in construction and sustainment of their facilities. Likewise, facility managers are increasingly mandated to track energy and carbon metrics using programs such as the Environmental Protection Agency's ENERGY STAR program.

To address these emerging requirements, new technologies are being developed and existing FM/integrated workplace management system (IWMS) technologies are incorporating these requirements into their platforms. Another important FM technology platform, building information modeling (BIM), has also gained momentum to support the life-cycle design of a building. These emerging FM technologies, explained in other chapters of this book, target critical facility management data requirements, but this addresses only half of the problem. These business requirements affect multiple people within and outside of the FM organization, on a daily basis, throughout the life cycle of their facilities. Workflow technology can enforce standardized record keeping about the asset and communicates that information to all necessary resources.

WORKFLOW EXPLAINED

Each FM organization has numerous processes required to support planning and operation. Workflow technologies effectively support processes that work well and can provide reinforcement for changed/improved processes recently established. The identification of activities within the organization that are repeatable and effective can assist in the determination of which processes to automate first. It is equally important to understand current workflow functionality within existing technologies already supporting the organization. If your current systems do not include a workflow engine but are considered "open systems," there are numerous workflow technologies available as commercial off-the-shelf (COTS) products that can be integrated.

Types

Most CAFM, IWMS, computerized maintenance management systems (**CMMS**), enterprise asset management (**EAM**), and ERP solutions already provide some level of enabling workflow technology. If your organization has not implemented this capability already, investigate the effort necessary to automate current manual workflows. During such an investigation, be cognizant that there are two primary process types: *transactional activities* and *systematic activities*. Although each contains different requirements and attributes, both are good candidates for automation.

Transactional Activities

These typically include requests and/or approvals of information passed back and forth between people; along the entire FM value chain from design to disposal, a sequence of requests and approvals are necessary to bring a facility from concept through construction, operation, and decommissioning (Figure 7.3). Thousands of requirements, requests, and approval cycles during an asset's operational life cycle can leverage workflow technology. These requirements include lease renewals, requests for proposals (RFPs), work orders, service requests, change orders, requests for information, and life-cycle monitoring requests to name a few. Workflow technology enhances the ability to effectively complete requests, communicate actions, and document events for regulatory audit control (Sarbanes-Oxley, International Organization for Standardization [ISO], Health Insurance Portability and Accountability Act of 1996 [HIPAA], etc.).

Systematic Activities

These include information typically passed between systems monitoring **conditions**. In some cases it is not, for example, just your human resources department making requests or providing information. We are in an era of machines and facilities that automatically provide information. This communication with building systems is a significant component of the OASIS Open Building Information Exchange (oBIX).[10] These systems feed essential data and knowledge about

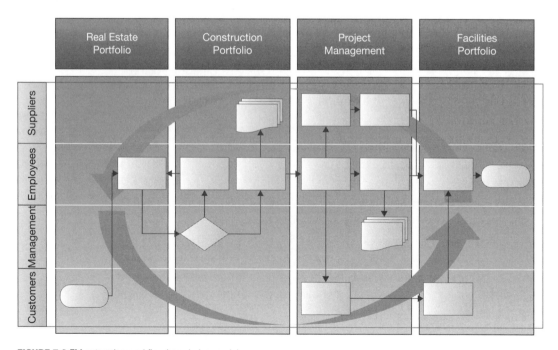

FIGURE 7.3 FM enterprise workflow knowledge model.

[10] OASIS Open Building Information Exchange (oBIX), Organization for the Advancement of Structured Information Standards, www.oasis-open.org.

our assets and facilities that enable us to make strategic and operational decisions. Once again, the basic elements of workflow technology and business process allow us to understand and respond accordingly. Based on our working knowledge of systems and conditions, we establish appropriate control limits and thresholds. When the system pushes beyond those thresholds, we receive communication and react accordingly.

Guidelines

Every implementation requires investment; time to capture processes effectively; cost to develop the workflows, notifications, and assignments; and resources to implement the project. Following are some guidelines to maximize your return on investment:

- **Leverage use of roles**. Defining **roles** in any process is important. Too often, individual assignments shift within the organization. When approvals and **assignments** are automatically generated, direct assignments are fallible. Roles provide flexibility and require less overhead to sustain the system as personnel changes occur.
- **Awareness of formal and informal decision points**. Identify the rigidity of all formal **decision points** during elicitation of activities and procedures. Can more than one person approve, is it always approved the same way, has someone created a work-around, are there requests that cause varying outcomes? Advanced planning can mitigate **risk** caused by process variation through formalized approval steps. Informal processes can cause just as many problems. Many organizations have introduced informal approvals into a workflow to accommodate fluctuating requirements. Eliminate flexible decision points (considered "waste" in a lean environment) if possible. If not, they should become formalized decision points and added to standard operating procedures.
- **Avoid broken processes**. If the process is discontinuous or broken in some other way, it must be fixed before applying workflow. Work with your team to reengineer the process manually before attempting to automate.
- **Methodically record your process**. Walk the process backward when working with your team to capture associated activities, **subprocesses**, **process delays**, and **resources**. Determine if the process contains parallel or **sequential activities**, requires **state changes** (e.g., draft, review, approved), **thresholds** or escalation requirements that may trigger additional processes and/or **messaging**. Process workers think thoroughly

through processes when proceeding from finished **output** to the starting requirement.

- ■ **Assess multisystem interaction (both manual and automated)**. Integrations between multiple systems are difficult. To determine how automation will provide the best return on investment, understand what each system contributes, supporting requirements, and process goals.

- ■ **Automation—success from the start**. Repetitive activities and critical support functions are good to automate. Repeatable steps are the easiest ways to ensure success and remove tedium from your workforce. Workflow technologies effectively support time-sensitive requirements through automated notification and routing. Customer transactions also benefit from automated routing and communication. Workflow technologies effectively support regulatory compliance and reporting requirements with systematic documentation and process consistency.

FM COMMUNITY WORKFLOW TECHNOLOGY CASE STUDIES

FM technology companies understand the importance of workflow within all business processes core to corporate real estate and facility management. Vendors have incorporated components of enterprise BPM technology into their applications and/or built custom BPM functionality, while other vendors have only developed limited workflow capability or none at all. The level of workflow automation varies greatly within the industry and technology providers. The latter mentioned includes vendors that focus on individual FM requirements, niche applications, and newly identified facility requirements. These vendors may not have the development bandwidth to address BPM and rely on manual changes to transact within the system. An example of this workflow substitution is the change of object-based "states" (e.g., inventory, operational, decommissioned) to progress an object (e.g., asset, part, room) through a business process. These technologies rely on a user to recognize the need for change and manually make the modification.

Another example would include construction- and facilities-focused applications, such as BIM technologies. While the focus of the technology comprises an important and dynamic aspect of the building life cycle, primary elements of the technology only manipulate and report data from the model within the application. Business requirements to encompass design, construction, change management, and commissioning processes are not supported within these applications. Many information points and decision requirements reside outside of the BIM model, and therefore require enterprise workflow and approvals to manage the entire process effectively. An overarching enterprise BPM technology could incorporate all business aspects, maintain process consistency, and inform people efficiently, thereby providing a conduit for information and decisions.

The following case studies illustrate effective use of workflow technology to support recurring facilities management activities.

Facilities Move Management

Organization: Government agency

Background: This organization utilizes one of the industry standard CAFM technologies to support space and property management functions for their headquarters and regional facilities throughout the United States. Their system serves as the primary method to provide reports, including housing plans, space allocation, and vacancy rates, and perform scenario planning for space and organizational realignments. In addition, they leverage the system for visitor access requests, employee on-boarding/off-boarding and move management, to name a few business processes.

The facilities move management process (Figure 7.4) facilitates requests, authorization, and relocation of employees/groups from one space/floor/building to another. In addition, there are multiple vendors involved to ensure that work systems/furniture, IT and phone systems, signage, personnel badging, electrical requirements, and employees' personal property are coordinated, moved, and operational.

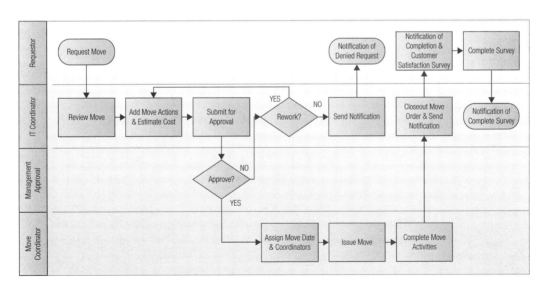

FIGURE 7.4 Move management process.

There are currently in excess of seven systems, four vendors, and six organizations that communicate and share information systematically to complete this process. Every workflow step transacts a notification of change or request for decision, or confirms a defined outcome. A communication and survey to capture the customer's satisfaction of the completed request to conclude the process.

An internal workflow engine within the CAFM system manages the majority of process requirements, but some extend beyond the available functionality of a single technology and require additional custom coding. Standards-based, open systems enable interaction and communication of data between systems.

Success is attributed to thorough documentation of the human and system touch points, collaboration between the organizations involved, and an understanding of the technologies applied. This provided the FM organization with a thorough understanding of how to leverage the database structure and workflow capability.

Vendor Bid and Selection Management

Organization: Financial services company

Background: This corporate real estate/facility management group manages office and retail space across North America. Their current IWMS supports the real estate, facilities, and construction departments of two major divisions within the corporation. Previously, the organization had two stovepiped (i.e., nonintegrated applications) systems that hindered an efficient integrated strategic operation. Sharing lease, facility, and project management data across the corporation was time consuming and made errors more probable. The organization created a common technology platform to consolidate real estate and facilities asset data, providing enterprise transparency and communication between the major divisions for owned/leased facilities and assets.

In addition to system-supported real estate functionality, a key business requirement for the construction management department was to maintain better control of construction management and vendor selection processes. The department identified a requirement to create a construction vendor bid management system to support the vendor selection for facilities construction, signage, and security projects.

The organization defined and mapped their bidding process from inception to supplier award. They focused on all vendor communications and internal organization to eliminate any information gaps that would cause undue delays. All information requests, additional requirements posting, or changes are automatically distributed as notifications to all members involved with the specific bid.

The design review process (Figure 7.5) is an internal requirement to consolidate design and costing documentation. The construction documentation phase diagram illustrates the estimation of construction costs as well as development of funding packages for other outsourced services. Once complete, the build package is forwarded for final design and cost approval, prior to bid release. After the project manager submits information, the workflow engine triggers an e-mail notification to the manager for approval. **Escalations** are time-limit threshold rules triggered by activities exceeding the threshold requirement.

During the bid release process (Figure 7. 6), all interested suppliers are required to submit contact information and select projects of interest. After bid information is posted to the site, the project manager officially issues an RFP release; notifications are pushed via e-mail to the interested parties. During the supplier's review, additional questions or clarifications may arise. The supplier submits a request via the bid site that in turn automatically sends an e-mail to the project manager for response. This workflow may also require the architect and engineer to provide supporting material to clarify or answer the request. Once suppliers are notified, they can request information from the web site.

After the initial bid period closes, the project manager reviews the response matrix of the prospective bidders' information.

The project manager and the project team complete their initial review of all bids (Figure 7.7). The project manager then contacts the bidders to discuss their

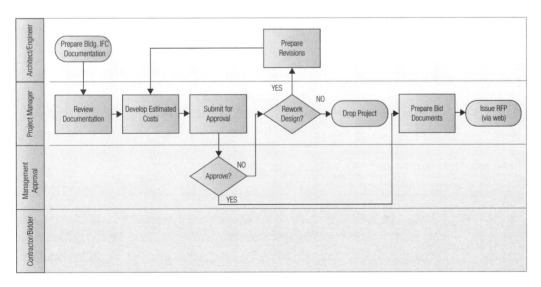

FIGURE 7.5 Design review process.

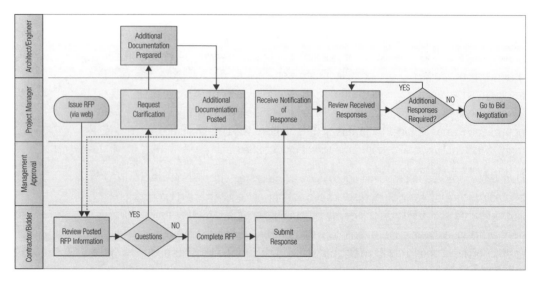

FIGURE 7.6 Bid release and review process.

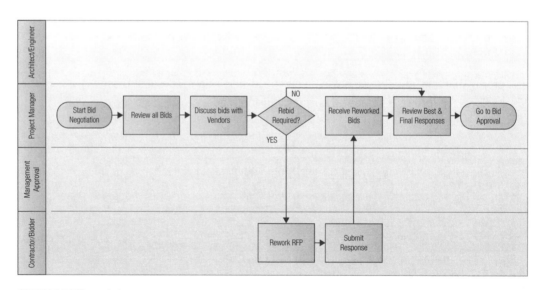

FIGURE 7.7 Bid negotiation process.

proposals, clarify any questions/concerns, and determine if clarifications require revisions to scope and/or pricing components of the bid. If the response is positive, suppliers respond accordingly to the changes required, repost the bid documents, and submit revisions. Again, notifications inform the project team that new documentation is available.

The project team prepares their findings and recommendations for management approval after all negotiations are completed with the bidders, and revisions are resubmitted to the system and reviewed accordingly. The project manager then submits documents for management approval (Figure 7.8). This invokes an approval subprocess and notifies the approving official to review the submission. The official can either request more information, additional scoping, or price adjustments, or approve the submission.

IWMS platform and workflow technology supports decision processes. Notifications support required project management–directed activities, advancing the project. The project manager is prompted to select the winning bidder for the project and invokes a purchase request/purchase order subprocess. Once completed within the department, notifications are sent to the selectee that the bid approval packet is available. The contractor reviews and completes the necessary information and submits their acceptance of the award. This submission notifies the project manager and initiates project kickoff.

The implementation of this centralized project bid repository, supported by well-thought-out repeatable processes, reduced cycle time of project bidding by a minimum of 30 percent and project bidding costs substantially. In addition, centralization of this program provides the transparency necessary for management to meet strategic mission objectives across the entire organization.

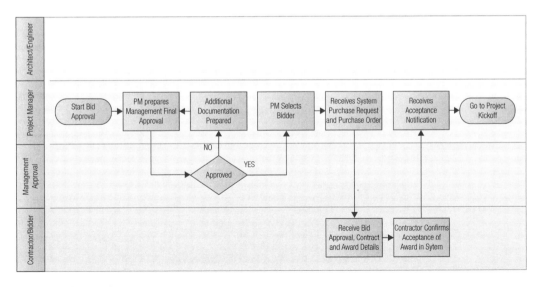

FIGURE 7.8 Bid award process.

KNOWLEDGE IN MOTION

Workflow technology facilitates the enactment of mature business processes, promoting strategic execution of organizational mission and objectives. Workflow technologies leverage enterprise and FM applications to support multiorganization processes and communication. Workflow platforms support enterprise standard processes through a combination of transactional, systematic, and human-centric requirements. Workflow standards and software enable corporate real estate and FM professionals to execute strategy through leveraged use of extended enterprise processes and knowledge.

ADDITIONAL RESOURCES

Articles

Adam Deane, Business Process and Workflow Blog, "Gartner BPM Cool Vendors," April 22, 2011, http://adamdeane.wordpress.com/2011/04/22/gartner-cool-vendors-business-process-management-2011/.

Ryan K. L. Ko, Stephen S. G. Lee, and Eng Wah Lee, "Business Process Management (BPM) Standards: A Survey." *Business Process Management Journal* 15(5) (2009): 744–791.

Web Sites

Business Process Management Initiative, www.bpmi.org/

Business Process Modeling Institute, www.bpminstitute.org/

Business Process Modeling Notation (BPMN), www.bpmn.org/

Drupal Workflow, http://drupal.org/project/workflow

Eworkflow Standards and Research, http://www.e-workflow.org/

Resource for Business Process Management, www.BPM.com

Windows Workflow Foundation, http://msdn.microsoft.com/en-us/netframework/aa663328

Workflow Management Coalition, http://www.wfmc.org/

Applications

Sustainability

8

Louise A. Sabol

OVERVIEW

Buildings significantly, and often negatively, impact the environment and consume natural resources. Building operation accounts for approximately 40 percent of U.S. primary energy use. This number increases to an estimated 48 percent when energy required to make building materials and construct new buildings is included. Building operations also contribute over 39 percent of the United States' carbon dioxide emissions and over 13 percent of its potable water consumption (Figure 8.1).

A well-crafted plan to improve the environmental performance of buildings will often result in cost benefits. Sustainability, **green building** goals, and energy efficiency programs, when planned intelligently, will have benefit for both the environment and the corporate bottom line.

Prioritizing environmental goals is an exercise that will yield a different result for different organizations. However, any sustainability plan will need to include ways to measure and collect data as well as software tools to support the sustainability initiative. Most organizations will discover that reducing energy consumption is a desirable goal.

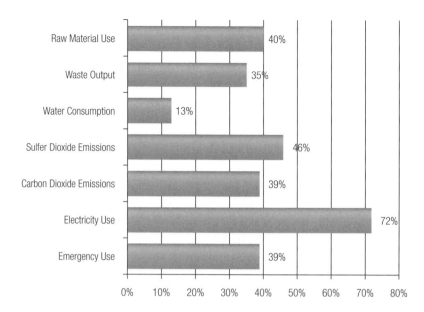

FIGURE 8.1 Buildings' impact on their environment.

Reproduced by permission of Design + Construction Strategies. Data from the U.S. EPA

Energy costs represent the largest operational expense for most buildings, contributing to at least 30 percent of a typical office building's expenditures.[1] The U.S. Green Building Council (**USGBC**) estimates that commercial office buildings use 20 percent more energy on average than necessary.[2] Organizations are seeing sustainability initiatives as a means to gain additional efficiencies in their operations, with building-based efforts being a key component to meeting organizational goals in this area.

SUSTAINABILITY FOR BUILDINGS

Sustainability seeks to reduce negative impacts on the environment and the health and comfort of building occupants, and improve building performance. To achieve improved sustainability, building managers reduce consumption of nonrenewable resources, minimize waste, and create healthy, productive environments. Many organizations are pursuing sustainable certification for their buildings, both to improve performance by pursuing a structured set of improvements and to connote progress and achievement.

Certification for Sustainability

There are several green building rating systems currently in use worldwide. The most widely used systems are: USGBC's Leadership in Energy and Environmental

---

[1] U.S. EPA ENERGY STAR for Commercial Real Estate, www.energystar.gov/index.cfm?c=comm_real_estate .bus_comm_realestate.

[2] Brandi McManus, "Monitoring Energy Use: The Power of Information," February 2009. www2.schneider-electric .com/documents/support/white-papers/WP_Monitoring-Energy-Use.pdf.

Design (LEED; United States), Building Research Establishment Environmental Assessment Method (BREEAM; United Kingdom primarily), Green Globes (Canada and the United States), and Green Star (Australia and New Zealand primarily). Achieving sustainability certification for both new construction and existing buildings involves a great deal of documentation, reporting, and activity tracking. Although there are software tools on the market to capture and manage the wide range of data accumulated on these initiatives, many organizations and project teams rely on customized spreadsheets (Figure 8.2) or simple databases

LEED CI v3 - Tracking Sheet

Green Interior Design and Construction 2009 Edition
Project Scorecard and Tracking Sheet
Certified: 40-49 Points; Silver: 50-59 Points; Gold: 60-79 Points; Platinum: >80 Points

February 2, 2011

74	24	3	9	TOTAL PROJECT SCORE		
Y	?+	?-	N	REQUIREMENTS	DOCUMENTATION	D/C
	Y			**PROJECT REQUIRED DOCUMENTATION**		
				Please upload a site plan, typical floor plan(s), typical building section(s), typical or primary elevation, and representative photos of the building (renderings are acceptable for Design Phase review; photos taken after substantial construction completion are needed for Construction Phase review) and a general project narrative (1-3 pages) that describes the background/history of the project, use(s) of the building in some detail, the location and surrounding area of the building, and any other project attributes you'd like to highlight for us beyond these requirements.	Please provide appropriate drawings, plans, sections, and other representative illustrations for both the design review (renderings will suffice) and the construction review (photos will suffice). Also provide a general project narrative (1-3 pages) that describes the project, history of the building, use of the building, etc. for evaluation.	D
19	2			**SUSTAINABLE SITES (21 potential points)**		
5	/	/	/	Credit 1: Site Selection Intent: To encourage tenants to select buildings that employ best practices systems and green strategies. *Due to the nat points or more being tracked in the "Y" column, the point total for "Y" will be limited to 5, and all columns will automatically display a forward slash		
				1-5 points. Choose from the following options:	Provide documentation proving that space exists inside a LEED certified building.	D
				OPTION 1, 5 points		
				Select a LEED certified building.		
				OR		
				OPTION 2, 1-5 points		
				Satisfy one of more of the following:		
				PATH 1. Brownfield Redevelopment, 1 point	Assemble information about the previous site contamination and remediation efforts undertaken. For further guidance please see SSc1 submittal template.	D
				A building developed on a site documented as contaminated (by an ASTM E1903-97 Phase II Environmental Site Assessment or a local voluntary cleanup program) OR A building on a site classified as a brownfield by a local, state or federal government agency. Effective remediation of site contamination must have been completed.		
	1			PATH 2. Stormwater Design—Quantity Control, 1 point	Please see SSc1 submittal template for documentation guidance.	D	O
				A building that prior to its development had less than or equal to 50% imperviousness and has implemented a stormwater management plan that is equal to or is less than the predevelopment 1 1/2 year 24-hour rate and quantity discharge. OR A building that prior to its development had more than 50% perviousness and has implemented a stormwater management plan that reduced predevelopment 1 1/2 year 24-hour rate and quantity discharge by 25% of the annual on-site stormwater load. This mitigation can be achieved through a variety of measures such as perviousness of site, stormwater retention ponds, and harvesting of rainwater for reuse. Stormwater values are based on actual local rainfall unless the actual exceeds the 10-year annual average local rainfall, in which case the 10-year annual average should be used.		

FIGURE 8.2 Example showing a portion of a customized spreadsheet to track information and progress for achieving a LEED certification for a commercial interiors renovation project (LEED CI).

Reproduced by permission of Design + Construction Strategies

to keep track of the information and progress accumulated during the course of the certification process.

The submission of project data to a certifying authority is primarily done via the Web (exclusively by the Web for LEED-EB). LEED Online is the Web-based application for managing the certification process and submitting required documentation for LEED projects to USGBC.

ENERGY STAR Building Certification

ENERGY STAR for Buildings is a voluntary energy efficiency program spearheaded by the U.S. Environmental Protection Agency (EPA) to foster improved energy efficiency in U.S. commercial and industrial buildings. First introduced in 1999, ENERGY STAR for Buildings provides a rating system to facilitate comparisons of the energy performance of commercial buildings and recognize the most efficient and cost-effective buildings in the country. Although sustainability certification systems such as LEED incorporate measures for improved building energy performance, there is no clear proof that a building with a sustainable certification is necessarily energy efficient. ENERGY STAR is the most well-known framework to provide a process and metrics to benchmark energy performance on a national basis with the specific goal of improving building energy performance. The ENERGY STAR program consists of a scorecard with a rating system of 1 to 100. Facilities that achieve a score of 75 or higher are eligible for the ENERGY STAR seal. An example statement of ENERGY STAR performance for a facility is shown in Figure 8.3.

ENERGY STAR Portfolio Manager is a free online tool that benchmarks and tracks the energy use of buildings, and provides a means for building managers and others to assess the energy performance of buildings. The tool's use is expanding while undergoing continuing enhancement. Data entered in the program is compared to national building performance metrics in the Department of Energy's Commercial Building Energy Consumption Survey (CBECS) database, a national sample survey that collects information on the stock of U.S. commercial buildings, their energy-related building characteristics, energy consumption, and expenditures. The tool's basic functionality also can calculate the greenhouse gas (GHG) emissions performance for a building.

Assessment and Planning

In order to determine whether to certify a building, which certification method to use, and how to create a sustainable building management plan, several types of information are particularly valuable to support the entire building life cycle

STATEMENT OF ENERGY PERFORMANCE
Office Sample Facility

Building ID: 2005550
For 12-month Period Ending: April 30, 2010[1]
Date SEP becomes ineligible: August 28, 2010

Date SEP Generated: July 02, 2010

Facility
Office Sample Facility
1234 Main Street
Arlington, VA 22201

Facility Owner
Sample Owner
1500 Test Avenue
Charlotte, NC 28227
555-555-5555

Primary Contact for this Facility
Jane Smith
1500 Test Avenue
Charlotte, NC 28227
555-555-5555
jsmith@jsmith.com

Year Built: 2000
Gross Floor Area (ft²): 53,232

Energy Performance Rating[2] (1-100) 90

Site Energy Use Summary[3]
Electricity - Grid Purchase(kBtu)	2,288,770
Natural Gas (kBtu)[4]	1,228,009
Total Energy (kBtu)	3,516,779

Energy Intensity[5]
Site (kBtu/ft²/yr)	66
Source (kBtu/ft²/yr)	168

Emissions (based on site energy use)
Greenhouse Gas Emissions (MtCO₂e/year)	413

Electric Distribution Utility
Dominion - Virginia Electric & Power Co

National Average Comparison
National Average Site EUI	114
National Average Source EUI	289
% Difference from National Average Source EUI	-42%
Building Type	Office

Meets Industry Standards[6] for Indoor Environmental Conditions:
Ventilation for Acceptable Indoor Air Quality	Yes
Acceptable Thermal Environmental Conditions	Yes
Adequate Illumination	Yes

Professional Engineer Stamp

Signature: _____

Based on the conditions observed at the time of my visit to this building, I certify that the information contained within this statement is accurate and in accordance with the Licensed Professional Guide.

Professional Engineer
License Number: 0000001
State: VA
John Doe
333 Old Sample Lane
Arlington, VA 22201
555-555-1234

FIGURE 8.3 Statement of Energy Performance, output from the ENERGY STAR Portfolio Manager application.
Reproduced by permission of Design + Construction Strategies

(Figure 8.4). Facility condition assessments[3] (FCAs), portfolio energy consumption data, information about existing heating, ventilating, and air-conditioning (HVAC) and building automation systems (BASs) or energy management systems

---

[3] See also Chapter.

FIGURE 8.4 Data support for sustainability is required in all phases of the building life cycle.
Reproduced by permission of Design + Construction Strategies

(EMS), and any existing computer-aided facility management (CAFM) or integrated workplace management systems (IWMS) are useful. Many organizations pursuing sustainable initiatives employ ad hoc tools, such as spreadsheets, to manage this information. Commercial software applications are rapidly evolving to accommodate the variety of data tracking, reporting, and analysis needs for sustainable requirements in all phases of the building life cycle.

SOFTWARE FOR SUSTAINABLE FACILITIES MANAGEMENT

Software applications can support an organization's sustainability efforts throughout the project life cycle, from initial assessments, to project planning, implementation, and into sustainable operations and maintenance. Many commercial building management software suites—IWMSs, CAFM, computerized maintenance management systems (CMMSs)—are well positioned to track this information and integrate the sustainability domain with standard building data and application functionality. Software vendors are incorporating sustainability and energy management features into their product lines to varying degrees. Application features and functionality supporting sustainability may not necessarily align to the specific demands of facilities organizations and warrant careful planning before selection and implementation. Figure 8.5 displays on overview of the green capabilities that facility management (FM) software applications are accommodating to various degrees.

Application tools can track sustainability-related data for key areas such as energy and water usage and costs, utility bill tracking, emissions data, solid waste generation, and system efficiencies. Integrated "smart building" systems can track real-time building information, and provide users with functionality to compare this data to business plan objectives, key performance indicators, or organizational **benchmarks**.

Advanced application features can perform what-if scenario planning, as well as provide capabilities to provide economic analysis, automating complex formulas to evaluate the financial and environmental impact of potential sustainability

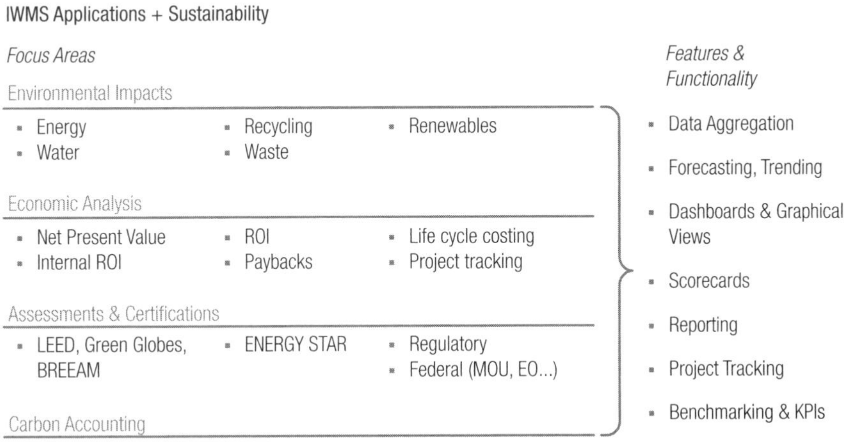

IWMS Applications + Sustainability

Focus Areas			*Features &*
			Functionality

Environmental Impacts

- Energy
- Water
- Recycling
- Waste
- Renewables

Economic Analysis

- Net Present Value
- Internal ROI
- ROI
- Paybacks
- Life cycle costing
- Project tracking

Assessments & Certifications

- LEED, Green Globes, BREEAM
- ENERGY STAR
- Regulatory
- Federal (MOU, EO...)

Carbon Accounting

- Data Aggregation
- Forecasting, Trending
- Dashboards & Graphical Views
- Scorecards
- Reporting
- Project Tracking
- Benchmarking & KPIs

FIGURE 8.5 Green capabilities of IWMS software.

Reproduced by permission of Design + Construction Strategies

investments and improvement initiatives. Some vendors offer the capability to track an organization's ongoing certification efforts for frameworks like LEED or ENERGY STAR. Software that has carbon accounting capabilities can offer the building manager a means to evaluate their buildings' carbon footprint using standard carbon accounting (GHG) methodologies.

Sustainability is becoming an important part of the FCA process. Software vendors in this arena are incorporating sustainability assessments and enhancements to their applications to help evaluate existing buildings' merits in this regard. An example of one such assessment—a building condition vs. energy efficiency analysis, is shown in Figure 8.6). Green FCA applications aim to provide building managers with a baseline of a portfolio's current state of sustainability, and identify opportunities, prioritize options, define metrics, and estimate costs for meeting an organization's goals and mandates.

The Importance of Visualization

Visualization features and the capabilities to display complex data graphically in facilities management software applications are improving. This benefits nontechnical users and decision makers alike, by providing the capabilities to understand performance data in easier, more intuitive methods. Application features such as dashboards, scorecards, comparative graphs and charts, geographic information system (GIS) mapping, 2D building diagrams, and 3D building models foster the display of complex, interdependent data and facilitate easier understanding among a broad range of stakeholders.

One of the more difficult areas of sustainability for organizations to manage involves baselining and strategizing reduction of a facility's carbon footprint. Software applications that have evolved beyond simple spreadsheets and incorporate

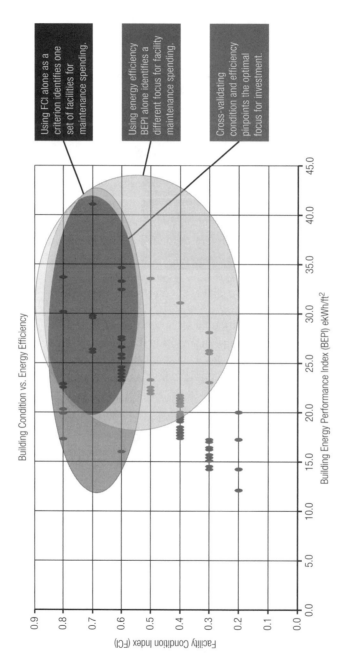

Building Condition vs. Energy Efficiency

Using FCI alone as a criterion identifies one set of facilities for maintenance spending.

Using energy efficiency BEPI alone identifies a different focus for facility maintenance spending.

Cross-validating condition and efficiency pinpoints the optimal focus for investment.

Facility Condition Index (FCI)

Building Energy Performance Index (BEPI) ekWh/ft²

FIGURE 8.6 Building analysis report, mapping energy efficiency (EUI) and building condition (FCI) to identify potential candidates for an increased level of investment to improve their condition and reduce energy costs.

Reproduced by permission of VFA Inc.

visual display of data will assist this complex endeavor and allow for more systematic views of environmental information. Figure 8.7 presents a sustainability assessment for a facility in a graphic scoreboard format, visually indicating the sustainability priority from "Unacceptable" to "Very Good."

Life Cycle Cost Analysis

Although design and construction of buildings is a critical area for achieving sustainability, organizations spend most of their infrastructure dollars operating and maintaining buildings over their life cycle. A life-cycle cost analysis, referred to as an LCCA, is a method for assessing the total cost of ownership (TCO) for a building. This analysis takes into account all costs involved in a building life cycle— acquiring, owning and operating, and disposing of a building or building system.

LCCA is especially useful to evaluate project alternatives that fulfill the same performance requirements, differing with respect to initial costs and operating costs, to determine the option that maximizes net savings. For instance, LCCA will help determine if a new high-performance HVAC system will pay back its initial cost by returning reduced operating and maintenance costs. Software for performing LCCAs is available from several sources, including public domain tools such as building life-cycle cost (BLCC) from National Institute of Standards and Technology (NIST) or life-cycle cost analysis (LCCA), an Excel-based tool from the Rocky Mountain Institute. An example of a life cycle cost analysis from

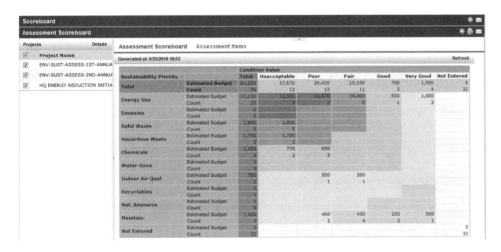

FIGURE 8.7 Sustainability assessment scoreboard, a graphical approach to evaluate high-priority environmental sustainability items, and drill down for more detail.

Reproduced by permission of ARCHIBUS, Inc., Facilities Management Techniques, Inc., and Bruce K. Forbes

the BLCC software tool is shown in Figure 8.8. Large organizations have also developed their own LCCA tools to reflect their particular methodologies and practices.

(Note that LCCA is not to be confused with a life-cycle assessment [LCA], a methodology that holistically evaluates the environmental impact of a product through its life cycle. Performing LCAs generally will be the province of the vendor, not the building manager.)

Comparison of Present-Value Costs

PV Life-Cycle Cost

	Base Case	Alternative	Savings from Alternative
Initial Investment Costs Paid By Agency:			
Capital Requirements as of Base Date	$0	$0	$0
Future Costs:			
Recurring and Non-Recurring Contract Costs	$0	$463,879	-$463,879
Energy Consumption Costs	$822,018	$372,060	$449,957
Energy Demand Charges	$191,804	$170,049	$21,755
Energy Utility Rebates	$0	$0	$0
Water Costs	$0	$0	$0
Recurring and Non-Recurring OM&R Costs	$861,220	$688,976	$172,244
Capital Replacements	$0	$0	$0
Residual Value at End of Study Period	$0	$0	$0
Subtotal (for Future Cost Items)	$1,875,041	$1,694,964	$180,077
Total PV Life-Cycle Cost	$1,875,041	$1,694,964	$180,077

Net Savings from Alternative Compared with Base Case

PV of Operational Savings	$643,956
- PV of Differential Costs	$463,879
Net Savings	$180,077

NOTE: Meaningful SIR, AIRR and Payback can not be computed for Financed Projects.

Comparison of Contract Payments and Savings from Alternative (undiscounted)

Year Beginning	Savings in Contract Costs	Savings in Energy Costs	Savings in Total Operational Costs	Savings in Total Costs
Nov 2000	-$16,940	$6,604	$16,912	-$28
Nov 2001	-$37,400	$26,707	$37,335	-$65
Nov 2002	-$44,000	$33,850	$44,807	$807
Nov 2003	-$44,000	$34,345	$45,643	$1,643

FIGURE 8.8 Comparative Analysis Report from the BLCC life-cycle cost analysis tool, available from National Institute of Standards and Technology (NIST).

Reproduced by permission of Design + Construction Strategies

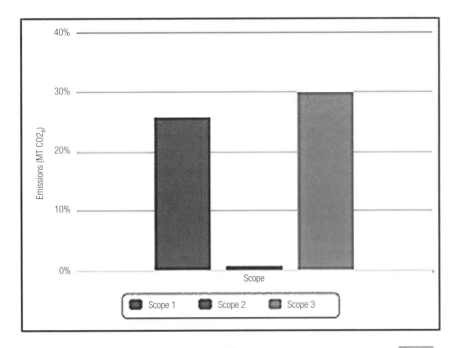

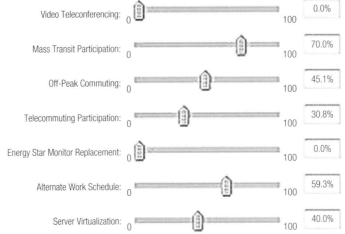

FIGURE 8.9 GSA carbon footprint tool, which allows federal agencies to use sliders to adjust parameters of building operations, altering its greenhouse gas performance. The GSA tool adheres to the World Resource Institute (WRI) GHG Protocol, an international standard on which most other protocols are based, and the International Organization for Standardization (ISO) 14064–1 Greenhouse Gases-Part 1: Specification.
Reproduced by permission of GSA

Carbon/Greenhouse Gas Calculations

Measuring and improving a building's carbon footprint (greenhouse gas emissions or GHG) is becoming an important metric for building owners and managers. This is especially the case in the federal government, which is mandating carbon reporting and significant performance improvement goals. There are multiple protocols for calculating carbon emissions. This sector of analysis is not only technical but changing rapidly as the discipline of sustainability is evolving. Carbon footprint calculators and carbon credits are also useful analysis tools to provide feedback and support planning for corporate sustainability reporting. The U.S. General Services Administration (GSA) has developed one such tool for evaluating a facility's carbon footprint, shown in Figure 8.9.

Enterprise Software Applications

Carbon management software and services is a rapidly growing area fueled by unpredictable energy costs, GHG compliance requirements, and more robust sustainability strategies within organizations. Software application suites that aim to manage this realm are alternately referred to as enterprise energy and carbon accounting (EECA) or enterprise carbon and energy management (ECEM) software platforms. Consolidation has been frequent in this sector in the past few years. Vendors are coming to this software market from a variety of directions, which include:

- **Environment Health & Safety** (EHS) vendors who have incorporated carbon modules (e.g., Enviance and IHS).
- **Traditional energy management vendors**, incorporating a carbon module in their application suites (e.g., Johnson Controls and EnerNOC).
- **Specialists**: Vendors that began with carbon applications and expanded to energy management (e.g., CarbonSystems, Hara, and ENXSuite).

ENERGY ANALYSIS TOOLS AND APPLICATIONS

Energy efficiency is a critical component of achieving sustainability for buildings. Energy analysis is a detailed technical discipline with many subcomponents that include simulation applications to model the performance of the building (whole-building simulation); software to engineer building systems to meet energy performance criteria (sizing programs); and focused tools to calculate specific performance aspects of building or component.

A good source for information on energy analysis software is provided by the U.S. Department of Energy.[4] The agency maintains a Web database that lists building software tools for evaluating energy efficiency, renewable energy, and sustainability in buildings. The database contains almost 400 applications and tools—almost every energy analysis application available to the general public. Both commercial

---

[4] See "Building Energy Software Tools Directory," http://apps1.eere.energy.gov/buildings/tools_directory/doe_sponsored.cfm.

and public domain software applications are listed. The tools vary widely in capabilities and scope, ranging from point solutions and simple calculators to comprehensive whole-building analysis suites. Categories of the tools in the directory are listed in Table 8-1. Many of these applications are directed toward design and engineering professionals, but the database also contains a few tools that are directed toward nonprofessional managers and policy makers, providing data support on energy issues for policy, planning, and general reporting.

Building Information Modeling

Building information modeling (BIM) software applications facilitate the creation and use of three-dimensional electronic building models along with a range of underlying building information. Along with supporting standard building design and documentation processes, BIM offers a means of analyzing building designs for sustainability requirements. BIM is an increasingly important tool for accomplishing energy analysis for a building project. Early in the design process, BIM can provide conceptual energy modeling, which provides early feedback on potential energy implications of a proposed project. The technology also supports the detailed engineering, which is crucial in determining the most viable energy-efficient alternatives for a project. Results for one such analysis, for evaluating MicroFlo ventilation, can be reviewed in graphical format within the model, as shown in Figure 8.10.

TABLE 8.1 Applications by subject listed in the online DOE Energy Software Tool Directory.

DOE Building Energy Software Tools Directory

Whole-Building Analysis

■ Energy Simulation	■ Renewable Energy	Sustainability/Green Buildings
■ Load Calculation	■ Retrofit Analysis	

Materials, Components, Equipment & Systems

■ Envelope Systems	■ Lighting Systems	■ HVAC Equipment and Systems

Focused Applications

■ Atmospheric Pollution	■ Solar/Climate Analysis	■ Validation Tools
■ Energy Economics	■ Training	■ Ventilation/Airflow
■ Indoor Air Quality	■ Utility Evaluation	■ Water Conservation
■ Multibuilding Facilities		

Codes & Standards

Reproduced by permission of Design + Construction Strategies

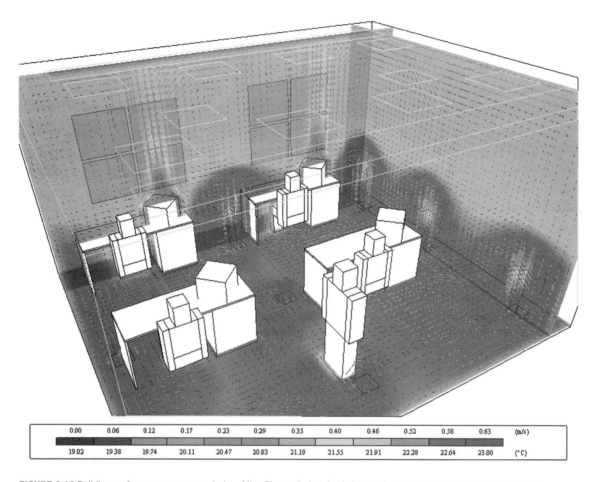

0.00	0.06	0.12	0.17	0.23	0.29	0.35	0.40	0.46	0.52	0.58	0.63	(m/s)
19.02	19.38	19.74	20.11	20.47	20.83	21.19	21.55	21.91	22.28	22.64	23.00	(°C)

FIGURE 8.10 Building performance energy analysis—MicroFlo ventilation. Analytics can be used in conjunction with and outside of a BIM model.

Reproduced by permission of Integrated Environmental Solutions (IES)

BIM capabilities are rapidly evolving. Many stand-alone energy and sustainable software applications are being integrated with BIM applications and supported by project workflows. There are several commonly used stand-alone software applications for evaluating energy usage in building projects, such as Energy-10, eQuest, EnergyPlus, DOE-2.1E, and BLAST. BIM software applications have incorporated capabilities to exchange data with these programs, as well as with other more vendor-specific software applications for energy analysis and component design (such as TRACE by Trane). gbXML (Green Building XML) is a standard data format that was developed specifically to support data exchanges for energy analysis between software applications, such as the interaction between BIM and energy modeling software.

BIM also offers the potential to affiliate and manage nongraphic data along with graphic representations of building components. This function offers great promise for tracking the range and breadth of information required for sustainable building design along with components visually represented in the model. Furthermore, BIM's capability to quantify components, affiliate real-world cost data, and track specifications and features allows for quicker cost estimations of sustainable alternatives and more rapid specifications of sustainable products.

The Future

Technologies to strategically manage energy use in building will become increasingly important, especially as smart grid technology gains broader utilization. Smart grid networks deliver electricity from suppliers to consumers with the assistance of digital technology that tracks power consumptions via two-way data networks. Owners will need to make informed decisions to control and reduce their buildings' energy use in sync with the pricing fluctuations resident in these new service systems. BIM promises to be a powerful technology to support the dynamic and complex information requirements for supporting buildings in the years ahead.

MANAGEMENT OF SUSTAINABILITY

Support for the operational management of sustainable and energy efficient buildings (high-performance green buildings) is another rapidly expanding area of technology development. Sophisticated software technologies to effectively manage the complex building components that directly control energy use and operational efficiency are integral to achieving higher performance goals. New systems or portals integrate data from multiple sources to give a unified picture of a building's real-time operation.

Building Performance and Monitoring

Building automation systems (BASs), when properly integrated into a building, can help optimize energy use, operations, and indoor comfort over the lifetime of a building. BAS vendors have historically maintained proprietary data formats and software applications to support their products. However, new open exchange standards and management mechanisms are emerging that integrate and manage building systems as a whole entity, creating what is being now termed a *smart building*.

Building Information Management			
Preliminary Review	**Project Development**	**Implementation**	**Operate & Maintain**
▪ Performance Discovery ▪ Baselining ▪ Identify Opportunities	▪ Design Decisions ▪ Regulatory Targets ▪ Building Performance Improvement	▪ Environmental Impact ▪ Tracking & Verification ▪ Performance Refinements	▪ Certifications ▪ Building Efficiency Tuning ▪ Portfolio Analysis & Prioritization

Building Commissioning

Building commissioning is a requisite activity for owners and operators who are serious about achieving sustainable, energy efficient buildings. Commissioning generally pays for itself through more efficient building operation and provides an improved working environment for occupants. Software applications that support building commissioning incorporate data retrieved from automated building systems for monitoring and evaluating performance. Smart building systems and intelligent software applications assist in improving building performance by integrating real-time decision support and the potential to support ongoing monitoring and continuous commissioning.

Data Management

Keeping track of the voluminous data generated by a sustainable management program can be a challenge. Many organizations hire consultants to provide systems integration that includes a data management dashboard. As shown in Figure 8.11, data management covers many categories and specialities, and supports the full building life cycle, from preliminary reviews through ongoing operations and management of the facility.

CASE STUDY: THE STATE OF MISSOURI BUILDING INFORMATION MANAGEMENT SYSTEM

One of the greatest difficulties in FM is the vast array of information that is generated, archived, and used in the practice, and the lack of mechanisms to summarize the information in a way that would provide a clear picture of past and present performance. The capability to do so will empower decision makers to make better decisions about critical facilities issues, especially energy management.

The state of Missouri was facing many rapidly escalating building issues, including increased energy expenditures, escalating real estate costs, and a growing backlog of deferred maintenance items. These issues propelled the state to embark on an enterprise-wide technology initiative to provide for improved management of its buildings with the goal of driving increased efficiencies from the portfolio. With approximately 32 million square feet in its real estate inventory, Missouri had been spending approximately $300 million annually to operate and maintain existing buildings.

A consortium of companies[5] came together to form Team CO-OP, bringing technology and application elements together to form an integrated solution under a $24 million contract. They were tasked with upgrading control and information systems in approximately 1,000 state-owned and -operated buildings. The first phase of the project included an assessment program that provided the state with its first comprehensive review of the performance of its real estate portfolio.

As part of the effort, the team needed to integrate a variety of disparate information silos into a common portal—a software application that provided a display of multiple data sources in order to provide a common operating picture of the facilities performance. This unified building information management system was christened the Global Access Facilities Portal. The application was comprised of several components, including a communications infrastructure, utility bill management, building automation controls, energy management, asset conditions management, business process and capital planning, work orders, and remote monitoring. Along with data management, the project included installation of Web-enabled building control systems and a low-cost, wireless communications network.

Project Details

The project's aim was to implement devices and systems that would provide a much higher level of monitoring, measurement, and interoperability of information to give a better picture of performance in the facilities. A key feature in the new system was providing real-time feedback of critical building data from multiple sources. This capability provides high-quality information to support decision-making for a range of users, from operations and maintenance staff to the executive suite, in a format not previously available.

In creating the unified portal view, the system developers needed to overcome the incompatibility of existing systems, proprietary architectures, outdated information, a lack of historical data, and ineffectual work processes—problems all too common in facility information management.

[5] Team CO-OP direct partners for the state of Missouri project include: Talisen Technologies, Johnson Controls, Inc., GridLogix, Appian, and ISCO International.

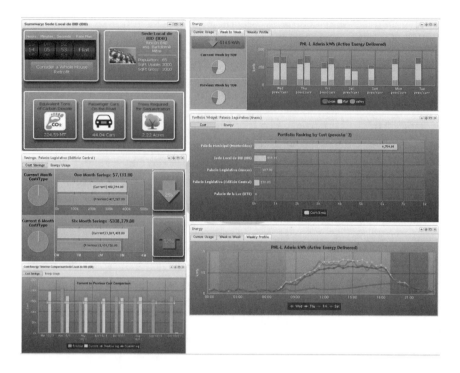

FIGURE 8.12 Facilities dashboard.

Reproduced by permission of Talisen Technologies, Inc.

The portal aggregates and presents data and control information from a wide variety of software applications and Internet-enabled devices, connected through secure communications. Users access information via the Web based on "role,"[6] and drill down for more detail on particular items, whether that be a particular site, building, or function. The system provides information on buildings' spaces, utilities, operations and maintenance, energy, and capital planning. An example of a facilities dashboard or portal, comprised of multiple data views and analyses, is shown in Figure 8.12.

Project Results

The estimated return on investment for the project was achieved in less than two years. The initiative returned annual savings from the combined projects of more than $35 million per year, $20 million from energy savings alone. Efficiencies were achieved through reduced energy usage, process improvements in building automation, monitoring and management, and more efficient real estate portfolio management. The carbon footprint was reduced significantly in GHG emissions.

---

[6] Within a computer system, roles are created to assign varying levels of permissions to users, so that they are allowed to perform certain functions, and are blocked from other activities not authorized for that role.

Further Development

Talisen, a key member of Team CO-OP, is working to extend the portal's concept which is poised to serve new constituencies that face the same issues as the state of Missouri, from city government to federal agencies. The Enterprise Sustainability Platform (ESP) incorporates access to a full system of applications, including IWMS, to provide data for a portfolio of facilities.

Notably, the portal incorporated visual, geographic display of data, as shown in Figure 8.13. For sustainability management, the application's carbon footprint analyzer displays carbon footprint data for sites and conducts what-if scenarios. The decision-making process is supported by multiple graphs and analyses, as shown in Figure 8.14.

FIGURE 8.13 Views of Talisen's ESP carbon footprint analyzer that delivers information to managers, displaying the expected annual net carbon emissions of a particular site—graphically displaying net carbon calculations and what-if scenarios.
Reproduced by permission of Talisen Technologies, Inc.

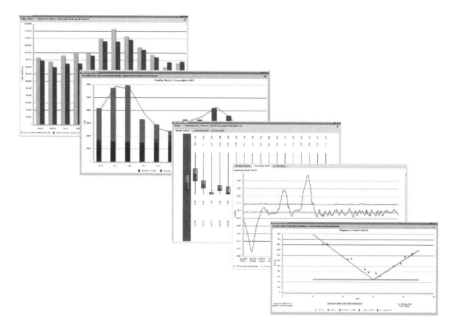

FIGURE 8.14 Talisen's enterprise energy management gives building owners technology tools to support measurement and verification of performance contractor's energy conservation measures, or simply put—did they really save what they were supposed to?

Reproduced by permission of Talisen Technologies, Inc.

For energy management, the application provides a utility dashboard, supporting portfolio analyses with graphical view of consumption and costs, plus the capability to reference a separate bin of data—historical utility bills. Real-time feedback of performance is a technological advance achieved through sensors and smart building technologies. The capability to serve up information to a common portal, from both historical data repositories and separate, real-time data streams provides decision makers with a broader view of facilities performance and better support decision making by providing a deeper information base throughout the portfolio.

ADDITIONAL RESOURCES

Buildings and Their Impact on the Environment: A Statistical Summary. U.S. EPA. Revised April 2009, www.epa.gov/greenbuilding/pubs/gbstats.pdf.

Commercial Buildings Energy Consumption Survey U.S. Energy Information Administration, www.eia.doe.gov/emeu/cbecs.

Energy Star Portfolio Manager U.S. Environmental Protection Agency, www.energystar.gov/index.cfm?c=evaluate_performance.bus_portfoliomanager.

Life-Cycle Cost Analysis (LCCA). Whole Building Design Guide. www.wbdg.org/resources/lcca.php.

Greenhouse Gas Protocol Initiative. Tools provided by the GHG protocol, www.ghgprotocol.org/calculation-tools/all-tools.

Christopher P. Hodges, "Getting Started—Sustainability." "How-To Guide" Series. IFMA Foundation. 2009. http://ifmafoundation.org/programs/sustain_wp.cfm.

"Evaluating the Sustainability of Existing Building Portfolios," a VFA white paper. VFA, Inc., 2010, www.vfa.com/wordpress/wp-content/uploads/2010/06/VFA_Whitepaper_Sustainability.pdf.

Ebenezer Hailemariam, Michael Glueck, Ramtin Attar, Alex Tessier, James McCrae, and Azam Khan, "Toward a Unified Representation System of Performance-Related Data," eSim, 2010.

"Managing Real Property—Spatially Enabling Executive Decision Support for FM." Presentation to the Federal Facilities Council. National Park Service, Park Facility Management Division, February 2010. http://sites.nationalacademies.org/DEPS/FFC/DEPS_047399.

Mayra Portalatin, et al. "Green Building Rating Systems," from the Sustainability "How-To Guide" Series. IFMA Foundation. 2010.

Team Co-Op Experience, The State of Missouri Building Information Management Solution, www.teamcoop.org/experience.html.

U.S. Department of Energy, Building Energy Software Tools Directory. http://apps1.eere.energy.gov/buildings/tools_directory.

USGBC LEED Online Certification U.S. Green Building Council, www.leedonline.com/irj/servlet/prt/portal/prtroot/com.sap.portal.navigation.portallauncher.anonymous.

Why Build Green? Building Impacts. A presentation by U.S. Green Building Council, www.usgbc.org/DisplayPage.aspx?CMSPageID=1720.

Condition Assessment in Facility Asset Management

9

James B. Clayton

"Those who manage and operate large physical plants, whether public or private, universally confront a conundrum: 'How do I satisfy the budgeters that I need certain resources to adequately maintain these facilities, without wasting those same resources on data gathering and analysis to build my case?'"[1]

BACKGROUND

Protecting a portfolio of facility assets against the ravages of time and keeping it fit for current use takes significant and continuous investment in repair and renewal of deteriorating components. Proposed expenditures must compete for money that organizations could put to other good uses. When there isn't enough money to go around, many valid and urgent needs remain untended, deterioration worsens, facility condition suffers, and organization performance degrades. Accumulated, deferred investment in repair and renewal creates an ever-accelerating, downward spiral of condition as breakdown maintenance depletes repair and renewal funds.

---

[1] G. R. Ottoman, W. B. Nixon, and S. T. Lofgren, "Budgeting for Facility Maintenance and Repair. I: Methods and Models." *ASCE Journal of Management in Engineering*, July–August 1999, 71–83.

For the past 50 years, facility professionals, chief financial officers (CFOs), governance boards, and legislatures have become increasingly aware of these realities and have been trying to deal with them by adapting a generic business process known as *asset management* to facility management. A key step in **facility asset management** is the continuous generation of data describing asset inventory, condition, and performance. Such data constitute the process "lifeblood," which feeds analytic tools and creates business intelligence of value to decision makers. The successful application of the generic process to any organization's facility portfolio therefore depends on the accuracy, granularity, and credibility of facility data available to that organization. Unfortunately, quality data comes at a price that few organizations can fully afford, making it necessary, at least until recently, to accept fewer benefits and reduced return on investment in facility asset management than first-rate data could otherwise render.

This chapter examines these issues by providing:

- A generic description of asset management
- A detailed description of facility asset management and the role played by condition assessment
- Comparisons of alternative techniques of **building condition** assessment
- Recommendations to help the reader decide which alternative technique is best for an organization

ASSET MANAGEMENT

Asset management is a broad term often used to signify the management of physical assets or financial assets. Physical assets encompass two main categories: fixed and nonfixed. Fixed assets include buildings, utilities, pavements, dams, locks, and so on, and nonfixed assets are rolling stock, vessels, automobiles, cranes, and the like. This chapter describes the management of only one subcategory of fixed, physical assets: buildings.

The American Public Works Association (APWA) Asset Management Task Force once proposed to define asset management simply as:

> [A] methodology to efficiently and equitably allocate resources among valid and competing goals and objectives.[2]

---

[2] American Public Works Association (APWA), "Asset Management for the Public Works Manager—Findings of the APWA Task Force of Asset Management" (Washington, DC: APWA, August 31, 1998).

The Institute of Asset Management recognizes that the management of physical assets plays a key role in determining the operational performance and profitability of industries that operate assets as part of their core business, and defines asset management as:

> [T]he art and science of making the right decisions and optimizing these processes (by cross disciplinary collaboration). A common objective is to minimize the whole life cost of assets but there may be other critical factors such as risk or business continuity to be considered objectively in this decision making.[3]

The Federal Highway Administration (FHWA) elaborates with a widely known definition:

> Asset Management is a systematic process of maintaining, upgrading, and operating physical assets cost-effectively. It combines engineering principles with sound business practice and economic theory, and it provides tools to facilitate a more organized approach to decision making. Thus, Asset Management provides a framework for handling both short- and long-range planning.[4]

And the Government Accountability Office (GAO) adds:

> At its most basic level, Asset Management involves the systematic collection of key data, the application of analytical tools, and the creation of business intelligence (BI), which managers can use to make sound investment decisions about their organization's physical assets.[5]

The process works as follows: First, performance expectations, consistent with goals, available budgets, and organizational policies, are established and used to guide the analytical process, as well as the decision-making framework. Second, asset inventory and performance data are collected and analyzed. This information provides input on future asset repair/renewal requirements (also called *needs*). Third, analytical tools and reproducible procedures produce viable cost-effective strategies for justifying budgets and allocating funds to satisfy organizational needs and user requirements, using performance expectations as critical inputs. Alternative choices are then evaluated, consistent with long-range plans,

---

[3] Institute of Asset Management, 2011, http://theiam.org/what-is-asset-management.

[4] Federal Highway Administration (FHA), *Asset Management Primer* (Washington, DC: FHA Office of Asset Management, 1999).

[5] Government Accountability Office (GAO), "Comprehensive Asset Management Has Potential to Help Utilities Better Identify Needs and Plan Future Investments," GAO-04-461, December 2004.

policies, and goals. The entire process is reevaluated periodically through portfolio and component performance monitoring and systematic feedback over time.[6]

Figure 9.1 illustrates one well-known generic asset management process. The process steps are indicated, as are the relationships among them. Various issues, tools, and/or activities are associated with each step. For example, alternatives evaluation would include the application of an array of engineering economic analysis (EEA) tools such as benefit/cost analysis, life-cycle cost analysis, and risk analysis.

The indicated steps would typically be included in any asset management approach, although the specifics would differ to suit a particular organization and asset type. Individual organizations and portfolio managers will define the parameters of their own processes based on organization-specific decision variables, such as policies, goals, asset types and characteristics, budgets, operating procedures, and business practices. Furthermore, any asset management process should be flexible enough to respond to changes in any of these variables or factors.

The assets likely to be included in an organization's initial asset management implementation efforts will depend on the organization's existing capabilities, particularly in the area of technical, financial, and human resources. What is needed to support the asset management approach is a logical sequence of decision steps, constituting a decision framework. The framework is supported by (1) information regarding organizational goals, policies, and budgets, (2) horizontal

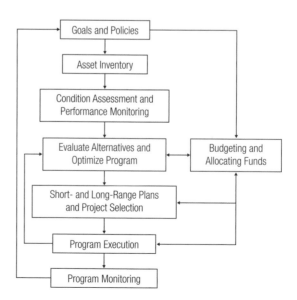

FIGURE 9.1 Generic Asset Management Process.

Reproduced by permission of Institute for Responsible Infrastructure Stewardship

[6] Federal Highway Administration, 1999.

and vertical organizational integration to implement the decision steps in practice, and (3) technical information to support the decision-making process.

ADAPTING ASSET MANAGEMENT PRINCIPLES TO FACILITIES MANAGEMENT

The application of asset management principles to facilities management (FM) began in the 1960s with comprehensive, annual inspections that produced lists and cost estimates of needed repairs and replacements. The focus of such inspections and information was on maintaining a "job jar" as a tactical, work scheduling tool, and the collected data had no clear strategic application. As facility condition assessment evolved, it both contributed to and derived benefit from parallel advances in asset management. The interplay of the two disciplines eventually converged to produce today's facility asset management.

This still-emerging discipline is a strategic approach to the optimal allocation of capital for the repair, renewal, and modernization of aging buildings, pavements, utilities, and other infrastructure. Like its generic forebear, facility asset management combines engineering and economic principles with business practices, tools, and a framework to facilitate organized, logical, and complementary decision making at strategic, operational, and tactical levels. Figure 9.2 illustrates a simplified framework with the basic elements of the generic process divided into four facility-specific activities. While Figure 9.1 presents a clearly divided, sequential flow chart of the process Figure 9.2 shows a grouping of interdependent

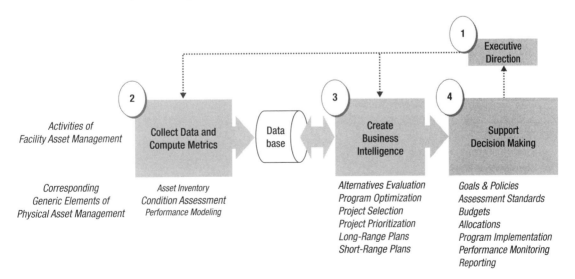

FIGURE 9.2 Simplified facility asset management framework.
Reproduced by permission of Institute for Responsible Infrastructure Stewardship

activities. The generic elements listed below each activity block in Figure 9.2 correspond to the boxes in Figure 9.1.

The process incorporating "facility asset management" goes by a variety of names including: *capital asset management, facilities capital planning and management*, or *capital renewal and deferred maintenance planning*. Whatever label is preferred, the promise of this process is that organizations using it will be rewarded with budget success, improved facility conditions and functionality, grateful users and stakeholders, and better mission support.

Advocates also claim that facility asset management can reduce long-term costs of ownership, prolong facility life, eliminate unforeseen demands on routine operation and maintenance activities and, thus, help optimize return on investment in facility condition and performance.

PHASES OF THE FACILITY ASSET MANAGEMENT PROCESS

Phase 1: Executive Direction

Phase 1 of facility asset management controls the overall rigor, effectiveness, and efficiency of an organization's process by setting goals, policies, and standards that regulate process quality, time frames, and cost. Executive direction should be set consciously and deliberately by the organization's management. If management does not fulfill this duty, lower-level employees and contractors will gladly substitute their own guides, which are not always in the best interests of the organization.

a. Goals and Policies

This ever-repeating action establishes goals and policies against which process steps and their outcomes can be measured and adjusted. Such goals and policies are used to guide the collection of data, the computation of metrics, the creation of business intelligence, and the decision-making framework that employs the business intelligence.

b. Standards

This action represents the creation and deployment of criteria and rules for regulating each process step and work products of process participants.

c. Schedules

This activity produces the calendar schedules for collecting data and computing metrics, creating various types of business intelligence products, and operating the decision-making framework.

Phase 2: Collect Data and Compute Metrics

The purpose of this phase is to systematically gather data and update metrics about individual facilities, their included systems and components. This information answers the questions:

■ What facilities do we have?
■ What are their physical characteristics, condition, and service utility?

Data and metrics describe the inventory, as well as its condition and performance, and are stored in one or more databases for future reuse in this and subsequent phases.

Phase 3: Create Business Intelligence

Phase 3 systematically answers questions such as:

■ What investments are needed in repairs, renewals, and modernizations?
■ Which investments should be made with limited funds?
■ What are the risks and outcomes of investments made and not made?
■ How can those risks be managed with proper investment?

Computer-based **parametric models** use inventory data and computed metrics from Phase 2 to compute many forms of business intelligence **(BI)**, which can be used by decision makers. Any comprehensive facility asset management software enables a trained analyst to forecast future behavior of metrics, create and rank work packages, and analyze alternative return on investment for individual projects—all based on data collected and metrics computed during Phase 2. Good parametrics also help the analyst develop both short- and long-range repair/replacement scenarios and plans, and many applications also enable analysts to forecast long-term renewal costs of building components over a building's entire lifetime.

Phase 4: Support Decision Making

This phase includes the activities that organizational managers conduct in order to set goals, policies, and standards; create and review budgets; allocate available resources; implement programs and projects; monitor spending and performance; and make reports. Managers work within a defined decision-making framework and use business intelligence produced by Phase 3, as well as other sources.

CONDITION ASSESSMENT IN FACILITY ASSET MANAGEMENT

"In an environment of tightly constrained spending, the decidedly un-glamorous business of facility maintenance, operating behind the scenes and producing subtle and distant outcomes, is an easy target for the cost-cutting knife. Defending M&R requirements means building a convincing case. Professional judgment and experience are essential, but lack the definitive edge of a hard, reproducible, computer-generated estimate."[7]

The activity in Figure 9.2 labeled "Collect Data and Compute Metrics" involves the gathering and treating of data pertaining to three facility-related factors: (1) inventory, (2) condition, and (3) performance. The activity's primary input is the output of the previous process step, "Executive Direction" and its purpose is to generate metrics and other data, which are in turn used in the subsequent process step "Create Business Intelligence." Business intelligence products of facility asset management include reports and projections on inventory, condition, performance, deferred maintenance, repair, and modernization; short- and long-range repair/renewal/modernization plans; funding alternatives, risks, and penalty costs attributed to deferring work items and projects; budget requests, fund allocation plans, spending evaluations, detailed project identification, return on investment calculations, project priority ranking lists, and execution plans.

This chapter deals only with the data collection and metrics of condition assessment.[8] Data collection and metrics pertaining to facility inventory and performance monitoring are separate, complex discussions not included in this discussion.

OVERVIEW OF FACILITY CONDITION ASSESSMENT

There are many different types of facilities, ranging from buildings, bridges, railways, and pavements to dams, locks, piers, and utility systems. Central to a comprehensive asset management program is the ability to evaluate and know the condition of all inventoried assets in an organization's real property inventory.

Specific condition assessment technologies have been developed for most of these facility types. For instance, there are at least 20 technical reports that

---

[7] Ottoman et al., 1999.

[8] The fascinating and quickly advancing field of facility performance assessment has a close but contrasting relationship to condition assessment. The remainder of this chapter concentrates on just the condition assessment aspects of facility asset management.

discuss development and provide details on using the various condition assessment techniques for a corresponding number of components and groups of related components of the U.S. Army Corps of Engineers Civil Works infrastructure. Due to space limitations, this chapter discusses the one technology of most interest to IFMA readers: building condition assessment.

BUILDING CONDITION ASSESSMENT METHODS AND TECHNIQUES

There are four main types of alternative techniques for accomplishing building condition assessment. All four draw upon building inventory data to varying degrees and supplement the processing of inventory data with various kinds and combinations of on-site visual observations and computerized parametric models.[9] All four techniques produce metrics and other condition-related data, which are used as inputs to the subsequent step in the **building asset management** process, "Create Business Intelligence."

As shown in Figure 9.3, each of the four building-related techniques can be classified into one of two main categories: (1) the **Monetary Method**, and (2) the **Engineered Method**.[10] It is important to understand the fundamental differences between these methods and techniques when choosing what is best for a particular organization.

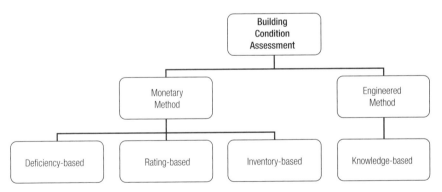

FIGURE 9.3 Building condition assessment methods and techniques.
Reproduced by permission of Institute for Responsible Infrastructure Stewardship

[9] The term *parametric model* as used in this chapter refers to a mathematical equation representing a relationship between a set of measurable factors (such as component type, age, and time) that defines another variable, such as condition, and determines the component's behavior regarding that variable.

[10] D. R. Uzarski and M. N. Grussing, "Building Condition Assessment Metrics: Best Practices." ASCE Special Publication Infrastructure Reporting and Asset Management: Best Practices and Opportunities (Reston, VA: American Society of Civil Engineers, May 2008), 147–152.

The four techniques are classified according to purpose, type of collected data, and metrics computed. All three techniques of the Monetary Method have one identical objective[11] and use dollar estimates of needed work to compute two, monetary-based metrics called backlog and facility condition index **(FCI)**. These three techniques differ only in how the dollar estimates are obtained. The deficiency-based technique gets cost estimates from engineers and technicians who conduct detailed visual inspections. The rating-based technique taps reports from people who record cursory visual observations. And the inventory-based technique employs preexisting databases of building attributes, usually without any visual input.

In contrast, the **knowledge-based technique**[12] of the Engineered Method has two additional objectives[13] and works in the opposite sequence, initially computing a **Building Condition Index (BCI) series** of metrics from which are derived dollar estimates of needed work and several other useful metrics, including the monetary-based condition metrics, backlog, and FCI. The following pages of this chapter define the key difference between the two methods and explain how it drives other significant variances between the four included techniques of building condition assessment.

Origin of the Monetary Method for Building Condition Assessment

The Monetary Method was conceived and developed by the U.S. Navy Bureau of Yards and Docks[14] in the 1960s in an effort to better manage shore base maintenance.[15] After years of refinement and use, the technique was eventually carried by ex-Navy people and a vendor to public higher education in the 1980s. Subsequently, the technique was further refined and successfully marketed by private vendors to other government agencies, educational institutions, the health care industry, and large corporations.

Foundation of the Monetary Method: Backlog and FCI

The classic description of the original Monetary Method is contained in a 1991 book written, in part, by the vendor who helped introduce it to public higher

[11] To produce information needed to manage estimated dollars of repair backlog.

[12] D. R. Uzarski, M. N. Grussing, and J. B. Clayton, "Knowledge-Based Condition Survey Inspection Concepts." *ASCE Journal of Infrastructure Systems* 13(1), March 2007, 72–79.

[13] To produce business intelligence needed to minimize life-cycle cost and to produce business intelligence needed to manage risk to mission.

[14] Now called the Naval Facilities Engineering Command.

[15] Naval Facilities Engineering Command (NAVFAC), *Facilities Management, NAVFAC MO-321*, NAVFAC 025-LP-173-2965 (Washington, DC: Department of the Navy, 1978).

education.[16] That book explained a detailed, systematic approach to visual inspection and helped establish the use of backlog and FCI as the first metrics of building condition assessment. Since then, the definitions of backlog and FCI have evolved in different directions to meet the needs of various organizations, thereby causing inconsistency and inability to compare different organizations in terms of the metrics.

For example, the original published equation for calculating FCI is shown in Equation 1:

$$FCI = \frac{\text{Cost of Deficiencies}}{\text{Current Replacement Value}} \tag{1}$$

where

Cost of Deficiencies is the total dollar amount to correct existing maintenance and repair deficiencies. The amount does not include any future maintenance and repair or other types of work such as alteration or new construction, and

Current Replacement Value is the amount required to reproduce a building in like kind and materials at one time in accordance with current market prices for materials and labor.

Equation 2 gives a different formula for FCI now sanctioned by a task force comprised of representatives of APPA, IFMA, FFC, and others[17]:

$$FCI = \frac{\text{Deferred Maintenance} + \text{Capital Renewal}}{\text{Current Replacement Value}} \tag{2}$$

where

Deferred Maintenance is "total dollar amount of existing maintenance, repairs (i.e., work to restore damaged or worn-out facility systems or components to normal operating condition) and required replacements (capital renewal), not accomplished when they should have been, not funded in the current fiscal year or otherwise delayed to the future. For calculation of facility condition index (FCI) values, deferred maintenance does not include grandfathered items (e.g., Americans with Disabilities Act compliance), or programmatic requirements (e.g., alterations)," and

[16] AME and S. C. Rush, *Managing the Facilities Portfolio* (Washington, DC: National Association of College and University Business Officers, 1991).

[17] APPA, FFC, IFMA, NASFA, and Holder Construction, Inc., Asset Lifecycle Model for Total Cost of Ownership Management Framework, Glossary & Definitions (Alexandria, VA: APPA, 2007).

Capital Renewal[18] is an exchange of one facility system or component for another that has the same capacity to perform the same function, and

Current Replacement Value is the total expenditure in current dollars required to replace any facility at the institution, inclusive of construction costs, design costs, project management costs, and project administrative costs. Construction costs are calculated as replacement in function versus in-kind.

Yet another equation 3 for FCI was adopted by the Federal Real Property Council (FRPP)[19]:

$$CI = (1 - \text{\$repair needs}/\text{\$PRV}) \times 100 \tag{3}$$

where

CI is the Federal Real Property Council's term for monetary condition index.

$repair needs is the amount necessary to ensure that the facility is restored to a condition substantially equivalent to the originally intended and designed capacity, efficiency, or capability

PRV is **Plant Replacement Value**: the cost of replacing an existing facility at today's standards.

Close study of just these three of the many available FCI equations makes it readily apparent why the Government Accountability Office (GAO) recently found that: "… condition indexes, which agencies report to FRPP, cannot be compared across agencies because their repair estimates are not comparable. As a result, "these condition indexes cannot be used to understand the relative condition or management of agencies' assets. Thus, they should not be used to inform or prioritize funding decisions between agencies."[20]

Additional factors add to the confusion over FCI both within and outside the federal government:

■ There are multiple ways to calculate CRV and PRV, and some officials don't recognize the difference between the two.

■ In some circles, FCI is called Asset Condition Index (ACI), Financial Condition Index, or, simply, Condition Index (CI).

---

[18] Minimum dollar threshold levels for capital renewal are set by the building owners/manager, typically in excess of $5,000 or $10,000.

[19] Federal Real Property Council (FRPC), *2011 Guide for Real Property Inventory Reporting*, (Washington, DC: Federal Real Property Council, Office of Management and Budget, October 2011), 11.

[20] GAO, *Federal Real Property—An Update of High Risk Issues*, GAO-09-801T, Washington, DC, July 15, 2009.

- The original FCI condition rating system employs a range of values to represent the condition categories of good, fair, and poor. (Good = FCI < .05, Fair = .05 < FCI > .10, Poor = .10 < FCI). However:
  - These categories and ranges are arbitrary and without any basis in science or economics.
  - Because this scheme is counterintuitive for many people (low indicator meaning good, high indicator meaning bad), some organizations define their condition index to be the quantity (1 minus FCI) in order to correlate higher values of the metric with better condition and, thus overcoming the counterintuitive shortcoming of the original FCI equation.
- Recently, certain officials of the GAO noted that a more appropriate term for FCI would be *Financial Condition Index* in recognition of the fact that, at best, FCI indicates only an organization's financial "health" regarding the ability to provide adequate facility services.[21]

The Deficiency-Based Technique

This chapter uses the term *deficiency-based technique* when referring to the refined, now widespread practice that evolved from the Navy and was described in the previously cited 1991 book.[22] The **deficiency-based technique** has been refined and augmented, and can be described in terms of the progression shown in Figure 9.4.

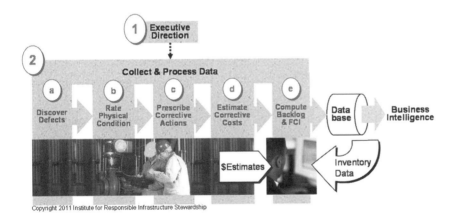

Copyright 2011 Institute for Responsible Infrastructure Stewardship

FIGURE 9.4 Deficiency-based technique relies on inspector opinion.

Reproduced by permission of Institute for Responsible Infrastructure Stewardship

[21] U.S. Army Engineering Research and Development Center—Construction Engineering Research Laboratory (ERDC-CERL), "Overcoming Challenges in Federal Facility Investments," paper presented at the Federal Facilities Council special committee on Predicting Outcomes of Investments in Maintenance and Repair for Federal Facilities, February 18–19, 2010, p. 6.

[22] AME and Rush, 1991.

Phases of the Deficiency-Based Technique

PHASE 1: EXECUTIVE DIRECTION

The ultimate purpose of condition assessment in facility asset management is to determine the present condition of an organization's facility assets and to provide data and metrics for use in subsequent process phases of creating and using business intelligence. Accordingly, Phase 1 of the deficiency-based technique sets the goals, policies, and standards that regulate assessment quality and establishes inspection schedules that determine data freshness and process cost.

a. Goals and policies for data collection and metric computation

Phase 1 begins with an organization's leaders establishing goals and policies against which data collection standards and schedules can be measured and adjusted. Such goals and policies are also used to guide the computation of backlog and FCI metrics.

b. Standards for collecting data and computing metrics

This action represents the creation and deployment of criteria and rules for regulating the assessment and work products of Phase 2 participants. Standards determine things such as:

i. When and how to inspect buildings.

ii. Which discovered physical conditions are acceptable and can be ignored versus which conditions are unacceptable and require correction.

iii. Whether an unacceptable condition warrants a repair vs. a replacement.

iv. What is the desired accuracy for cost estimates associated with corrective actions?

c. Inspection schedules

In the deficiency-based technique, teams of specially trained, highly skilled engineer-inspectors receive schedules that tell them which buildings to tour and comprehensively inspect. Schedules are usually based on a calendar frequency of inspection that management can afford rather than on component condition or organizational need for information.

PHASE 2: COLLECT DATA AND COMPUTE METRICS

The purpose of this phase, as related to deficiency-based technique, is to collect and aggregate monetary cost data to system, building, and portfolio levels in order to compute backlog and FCI metrics. Phase 2 of the deficiency-based technique is comprised of the following actions:

a. Identify **defects**

Inspectors tour the entirety of each assigned building, observing all systems and components within their own specialty fields (mechanical, electrical, structural, etc.), and looking for the presence of conspicuous defects. A defect is a visual clue (e.g., corrosion) that a building component (e.g., gutter), is deteriorating or even is in potential or actual failure mode. The deficiency-based technique relies on the individual inspector's training, skill, experience, and situational awareness to detect defects, but does not require the inspector to catalog, record, or report the attributes of detected defects, per se. Instead, whenever the inspector detects one or more defects on a particular component he simply initiates the next action of Phase 2.

b. Rate physical condition

Deficiency-based inspectors are not required to rate physical conditions per se. Nonetheless, inspectors view defective components and form opinions regarding which conditions are "acceptable" and which are "below standard." This subjectivity plays a big role in influencing the next steps of prescribing corrective action, and the fact that such ratings are unwritten makes the process opaque and untraceable.

c. Prescribe corrective actions

The deficiency-based technique does not require inspectors to formally catalog, record, or report defect data or condition ratings. Instead, inspectors use mostly unwritten, heuristic standards and unstructured personal decision-rules to:

i. Decide whether components should be repaired, replaced, or left alone until the next inspection.
ii. Write and report descriptions of needed repair and replacement actions.
iii. Record and report opinions on needed work type, work quantity, craft classification, urgency, life/safety, funding source, etc.
iv. Predict and report a component's remaining useful life.

d. Estimate corrective costs

The deficiency-based technique requires inspectors to estimate, record, and report a cost for each reported corrective action. The accuracy of such estimates varies greatly according to inspector training, skill, experience, and situational awareness as well as the quality assurance processes used by the inspecting organization.

    e. Compute backlog and FCI

This action is normally performed by automated parametric models designed to support the deficiency-based technique. There are many commercial versions of such software, including web sites that let clients conveniently access and manipulate their own data. All versions use inspectors' cost estimates to compile and compute the estimated corrective costs in a given system, building, or group of buildings. The various sums are called deferred maintenance backlogs, **deferred maintenance and repair (DM&R)**, backlogs of maintenance and repair (BMAR), or simply backlogs of the respective system, building, or group of buildings. Parametric models also combine backlog data with facility inventory data to compute FCI.

PHASE 3: CREATE BUSINESS INTELLIGENCE

Deficiency-based parametric models use backlog, FCI, and facility inventory data to compute many forms of business intelligence that can, in turn, be used by decision makers. Any deficiency-based technique software worth considering enables the trained analyst to forecast future backlog and FCI; create and rank work packages; and analyze alternative return on investment for individual projects—all based on inspector cost estimates, predictions of remaining useful life (RUL), and selected inventory data.

Good deficiency-based technique software also helps the analyst develop both short- and long-range repair/replacement scenarios and plans. Short-range (five-year) "what if" scenarios and work plans are computed by formulas that estimate levels of backlog and FCI based on projected funding levels and indicate necessary funding levels to achieve targeted backlog levels and FCI.

Most deficiency-based technique applications also enable analysts to forecast long-term renewal costs of building components over a building's entire lifetime using a combination of inspector RUL predictions and life-cycle concepts. According to the law of large numbers, projections of this nature are more meaningful for a portfolio as a whole than for any one component or facility.

Dissatisfaction with the Expense of Deficiency-Based Techniques

Despite inspectors' use of hand-held data collection devices, the labor-intensive requirement for comprehensive, annual facility touring and cost estimating by skilled labor make the deficiency-based technique very expensive and time consuming. Resources are often wasted by inspecting items that don't warrant scrutiny and preparing cost estimates that will never be used. Furthermore, data collected by deficiency-based techniques represent a snapshot in time and therefore provide limited future visibility and quickly grow stale as building components deteriorate through age and wear.

In recent years, organizations that initially employed the deficiency-based technique have made numerous attempts to reduce the inherent expense of obtaining inspector cost estimates in order to produce backlog and FCI. Three modified deficiency-based techniques have been tried:

1. **Reducing frequency of entire building inspections**. The first and most common practice used to ease the cost of gathering cost estimates is to reduce the frequency with which individual buildings are inspected. The original deficiency-based technique schedules inspections for entire buildings at yearly intervals. When the reduced frequency technique was devised, a building that normally would be inspected annually might have been inspected only once every three to five years. The reduced frequency technique slashes inspection cost but exacerbates inherent credibility problems of the backlog and FCI metrics by allowing cost data to stagnate during extended periods of no inspection. The reduced frequency technique also misses opportunities to assess critical components in uninspected buildings that need at least partial inspection. Furthermore, extending the inspection cycle to three to five years leads to increased breakdowns, negative impact on operations, and, ultimately, the harmful siphoning of funds from proactive stewardship. Cost estimates gathered by the reduced frequency technique are fed into deficiency-based technique parametric models for computing backlog and FCI. It is also one of the few building assessment techniques that produce cost information granular enough to create and prioritize actionable work items and projects.

2. **Scheduling inspections of systems, not buildings**. This variation of the deficiency-based technique schedules detailed inspections of selected building systems (such as roofing) rather than whole buildings. Schedulers identify and tag each system in the inventory according to perceived need for inspection, and then schedule system inspections by frequencies set according to system attributes such as mission criticality, age, condition, and backlog. Reduced frequency system scheduling further slashes inspection cost, but also exacerbates inherent credibility problems of the backlog and FCI metrics by allowing cost data to stagnate during extended periods of no inspection. The system inspection scheduling practice is an improvement over the reduced frequency, whole-building practice because it misses fewer opportunities to assess needy systems and, thus, avoids more breakdowns, negative operational impact, as well as the harmful diversion of funds from

proactive stewardship. Cost estimates gathered by the system inspection practice are fed into deficiency-based technique parametric models for computing building- and portfolio-level backlog and FCI metrics. It also produces cost information granular enough to create and prioritize actionable work items and projects.

3. **Inspecting a statistical sample of systems**. Another technique for lowering the cost of the deficiency-based technique is to limit the number of detailed inspections to statistically sampled building components and inferring the results to entire portfolios. This method was used in lieu of comprehensive inspection of all buildings for assessing the condition of public higher education facilities in Virginia.[23] It achieved credible results at significantly lower cost compared to the full-blown deficiency-based technique. At the statewide portfolio level, this sampling technique produced backlog, FCI, and "what if" funding scenarios. It was not designed to yield any metrics at the institution or building level, but could have if funds had been available for additional sampling.

Sampling methods such as this cannot produce work items or project details except for the limited number of building components that are actually inspected. A major flaw is that few portfolio owners know enough about statistical sampling and, consequently, engage the lowest priced inspection vendor whose low price invariably is based on inadequate sampling. Unsuspecting officials accept the analyses because they're deemed scientific in nature. The officials then unwittingly treat the results of inadequate sampling as though they are "statistically significant" and use the faulty data to support financial decisions.

This variation of the deficiency-based technique is useful in determining portfolio-level backlog and FCI metrics, but the portfolio steward must still expend additional resources to acquire data for identifying work items and projects.

Description of the Rating-Based Technique

In other attempts to avoid the expense of the deficiency-based technique, some organizations have tried substituting cursory field observations in place of detailed inspections and feeding subjective ratings of condition into parametric models, which compute estimated costs, backlog, and FCI. This alternate practice, called the rating-based technique, is depicted in Figure 9.5, which, for easy comparison, is located adjacent to the picture of the deficiency-based technique.

[23] J. B. Clayton, "Facility Condition Assessment of Virginia's Public Higher Education Institutions." Working paper, ANADAC, Inc., Arlington, VA, 1993.

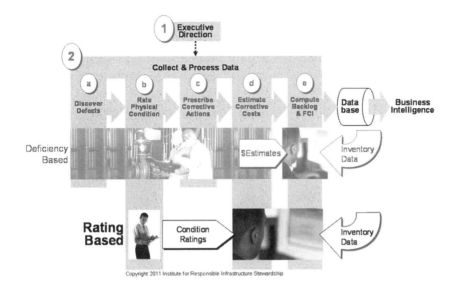

FIGURE 9.5 Rating-based technique—substitutes questionnaires or cursory observations for detailed inspections.
Reproduced by permission of Institute for Responsible Infrastructure Stewardship

There are two subcategories of the rating-based technique: (1) questionnaires, and (2) visual surveys. Both have been designed to limit expensive data collection and both yield macro indicators of backlog and FCI without prescribing corrective actions or identifying work items or projects.

1. **Questionnaires.** This subcategory of the rating-based technique uses parametric modeling to produce a macro-level, portfolio summary of corrective costs by sending questionnaires to building managers and/or occupants rather than conducting detailed inspections by qualified engineers and technicians. This method is relatively inexpensive but does not render actionable work and project requirements and often relies on untrained people to answer the questions, resulting in inconsistencies between portfolios.

2. **Cursory observations.** An example of this practice is the Army Installation Status Report (ISR), where either qualified technicians or nontechnical administrative people use written and pictorial guidance to visually observe and rate the general appearance of building systems and record ratings on an ordinal "red, yellow, green" scale. A parametric model calculates an overall quality rating for each type of building in the portfolio from the distribution of "color" ratings for all buildings within that type group and estimates portfolio-level backlog and FCI. This method is relatively inexpensive but does not render specific work and project requirements.

The NASA deferred maintenance estimation methodology is another example of this subcategory of the rating-based technique. It also uses a parametric model to compute an overall assessment of the general condition of facilities and a dollar estimate of deferred maintenance costs. It typically begins with a rapid visual inspection of all systems in each building. Trained assessors follow a pro forma that captures consensus impressions of conditions in a numerical rating (1–5) for each system. The ratings are used in conjunction with overall system costs on a square foot basis and percentage of current plant value (CPV) to estimate corrective costs and calculate backlog and FCI. NASA headquarters uses cursory observations to determine budget requirements, but the executing NASA centers must still spend considerable resources to acquire data needed to identify and prioritize work items and projects.

In 2006, the Wyoming School Facilities Commission employed the NASA "shortcut" to identify $331 million in deferred maintenance at a cost of just 17 percent of the estimated cost of the traditional method. The technique does not produce details of specific work items or projects.[24]

Description of the Inventory-Based Technique

By the early 1990s, dissatisfaction with the cost of deficiency-based techniques, as well as failure of deficiency-based and rating-based techniques to overcome inherent issues of credibility, led the office of Secretary of Defense to seek yet another approach. As a result, a consultant devised a technique that completely eliminates inspectors and observers as sources for portfolio-wide backlog and FCI estimates. The commercial offspring of this work is called "Whitestone MARS Facility Cost Forecast System." It estimates future macro-level funding necessary to restore and maintain entire building portfolios by loading parametric models with just building system inventory data and no inspection or rating data.

As the main focus of analysis, the models employ building metadata (e.g., type of building and date of construction) to speculate on current component age and average service life (as determined by actuarial practice) and use that data to produce portfolio-level estimates of backlog and FCI. Figure 9.6 is a graphic comparison of the inventory-based technique with the deficiency-based technique.

The reader should note several important similarities and differences between the two techniques.

- Both techniques compute backlog and FCI; neither rates physical condition directly.

[24]N. Thomson and J. Whittaker, "The BMAR Approach to Asset Management." *Military Engineer*, January–February 2008, p. 62.

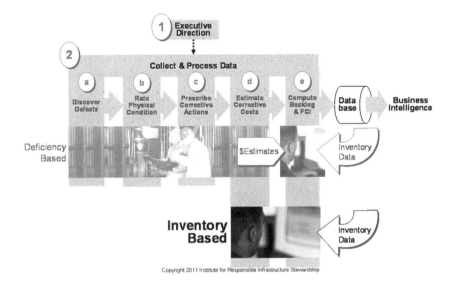

FIGURE 9.6 Inventory-based technique—eliminates inspections, questionnaires, and field observations.

Reproduced by permission of Institute for Responsible Infrastructure Stewardship

- Unlike the deficiency-based technique, the inventory-based technique: ". . . relies on several general assumptions about building configuration, materials, and conditions based on the 'law of averages,' which perform adequately for a large portfolio of buildings as a whole. However, these inventory-base tools lack the connection to specific real world buildings, their localized conditions, and operating environments, thus preventing the critical transition from budgetary decision making to work plan execution."[25] In other words, the inventory-based technique can be used only on portfolios comprised of many buildings and yields backlog and FCI only at the portfolio level and not at the individual building level. Neither does the inventory-based technique identify or price individual work items and projects that constitute the backlog and FCI.

- The inventory-based technique is substantially less expensive than the deficiency-based technique; $0.01 to $0.02/square foot for the former and at least $0.15/sf for the latter. Results are more consistent, as well, because the inventory-based technique derives backlog from stable inventory and statistical data rather than from inconsistent, widely variable cost estimates or condition ratings produced by different inspectors and observers.

---

[25] L. R. Marrano, "Using Performance Metrics for Making Facility Investment Decisions." Working paper, ERDC-CERL, Champaign, IL, March 2011.

■ Both inventory-based and deficiency-based techniques yield backlog and its derivative FCI as proxy indicators of physical condition. It is important to note that this practice is widespread despite the fact that there is no scientific study or any data showing backlog or FCI to be reliable indicators of building condition. To the contrary, as discussed in a subsequent section of this chapter, there is a large body of study and research to resolve the longstanding concerns about the advisability of using backlog and FCI for assessing physical condition.

A recently created variation of the inventory-based technique is called *age-based scalable modeling*.[26] Like the inventory-based technique, it estimates backlog and a "theoretical FCI" by entering building system age and standard life expectancy data rather than **deficiency** or rating data into parametric models. It differs from the basic inventory-based technique in that it employs nonlinear deterioration curves and field observations to periodically update system inventory data rather than taking such data at face value from actuarial tables.

It also uses a parametric model to reduce deficiency-based inspection frequency and cost by inspecting in a given time period only those building systems meeting pre-set criteria for age and remaining useful life. Data gathered by deficiency-based inspections are used to calibrate deterioration curves, which are used to compute repair-need percentage for every building system and building in the portfolio. Like all rating- and inventory-based techniques, age-based scalable modeling does not identify work items and projects, which comprise the backlog and FCI metric, so portfolio stewards must invest additional resources to acquire such additional detail.

DISSATISFACTION WITH THE MONETARY METHOD SPURS RESEARCH

In the early 1980s, Navy leaders decided that their monetary method was not satisfactory. The organization could not afford comprehensive, annual inspections. Additionally, inspection data were inconsistent, unverifiable, often proved inaccurate, and quickly became outdated. Metrics behaved illogically and didn't withstand budget scrutiny. The Navy had learned that, contrary to popular theory, increased funding actually promoted significant backlog growth while reduced funding shrank reported backlog. This converse effect was attributed to the subjectivity and nonrepeatability of the inspection process. More importantly,

[26] E. Teicholz and G. Evans, "Assessing Facility Conditions: A Cost-Effective Strategy," 2007, available at www .graphicsystems.biz (accessed January 1, 2012).

actual physical condition of Navy buildings continued to deteriorate despite increased investment in backlog reduction in doses prescribed by backlog and FCI theories.

The Navy needed a better technique. It was already reducing frequencies of building inspections to cut inspection costs only to realize that longer times between inspections eroded data credibility, increased breakdowns, disrupted building operations, and siphoned money from planned repairs. The Navy also rejected the rating-based and inventory-based techniques because these approaches could not identify individual work and project requirements.

Consequently, the Navy joined with the Air Force (which was experiencing similar issues) in funding Army research for next-generation building condition assessments. Their goals were to reduce inspection costs; improve credibility of inspections and repair budgets; enable more productive funding allocation and project selection; and allow meaningful tracking of spending impact on mission performance. Another objective of this initiative was to create a condition metric that was so reliable and consistent it could be used to regulate the outsourcing of installation maintenance functions.

The Engineered Method—Product of Published Government Research

Subject matter experts at the U.S. Army Engineered Research and Development Center, Construction Engineering Research Laboratories (ERDC-CERL) took the same scientific approach to restructuring building condition assessment that they had previously used to develop advanced assessment methods for roofing, pavements, and railway tracks.[27] In keeping with the principles of asset management, they also integrated their restructured building condition assessment technique into a comprehensive facility asset management process for assessing both building condition and performance, computing metrics for each, and using the metrics to create useful business intelligence.[28]

While ERDC-CERL was conducting its research on building condition assessment, a 1998 National Research Council (NRC) report[29] reiterated the many shortcomings of existing federal condition assessment programs and

---

[27] e.g., ASTM D6433-03, *Standard Practice for Roads and Parking Lots Pavement Condition Index Surveys*, and ASTM D5340-04e1, *Standard Test Method for Airport Pavement Condition Index Surveys*.

[28] Grussing, Uzarski, and Marrano, 2009.

[29] National Research Council (NRC), *Stewardship of Federal Facilities* (Washington, DC: National Academies Press, 1998).

recommended that the programs be restructured to (1) optimize available resources, (2) provide timely and accurate data for formulating maintenance and repair budgets, and (3) provide critical information for the ongoing management of facilities.

In 1997, ERDC-CERL began publishing its research[30] and in 1999 the engineered method was rated "preferable choice" among 18 alternative methods by a peer-reviewed American Society of Civil Engineers (ASCE) paper.[31] More important, the Army's Engineered Method met the aforementioned Navy and NRC specifications, thereby affording its potential users "considerable savings and benefits in building condition assessment as well as reducing total maintenance and repair costs by nearly half over a 50-year lifecycle."[32]

The Engineered Method for building asset management evolves around a different kind of data that can be gathered at significantly less cost than the deficiency-based technique[33] and has been shown by researchers to produce more credible and useable information than produced by the Monetary Method. Federal organizations such as the NRC[34] and the Federal Facilities Council (FFC)[35] also have recognized this body of research, and several federal agencies are currently implementing the Engineering Method as the basis for agency-wide building asset management.[36]

DIFFERENCES BETWEEN KNOWLEDGE-BASED AND DEFICIENCY-BASED TECHNIQUES

Figure 9.7 compares the restructured, knowledge-based building condition assessment technique with the deficiency-based technique. Both techniques employ the same steps in the same order, but, as discussed in several

[30] D. R. Uzarski and L. A. Burley Jr. "Assessing Building Condition by the Use of Condition Indexes." In the proceedings of the ASCE conference on *Infrastructure Condition Assessment: Art, Science, and Practice Proceedings,* ASCE, Reston, VA, 1997.

[31] Ottoman, Nixon, and Lofgren, 1999.

[32] M. N. Grussing and L. R. Marrano, "Building Component Lifecycle Repair/Replacement Model for Institutional Facility Management." In *ASCE Conference Proceedings*, Reston, VA, July 24, 1997, pp. 550–557.

[33] M. N. Grussing and L. R. Marrano, "Knowledge-Based Inspection Capabilities," Report No. ERDC/CERL TN-06-1, January 2006.

[34] NRC, Predicting Outcomes from Investments in Maintenance and Repair for Federal Facilities (Washington, DC: National Academies Press, 2011).

[35] Federal Facilities Council (FFC), "Key Performance Indicators for Federal Facilities Portfolios: Federal Facilities Council Technical Report Number 147," National Research Council, 2005, p. 17.

[36] As of this writing, the USMC has selected the Engineered Method as its enterprise condition assessment program; the Navy has selected the Engineered Method as its enterprise life-cycle analysis and long-range work planning tool, and the Army, USAF, and Defense Logistics Agency are engaged in Engineered Method trials.

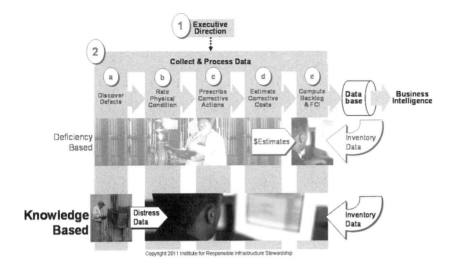

FIGURE 9.7 Knowledge-based technique—replaces inspector opinion with management-driven parametrics.
Reproduced by permission of Institute for Responsible Infrastructure Stewardship

ERDC-CERL papers cited in this chapter, differ significantly in who accomplishes each step and how each step is accomplished.

Specifically, the knowledge-based technique[37]:

- Capitalizes on inspector skills in identifying distresses while eliminating inspector subjectivity in prescribing and estimating the cost of corrective actions.
- Standardizes the way in which inspectors classify and record identified distresses.
- Replaces inspector subjectivity with transparent, consistent, and auditable parametric models, which are constantly and precisely regulated by executive direction.
- Produces a family of metrics, the BCI (series)[38] that depicts true physical condition while also yielding more accurate and dependable monetary metrics (backlog and FCI).
- Includes an accurate condition prediction tool that can help significantly reduce or eliminate critical breakdowns and bolster credibility of budget requests.

Here's a brief summary of the similarities and differences between knowledge-based and deficiency-based techniques:

---

[37] D. R. Uzarski, *Knowledge-Based Condition Assessment Manual for Building Component Sections* (Champaign, IL: U.S. Army Research & Development Center, Construction Engineering Research Laboratory, 2004).

[38] Uzarski and Burley, 1997.

Phase 1: Executive Direction

Similar to Phase 1 of the deficiency-based technique, Phase 1 of the knowledge-based technique controls the overall rigor, effectiveness, and efficiency of an organization's process by setting goals, policies, and standards that regulate assessment quality and by establishing inspection schedules that determine data freshness and process cost. Unlike Phase 1 of the deficiency-based technique, Phase I of the knowledge-based technique requires that the organization's management set Executive Direction consciously, deliberately, and in precise detail. The knowledge-based technique cannot be deployed until management fulfills this obligation. After management sets and deploys the necessary goals, policies, and standards, inspection groups cannot substitute their own assessment goals, policies, and standards.

1. Assessment goals and policies

    The first action of both techniques is to establish goals and policies against which data collection standards and schedules can be measured. Such goals and policies are also used to guide the collection of data as well as the computation of metrics.

2. Standards

    Deficiency-based standard-setting is frequently relegated to technical employees or inspection vendors. The knowledge-based technique requires responsible managers to consciously set these standards.

3. Inspection schedules

    Organizations using the knowledge-based technique do not schedule teams of highly skilled engineers to tour buildings looking for defects. Instead, they can use trained service technicians and even integrate scheduled distress surveys into technicians' daily preventive maintenance (PM) assignments and service calls. This capability limits the time demand on technicians and further reduces the cost of data collection. In keeping with the cost-cutting goal of its research, ERDC-CERL designed the knowledge-based technique so that trained service technicians can produce distress data as accurately and proficiently as engineers inspecting the same components or predetermined group of components called a "component section."[39]

---

[39] Building component sections are the "management units" upon which work decisions are made. Example: a group of four 50-lb/hr central humidifiers, same model and age. A component section's condition establishes work item scope and cost for that section.

Knowledge-based parametrics, such as physical condition forecasts for specific building components, generate schedules that tell trained technician-inspectors which limited number of selected components to inspect and which of three progressively rigorous inspection types to use on each component. Component selections and inspection types are based on actual need, as determined by forecasted component conditions and standards set by management. Knowledge-based scheduling skips inspections when not warranted or cost-effective, such as very early or very late in a component's life cycle.

Knowledge-based parametric models select and schedule the type inspection that is most cost effective for each component's condition as predicted by the models' automatic condition index updating feature and preprogrammed risk tolerances of the organization's management. The least costly inspection (called *direct rating*) simply tracks a component's general condition, serving as a watch-dog until the component's general condition indicates that it is time to obtain more granularity by scheduling the second, more detailed type inspection (called a *distress survey*). Then, when the second type inspection indicates that the time for component repair or replacement is on the planning horizon, the software schedules the third type inspection (*distress survey with quantities*), which produces actionable work packages and project-level detail sufficient for program planning purposes. When projects become serious candidates for funding, they receive the fourth and most detailed inspection, which becomes the basis for execution planning.

Knowledge-based inspectors do not tour buildings. Instead, they go directly to the components listed on their schedule and conduct the prescribed type inspection. This "just-in-time" scheduling approach and the use of technician-inspectors rather than engineer-inspectors are major factors in cutting the cost of knowledge-based inspections to less than 25 percent of those required for comprehensive, calendar-derived deficiency-based inspections.

Phase 2: Collect and Process Data

The purpose of this phase is to gather and treat component distress data in order to rate physical condition, prescribe corrective actions, estimate costs of corrective actions, and compute backlog and FCI metrics. Phase 2 of the knowledge-based technique is comprised of the following actions:

1. Identify defects

   Both deficiency-based and knowledge-based techniques rely on the individual inspector's training, skill, and experience to initially detect physical defects in building components. But while the deficiency-based inspector does not catalog, record, or report such defects, knowledge-based inspectors follow a standard, engineered procedure to perform this task.

The inspector records each defect and tags it with various attributes: component identity, **distress** type, severity, and **density** or quantity. He neither formulates nor records any of the opinions or estimates needed to specify a corrective action or to predict remaining useful life. These calculations are done later by the knowledge-based parametrics. Consequently, researchers' field tests and user experience shows that the knowledge-based inspection process is quicker and much less costly than deficiency-based inspections, and data are virtually independent of inspector bias, guesswork, and inconsistency. Limiting inspector participation to Steps 2a and 2b and not using inspectors to accomplish the subsequent steps of data processing is another major factor in cutting the cost of a knowledge-based inspection program to 25 percent of that required for labor-intensive deficiency-based inspections.

2. Rate physical condition

    Inspector opinion of physical condition does not influence knowledge-based condition ratings for building components. Instead, a parametric model uses inspector distress data to directly compute a science-based condition index for each *building component section* and subsequently keep each index constantly updated in real time with deterioration projections calibrated with refreshed inspection data. However, whenever an inspected component is free of reportable defects, the knowledge-based inspector is trained and required to assign, record, and report one of nine possible, predefined "direct condition ratings" for that component.

    The parametric model also rolls up refreshed component section condition indexes into a BCI (series) of condition indexes for parent systems, facilities, and portfolios. Army research shows that condition indexes computed and updated in this manner achieve a consistency among inspectors of plus or minus 5 points on a scale of 1 to 100 (100 = distress free) with 95 percent confidence regardless of the profession or trade of properly trained inspectors.

3. Prescribe corrective actions

    Deficiency-based inspectors use mostly personal opinion to prescribe corrective actions. The knowledge-based technique prescribes impartially and consistently by using a component's computed condition index and other parametric models regulated by specific, preset management preferences and risk tolerances. Individual, prescriptive work items and projects are produced quicker, at much less cost, and independently of inspector bias, guesswork, and inconsistency.

4. Estimate corrective costs

The knowledge-based technique minimizes estimating variability by relieving the inspector of estimating duties and relying, instead, on computerized parametric models consisting of unbiased work scopes, reliable commercial cost data, and management-set standards.

5. Compute backlog and FCI

Both deficiency- and engineering-based techniques compute backlog and FCI using inspection data. The major difference is that the Engineered Method operates on objective "distress" data while the deficiency-based technique operates on subjective work scopes and cost estimates.

ADDITIONAL BENEFITS OF THE ENGINEERED METHOD

The Engineered Method includes all the functions and yields all the business intelligence produced by the best-in-class techniques of the Monetary Method—plus much more. By capturing and analyzing objective, consistent component "distress" data rather than work scopes and cost estimates contaminated with subjectivity and variability, the Engineered Method is able to produce many additional, high-value business intelligence products that are impossible to duplicate with the Monetary Method. These include:

■ Accurate and dependable forecasts of future condition at various funding levels; triggering the creation and prioritization of corrective actions by management-set standards of mission performance and risk tolerance; selection among alternative corrective actions based on return on investment; forecasted penalty costs for deferring repairs beyond their most advantageous execution time; risk-informed decision making and multicriteria decision making; precise analysis of alternative funding scenarios; and creation of actionable short- and long-range capital repair and renewal programs.

■ Unlike results turned out by techniques of the Monetary Method, the results of the Engineered Method are scientifically derived from objective, constantly refreshed physical condition data supplemented with management's pre-programmed risk tolerances and, therefore, are highly credible and consistent. Minimum cost, need-based inspection schedules are also derived from the same condition data and risk tolerances.

DECIDING WHICH TECHNIQUE IS BEST FOR YOUR ORGANIZATION

"Condition assessment can only meet the need if the metric used meets the objective of the user. A single condition assessment procedure, no matter how robust, cannot meet all needs of all users. A particular condition assessment technique should not be denigrated for not meeting an objective it was not designed for."[40]

The following list summarizes the pros and cons of the varied methods described in this chapter, suggesting that there is a place in facilities asset management for each of them.

- Deficiency-based technique (currently employed by the U.S. Department of Energy and National Park Service, inter alia)
    - Pros
        - Generates financial backlog and FCI for portfolio, facility, and systems
        - Identifies and prioritizes individual work items
    - Cons
        - Expensive ($0.15+/sf)
        - Wasteful overinspection, risky underinspection
        - Inconsistent results, credibility issues
        - Unproven financial condition forecasting
        - No physical condition indexing or forecasting
        - Expensive and proprietary commercial software
        - Vendor lock on software
- Rating-based technique (Army, NASA, Smithsonian, inter alia)
    - Pros
        - Generates financial backlog and FCI for large portfolios
        - Affordable (~ $0.02/sf)
        - Low cost of custom software development by agency consultants
        - No vendor lock on in-house agency software
    - Cons
        - Does not identify or prioritize individual work items
        - Wasteful overinspection, risky underinspection

[40]S. D. Foltz and D. T. McKay, "Condition Assessment Aspects of an Asset Management Program." U.S. Army Engineering Research and Development Center, January 2008.

- No physical condition indexing or forecasting
- Inconsistent results, credibility issues
- Inventory-based technique (OSD [now transitioning to the engineered method], GSA)
  - Pros
    - Generates financial backlog and FCI for large portfolios
    - Affordable (~ $0.02/sf)
    - Low cost of custom software development by agency consultants
    - No vendor lock on in-house agency software
  - Cons
    - Does not identify or prioritize individual work items
    - No physical condition indexing or forecasting
    - Credibility issues
- Knowledge-based technique (USMC, Navy, Defense Logistics Agency; Army and USAF transitioning)
  - Pros
    - Generates both physical condition index and work/project backlog and FCI for portfolio, facility, and systems
    - Both physical and financial condition indexing and forecasting
    - Generates physical condition index for portfolio, facility, and systems
    - Affordable (~ $0.02/sf)
    - Identifies and prioritizes individual work items
    - Eliminates waste and breakdowns from over- and underinspection
    - Proven and accurate physical and financial condition forecasting
    - Consistent and credible—based on published, peer-reviewed science
    - Government software free to federal government agencies
    - No vendor lock on government software
  - Cons
    - May require $0.02 to $0.06/sf one-time start-up cost to gather component inventory data
    - Requires a solid understanding and thoughtful application of asset management principles
    - Vendors selling counterfeit processes and software

A facility manager would be well-advised to thoroughly evaluate the applicability of each available practice to his own organization's particular needs and pocketbook before making a commitment to any one of them. The following sections provide a starting point for such an evaluation.

Organizations that Should Consider Using the Deficiency-Based Technique

The deficiency-based technique is best for organizations with few buildings to manage and/or those that need and can afford a good tactical system for near-term project-level functions such as: identifying and pricing specific corrective actions, packaging them into executable projects, and prioritizing the projects; allocating available funds among the current list of backlogged projects; supporting requests for next year's funding of pricing specific projects; and tracking results of near-term spending on individual work items and projects.

Eroded credibility of its primary FCI metric as well as use of "book value" average service life of building components render use of the deficiency-based technique extremely limited for organizations that also need a long-range tactical system for project planning or a good strategic system for near-term and long-range portfolio-level functions such as: ascertaining current and possible future portfolio condition and preparing portfolio-level budget requests and "what-if" scenarios. One-time start-up costs for the deficiency-based technique can be expensive, and recurring annual costs of building inspection and data upkeep are very high.

Organizations that Should Consider Using Rating-Based or Inventory-Based Techniques

Rating- and inventory-based techniques are best for organizations with large building portfolios and/or those needing only a strategic system for supporting near-term budget requests and funding allocations at the macro level. Rating- and inventory-based techniques do not provide business intelligence at the work item or project level. Questionable credibility of the primary FCI metric renders both techniques limited for ascertaining current portfolio physical condition and forecasting future conditions. The use of "book value" average service life of building components also reduces credibility of long-range budget requests. On the plus side, there are usually no one-time start-up costs, and annual costs of building inspection and data upkeep are very low compared to the deficiency-based technique.

Organizations that Should Consider Using the Engineered Method

The engineered, knowledge-based technique is best for organizations that need a system for comprehensively and credibly supporting all strategic and tactical functions associated with *building asset management*, both near and long term. Annual costs of building inspection and data upkeep for the engineered method are very low compared to the deficiency-based technique, but there may be an initial, one-time investment required to gather and organize detailed component inventory data. Protocols are available for reducing up-front investment by initially employing inventory templates and modeling and spreading the cost of detailed data collection over the long term on an as-needed basis. Using the engineered method also requires a solid understanding and thoughtful application of asset management principles.

CONCLUSION

The emerging discipline of facility asset management provides a strategic approach to the optimal allocation of capital for the repair, renewal, and modernization of aging buildings, pavements, utilities, and other infrastructure. It combines engineering and economic principles with business practices, tools, and a framework to facilitate organized, logical, and complementary decision making at strategic, operational, and tactical levels.

The successful application of facility asset management depends on the accuracy, granularity, and credibility of facility data available to that organization. This chapter examined the role played in data collection and creation of business intelligence by the process of physical condition assessment and compared four alternative techniques of assessing physical condition of buildings.

It also provided recommendations to help the reader decide which alternative technique is best for an organization. A facility manager would be well-advised to thoroughly evaluate the applicability of each alternative to his own organization's particular needs and resources before making a commitment to any one of them.

Computer Modeling

10

Eric Teicholz

INTRODUCTION

This chapter presents an overview of computer modeling and simulation related to facility management applications. Following a brief review of computer models and simulation, the chapter describes four areas in which models have been successfully used: visualization, space allocation and management, facility asset management, and energy.

COMPUTER MODELS AND SIMULATION—A BRIEF OVERVIEW

Every model involves some simplification of a more complex reality to allow for calculation of desired relevant variables (heat flow, stress, cost, energy utilization, etc.). Some models are mathematical, others are not. Mathematical models representing physical processes have been in use since the mid-eighteenth century. But it was the advent of the digital computer that enabled mathematical models to be more easily developed and tested. Today, mathematical representations of most facility management functions are possible and a number of tools and programming languages have facilitated the development and testing of models for just about any application.

A computer model consists of two primary components: the computer-based mathematical representation of a physical process (e.g., how a system behaves) and the definition of conditions for testing that representation against desired criteria. Such models attempt to calculate solutions that predict how systems behave based on various parameters and the model's initial conditions.

Some models do not converge to a single quantifiable solution (e.g., space adjacency optimization). A number of approaches have been developed for predicting system behavior in systems that incorporate such over-constrained problems.[1] Many overconstrained facility management problems employ user feedback (heuristic techniques) to improve the model's performance.

Simulation

Simulation models require external data input into the model because the universe of possible solutions for the model cannot be computed without such input. For example, an energy model designed to calculate an ENERGY STAR score for a building might have initial input from a variety of sources: the user (e.g., building type, address, age), prestored tables (weather conditions, energy costs for that location), or the building automation systems (BAS) that have the ability to automatically track and control energy usage for various assets.[2]

A simulation model manages model events over time. Therefore, the model must possess information on how the model might change at discrete points in time. Using condition assessment as an example, the simulation model must have information on the relevant variables such as how building systems degrade over time, the estimated useful lives (EULs) of the various building components and their replacement costs over time. For example, a certain type of roof might have an EUL of 20 years and must be completely replaced at the end of its useful life, whereas a foundation might have a 100-year EUL and a 5 percent replacement value. Using such degradation and cost curves related to building systems, a condition assessment simulation model can calculate the amount of projected investment required to maintain the asset at a certain condition level. Such models can be used to predict estimated levels of preventive maintenance costs for specific building systems or for an entire building. Organizations are using the output of such models for capital planning.

---

[1] P. Meseguer, N. Bouhmala, T. Bouzoubaa, M. Irgens, and M. Sanchez, "Current Approaches for Solving Over-Constrained Problems," *Constraints Journal* 8(1) (January 2003), 9–39.

[2] See Chapter 3 for a more detailed discussion of building automation systems.

MODELS IN FACILITY MANAGEMENT

Software developers have modeled almost every facet of facility management functions including space planning and forecasting; lease administration; budgeting; real estate acquisition and disposal; energy benchmarking; facility asset management; move, add, and change (MAC) management; asset maintenance and reporting; emergency preparedness; security; health and safety; risk analysis; and administrative services.

To develop such models, a building normally is defined in the computer as a hierarchical set of spaces (e.g., campus, building, floor, room) that consist of systems, occupants, equipment, building components, properties, and so forth. This integrated data model enables the development of applications that reflect the facility management life-cycle activities performed on the building.

Building Visualization: CAFM and BIM Models

Computer-aided facility management (CAFM) and building information modeling (BIM) are a combination of geometry, data about an object, and, in the case of BIM, parametric rules that govern the geometry of that object and its relationships to other objects.[3]

CAFM systems have tools to model the geometry of buildings as well as the nongraphical building data. Geometric **input** tends to be two-dimensional and built on traditional computer-aided design (CAD) software augmented by a variety of interactive graphic functionality that supports drafting and editing of plans and layouts. Besides the geometric model, CAFM systems also provide a database management system (DBMS) that has nongraphic data populated from the CAFM software itself or by data input from external data sources. Current CAFM systems often populate the data model by pulling asset, personnel, energy, and other types of data from a variety of sources—both real-time (e.g., sensor data from BAS) and passive (e.g., asset barcodes, external databases). Another important component of the facility model is the documentation (specifications) for the **facility assets** and building components. Assets often are classified into groups and assemblies by using standards, such as **Uniformat** II,[4] to ensure consistency and facilitate communication between applications.

[3] C. Eastman, E. Teicholz, P. Sacks, and K. Liston, *A Guide to Building Information Modeling for Owners, Managers, Designers, Engineers and Contractors* (Hoboken, NJ: John Wiley & Sons, April 19, 2011).

[4] UNIFORMAT II is a classification system for building elements and associated site work. It provides for the integration of a building's program, specifications, and building estimates (see www.uniformat.com/uniformat-ii.html).

Most current CAFM systems also enable geometric data to be kept in a format that is compatible with the geospatial data defined in geographic information systems (GIS) to allow for the bidirectional transfer of data between GIS and CAFM models.[5]

Building information models[6] also integrate geometric and associated facility management data but create models that are fundamentally different from CAFM models. BIM is a three-dimensional digital representation of the physical and functional characteristics of the objects (also called elements or components) in a building. It facilitates the exchange and interoperability of digital information about the building and forms a reliable basis for design, construction, and operational decisions. A fundamental goal of BIM is to enable collaboration by different stakeholders at different phases of the building life cycle. This includes a stakeholder's ability to insert, extract, update, or modify information in the BIM model to support and reflect the roles of that stakeholder. Using this definition, BIM acts as a collaboration and facilitation resource for stakeholders and is updated at various times during the building's life cycle.

The BIM integrated 3D model can access and process all pertinent graphic and nongraphic data about a facility and present it as an integrated coherent model. As mentioned, it not only contains information about the 3D geometry of the building's elements but also the types of topological relationships that exist between elements. Thus, if a user makes a change in one view, it automatically is reflected in all views. BIM's goal for facility managers is to inherit relevant geometric and attribute data from previous stakeholders (e.g., architects, engineers, and contractors) and avoid having to reenter or reformat this information. Nongraphic data in BIM models might include asset attributes such as material data, fabrication information, and even asset behavior under different conditions.

Some traditional CAFM vendors accept BIM files as input but then strip away much of the intelligence and integrity of the model after it is imported into the vendor's software CAFM environment. Other CAFM vendors import a BIM model and have the capability to maintain the integrity of the BIM geometric model to coexist with the CAFM model. The CAFM software vendor will develop links to BIM such that information about an asset that resides within CAFM can be queried from the BIM model.

However, at present, BIM modeling is just beginning to be used by building owners and facility managers. Creation of a detailed BIM for an existing building is

---

[5] See Chapter 4 on geographic information systems.
[6] See also Chapter 2.

often a time-consuming and expensive process. If drawings do not exist, either conventional surveys or laser scanning of digital pictures of the building can be used for the creation of as-built BIM data. If current and accurate as-built drawings or CAD files exist, then the input process becomes less tedious and expensive. Additionally, few BIM data exchange standards exist for the incorporation of the required data and functions needed to support the wide scope of decisions made by facility managers.

Eventually, BIM shows great promise for FM applications—especially if facility managers get involved earlier in the life cycle of buildings. As the architectural, engineering, and construction (AEC) industries increasingly use BIM as their development platform, as facility managers become more aware of the richness of the BIM model, as FM/BIM integration standards are developed and as software vendors develop better ways to integrate CAFM and BIM models, facility managers will increasingly endorse this technology.

Space Allocation Models

The forecasting, planning, allocation, and management of space is among the most important and basic functions performed by facility managers.[7] In developing and supporting space models, one or more of the following data elements are used in the model:

- The current people and assets that occupy the space.
- The physical constraints of the building (e.g., number of floors, size of spaces).
- Budgetary constraints (e.g., costs of various types of moves).
- Regulatory constraints.

Desired Adjacency Requirements Between Spatial Elements

As indicated earlier, there are few instances where the computer model can converge on a single optimal solution. As such, space planning and management is an overconstrained process whereby the model often incorporates some form of heuristic modeling solution.[8]

Space allocation models normally incorporate four discrete phases.

---

[7] J. A. Demkin, *The Architect's Handbook of Professional Practice* (Hoboken, NJ: John Wiley & Sons, 2008).

[8] M. Lennette, "Why Use a Heuristic Programming Technique," www.odf.state.or.us/DIVISIONS/Management/Asset_Management/HH/11_WhyUseHeuristics.pdf (accessed December 20, 2011).

Space Inventory Phase

Space inventory components, such as buildings, rooms, personnel, organizational structure, space standards, equipment and furniture, are the first inputs considered. It is important to note that the level of "granularity in the data" needs to be determined. For some organizations, space may need to be monitored at a cost-center level in order to accommodate finance-driven space charge back procedures. Other organizations may want to keep an inventory that tracks personnel, equipment, and furniture in specific rooms.

Requirements Phase

The second phase of space planning defines space requirements and standards that are to be considered by the allocation model. Each computer solution would be compared with the desired space standards. Space standards for workstation layouts might include furniture, fixtures, and equipment (FF+E) and typically are associated with personnel classification levels.

The heuristic employed might require the user to define a starting point for the model or random number generators might be used to place spaces and solutions compared to the desired standards. Requirements would be the same data categories that exist in the inventory:

- **Organizational area requirements**. To begin to plan the layout of space, the facility planner first must know which operating groups to plan for and how much space each requires.
- **Locational and adjacency requirements**. The physical layout of workstations, workgroups, and business units influence the overall productivity of the organization. Adjacency requirements often are depicted as numbers that reflect the desired relative adjacencies of the spaces being considered. Thus, the model would attempt to organize groups that have a high degree of interaction in spaces that are contiguous. Likewise, other organizational units should be farther apart if there is a risk that productivity would be hindered by proximity. Both positive and negative relationships, reflecting the interaction among operating groups, ideally should be considered by the allocation model.
- **Future growth or reduction**. To the greatest extent possible, location and layout decisions should consider possible future scenarios for change. For example, operating groups may grow or be downsized. If such information can be projected, the model should include not only current requirements but also anticipated future needs as well.

Allocation Phase

Space allocation modeling involves assigning activities (business units, workgroups, individuals, assets, etc.) to a location (sites, buildings, floors, etc.). The model generates solutions and compares the solution to the adjacency requirements specified in the previous phase. Adjacency requirements (whether they relate to people, cost centers, assets, or other organizational units) usually are represented by an **adjacency matrix**.[9]

In Figure 10.1, the adjacency matrix is symmetrical and indicates desired spatial relationships between three spaces (i.e., rooms, departments, cost centers, buildings, etc.). In this example, a low number indicates desired proximity. Thus, the space planner has indicated a 1 as the adjacency between space 1 (column 1) and space 3 (column 3). Similarly, the planner has indicated that space 3 and space 2 should not be adjacent.

Allocation can be performed manually or automatically. Space allocation models might use random number generators (i.e., stochastic procedures) to generate solutions and then compare the solution to input criteria such as an adjacency matrix. Alternative solutions can be given a scored rating which is based on the adjacency and locational requirements of the affected workgroups. Solutions can be graphically presented as stack plans, block plans, and bubble diagrams.

In the stacking plan in Figure 10.2, the thickness of the lines between spaces show the degree of desired adjacency between departments in this four-story building. Cross-hatching is used to depict various departments. For the forecasting period selected, some departmental areas do not fit within the existing building envelope. The blocking plan in Figure 10.3 depicts the optimal relationship of spaces on a floor based on the adjacency matrix coefficients. The size of the space polygons reflects the area of the space, cross-hatching depicts the space

	SPACE 1	SPACE 2	SPACE 3
SPACE 1	✕	2	1
SPACE 2		✕	3
SPACE 3			✕

FIGURE 10.1 Adjacency matrix.
Reproduced with permission of Graphic Systems, Inc.

[9] For a depiction of various adjacency matrices, see Wolfram's Mathworld, http://mathworld.wolfram.com/AdjacencyMatrix.html.

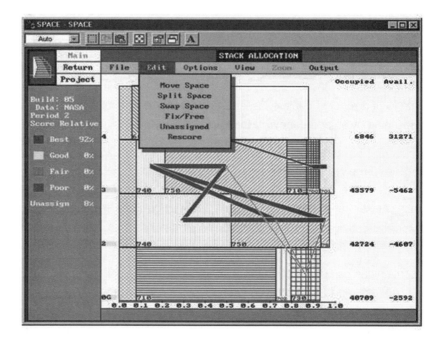

FIGURE 10.2 Stack plan showing occupancy, adjacency, and forecasting requirements.

Reproduced with permission of Graphic Systems, Inc.

ownership, and the width of the line connecting the two spaces indicates the strength of the desired adjacency between the spaces.

Planning Phase

Space planning is fundamental to each stage of the space allocation process. Planning requires a continual examination of the variables that affect the alternative solutions at future points in time. These variables include organizational growth or shrinkage patterns; leasing options; cost factors associated with space, renovation, construction, or moving employees; changes in required adjacencies; or revised space needs from the addition of new equipment.

The most generally used forecasting method applies annual growth rates to historical trends. However, this approach cannot be effectively used to identify the amount of space required by individual work groups. A second method of forecasting multiplies a net usable area by the number of employees occupying the space, (e.g., a department's total usable area—taking into account departmental circulation space and support areas). The result gives an average area/person figure, which then is multiplied by the projected personnel count in the department. A third, and perhaps more accurate, method of forecasting uses categorized space standards multiplied by forecasted personnel levels to calculate anticipated space requirements.

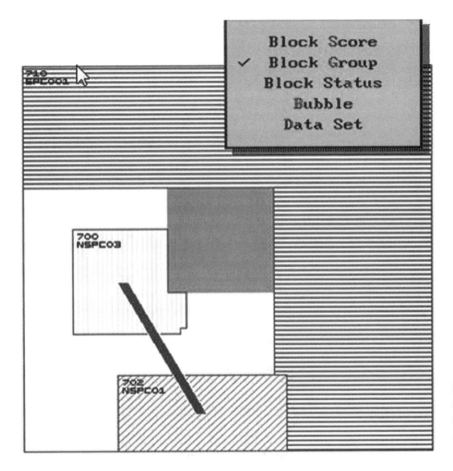

FIGURE 10.3 Block plan showing departments, areas, and adjacencies.
Reproduced with permission of Graphic Systems, Inc.

Facility Asset Management Models*

Facility asset management (FAM)[10] is an emerging, strategic approach to capital budgeting and optimal allocation of scarce funds for the **repair, renewal**, and modernization of aging facilities. FAM can control operational risk, reduce cost of ownership, prolong component life, and eliminate unforeseen dollar demands and, thus, help optimize return on investment in facility performance.

The FAM process entails systematically collecting key data and delivering the data to computer models and analytic tools to create business intelligence (BI).[11]

---

* This section of the chapter was written by James Clayton.

[10] See Chapter 9 for a detailed description of facility asset management.

[11] Business intelligence, as it relates to facility management, refers to the use of computer techniques for extracting and analyzing facility data for making business decisions.

Facility managers can use the BI to facilitate organized, logical, and complementary decision making at strategic, operational, and tactical levels.

Computer modeling enables the FAM process by making data collection more affordable, computing key **metrics** with collected data, and creating useful BI from computed metrics and other collected data.

Computer Models that Make FAM Data Collection More Affordable

The FAM process needs a constant stream of accurate data about the physical characteristics,[12] business relevance,[13] and performance[14] of individual facilities. Data collection done in traditional manual ways is labor intensive, employs teams of specially trained, highly skilled people, and therefore makes FAM too expensive for many organizations that could otherwise benefit from using it.

Computer modeling significantly cuts the cost of collecting FAM data in two ways: by creating data of physical characteristics with tools such as building templates and automatically generating facility performance assessment schedules.

CREATING PHYSICAL CHARACTERISTIC DATA
WITH BUILDING TEMPLATES

An organization's FAM process employs general data about the physical characteristics of each facility as a whole as well as each facility's constituent systems. The more sophisticated FAM processes also use detailed data about each system's components and component life-cycle attributes (e.g., type, material, and actual age) or other attributes deserving special management attention (e.g., identical components with different weather exposures or access constraints).

USING TEMPLATES TO CREATE WHOLE FACILITY INVENTORIES

A facility inventory database describes each managed facility as a whole and includes data elements related to its physical characteristics such as individual facility identifier, location, construction type, footprint dimensions, number of floors, functional areas, and replacement cost.

A FAM model might import facility attribute data from an existing source such as a real property database. If data are not available or of questionable quality, new data would have to be created from the most economical combination of three

---

[12] Identification designator, location, type, size/capacity, initial cost, year constructed/replaced.

[13] Relative importance and impact of an asset's performance on the organization's mission.

[14] Physical state (condition) and functionality (service utility).

techniques including manual review of drawings, specifications and records, site visits, and computer templates. The first two techniques are costly but accurate, while the latter is relatively inexpensive but less accurate. For every situation, there is at least one combination of the three techniques that produces usable data at lowest cost.

A template generates approximate physical characteristics of a building based on known, key characteristics of another similar building. A building template can include a little or a significant amount of data depending on the need for which the template was created.[15]

Using building templates is a quick way to create an inventory, but the quality of the estimated inventory is only as good as the data from which the template was first created and how similar the target building is to the original. Differences may exist between the "true" building inventory and the inventory estimated from the template. These inaccuracies may be minimized with field data on an "as-needed" basis.[16]

In many cases, due to cost and logistical limitations, large geographically dispersed organizations may be unable to generate detailed building templates using any detailed information beyond the type of building and date of construction. In these circumstances, it is still possible to generate a template using available industry sources, such as RS Means.[17] These templates used in conjunction with system ages, deterioration curves, and objective questionnaires can even generate high-level performance metrics.[18]

USING TEMPLATES TO CREATE SYSTEM INVENTORIES

System inventories identify which systems are present in a specific facility (e.g., "exterior closure") and which components comprise each system (e.g., exterior walls, doors, and windows). Most computer models employ standard taxonomies such as Uniformat II (ASTM E 1557–97) for this purpose.

Subgroups of components having the same physical attributes (e.g., "exterior wooden personnel doors") or deserving special management attention (e.g.,

---

[15] D. R. Uzarski, *Knowledge-Based Condition Assessment Manual for Building Component Sections* (Champaign, IL: U.S. Army Research & Development Center, Construction Engineering Research Laboratory, 2004).

[16] Uzarski, 2004.

[17] See www.rsmeans.com.

[18] E. Teicholz and G. Evans, "Theoretical Condition Indices," *IFMA Facility Management Journal*, July 2007.

exterior wooden doors on the building's weather side) are called "component sections." Every component in a facility is grouped into one or more "sections," using the fewest sections possible to achieve desired granularity of management decisions.

Component-section data are rarely available from existing databases, and gathering them by manual review of drawings, specifications, and records and site visits can be cost prohibitive. Therefore, new data often have to be created from computer templates based on similar buildings. System and component-section data generation capabilities often are included in the whole-facility templates described above.

Generating Lean, "Just-in-Time" Data Collection Schedules

In attempts to avoid the expense of traditional data collection methods, some organizations have tried reducing facility assessment frequency, skipping assessments, and even substituting layman questionnaires and cursory field observations in place of comprehensive, skilled-based condition inspections. These substitute methods cut costs but sacrifice detail and utility of BI produced from the data.

Computer models are available that minimize unnecessary data collection. In general, these models monitor building component sections with predictive technologies until there are clear signs that an inspection is needed. Doing inspections only when needed reduces wasted time and money. The higher the percentage of inspection that's done "as needed," the lower the overall cost of inspection will be.

A promising approach to making FAM data collection more affordable involves "knowledge-based" computer models that generate lean, just-in-time condition inspection schedules as well as tell inspectors the most cost-effective inspection types[19] to use on each scheduled component. Thus, inspections are planned and executed based on knowledge, not the calendar. Because different building components have unique service lives, and some may be more important than others with respect to outcomes and risks, some components are inspected more often than others and at different levels of detail. By tailoring the frequency and level of inspections, a knowledge-based approach makes better use of

---

[19] FAM uses three progressively rigorous (costly) types of inspection: direct ratings, distress surveys, and distress surveys with quantities.

the available resources and provides more timely and accurate data to support investment-related decisions.[20]

Models that Efficiently Compute FAM Metrics

The FAM process uses two distinct types of metrics: performance metrics and business relevance metrics. Performance metrics indicate an asset's condition (monetary, physical, and functional) while business relevance metrics denote the importance an asset has to organizational operations and the likely impact on organizational mission of its possible degradation or failure.

PERFORMANCE METRICS

Sound FAM decision making calls for a full picture of asset condition in three dimensions: monetary, physical, and functional. Considering all dimensions together generates the most accurate results.

One well-known and widely used monetary condition metric is the facility condition index (FCI). It is the calculated ratio of an asset's deficiency costs (estimated maintenance/repair costs) to the asset's **current replacement value**.[21] Estimated repair costs for FCI numerators (estimated deficiency costs) usually are created by parametric models using data created in one of three ways: by engineers and technicians who conduct detailed visual inspections; by people who perform cursory visual observations; or by analysts who harvest pre-existing databases of building attributes, sometimes without any visual observation. Replacement values for FCI denominators are calculated in a multiple of different ways, including the insured value method, market resale value method, and parametric construction cost estimating methods available from commercial sources (e.g., R.S. Means). FCI represents an asset's projected financial condition (cumulative deferred **maintenance and repair** costs over time) rather than its actual physical condition.[22]

Empirical engineering research has produced an array of physical condition metrics for specific facility types such as pavements, railroad tracks, and building components. Each index represents actual physical condition on a scale of 0 to 100 and is produced by a mathematical model that deducts points from a like-new condition of 100. Models calculate points that are deducted from

---

[20] NRC, Predicting Outcomes from Investments in Maintenance and Repair for Federal Facilities (Washington, DC: National Academies Press, 2011), 6–5.

[21] AME and S. C. Rush, *Managing the Facilities Portfolio* (Washington, DC: National Association of College and University Business Officers, 1991).

[22] Ibid.

a like-new condition for a given asset based on distress attributes that are observed and recorded by trained technicians according to standard protocols. Attributes include distress types (such as broken, cracked, or otherwise damaged systems or components), distress severity (effect), and distress density (extent). The mathematical models reflect consensus of many building operators, engineers, and other subject matter experts. Inspectors only need to collect distress data, and they do not make judgments concerning the physical condition of the asset other than the distress categories. The computed building condition index (BCI) will be plus or minus five points of the expert group consensus with 95 percent confidence on a 0-to-100 scale.[23]

Functionality is a broad term that applies to an entire facility and its capacity to support an organization's programs and mission effectively. Functionality is related primarily to user requirements (mission), technical obsolescence, and regulatory and codes compliance, and it is independent of condition. A building functionality index (BFI) for buildings and building functional areas (such as administration, laboratory, storage, and production) has been developed by the U.S. Army.[24] It follows the same form, format, and rating scale development theory as engineering-based physical condition indexes. However, rather than accounting for distresses, functionality issues are considered with severity (effect) and how widespread the issue is. The numerical BFI scale (0–100) is correlated to modernization needs. The model addresses 65 specific functionality issues which are grouped into 14 general functionality categories such as adequacy of building size, configuration and operating efficiency, and level of compliance with the Americans with Disabilities Act, Antiterrorism and Force Protection requirements, and Efficiency, Environmental and Life Safety standards.[25]

BUSINESS ALIGNMENT METRICS

All facilities are not created equal. Some are more important to an organization than others and, therefore, equal deterioration or obsolescence of two facilities does not necessarily present the same operational risk to the parent organization.

The FAM process employs several metrics to account for these differences in producing BI for allocation of scarce repair/modernization resources. Two are described here:

[23] Ibid.

[24] M. N. Grussing, D. R. Uzarski, and L. R. Marrano. (2009). "Building Infrastructure Functional Capacity Measurement Framework." *ASCE Journal of Infrastructure Systems*, 15(4), pp. 37–377

[25] NRC, 2011.

- **Mission Dependency Index (MDI).**[26] Management-assigned, relative importance of facility in supporting its predominant mission element compared to the importance of all other facilities in the same portfolio in supporting their respective predominant mission elements.
- **Relative Mission Importance Index (MEI).**[27] Management-assigned, relative importance of a facility's predominant parent mission element compared to all other mission elements of the organization.

Computer models can generate and compile these metrics from structured interviews, questionnaires, and an analytic hierarchy process (AHP) that captures collective judgments of engineers, operators, and decision makers.

Models that Create Business Intelligence from Computed Metrics and Other Data

Computed metrics and other collected data describing building inventory and its performance and business alignments are stored in one or more databases for reuse in creating **business intelligence**. Business intelligence produced by computer models includes reports and projections on performance metrics, probability of component failure, and remaining service life; backlogs of deferred maintenance, repair, and modernization costs; short- and long-range repair/renewal/modernization plans; funding alternatives, mission risks, and penalty costs attributed to deferring work items and projects; and budget requests, fund allocation plans, spending evaluations, detailed project identification, return-on-investment calculations, project priority ranking lists, and execution plans.

FAM Modeling Summary

Computer models using BI solutions promise visibility, insight, and performance improvements in facility asset management when deployed efficiently. Too much waste in creating BI data can lead to unnecessary cost and time expenditures. Best practices that employ readily available computer models to collect data and generate BI data can save money and achieve effective asset management.

Energy Models

We continue to see increases in energy costs. At the same time, we know that buildings are major consumers of energy, accounting for more than 40 percent

---

[26] A. Antelman and C. Miller, Special Publication SP-2113-SHR, Mission Dependency Index Validation Report, Naval Facilities Engineering Command, Naval Facilities Engineering Service Center, Port Hueneme, CA, 2004.

[27] U.S. Coast Guard, "Relative Mission Importance Index Process Guide," U.S. Department of Homeland Security, U.S. Coast Guard, CGTO PG-43-00-40, March 16, 2007.

of global energy usage and landfill waste, and in the United States, almost 75 percent of electricity usage and 40 percent of carbon emissions. Consequently, the energy models that recommend required (i.e., mandated) or cost-effective retrofits are of great importance to facility managers.

Computer-based building energy modeling[28] and the determination of cost-effective energy conservation measures **(ECMs)** currently are receiving a great deal of attention. The drivers for this focus are not only the current energy mandates[29] but also financial and environmental concerns. Models exist that take into account a number of variables, including location, building type, occupancy patterns, available energy rebates, and electrical and lighting loads. Models can suggest recommended retrofits based on factors such as return on investment (ROI), benchmarks, or standards (e.g., Leadership in Energy and Environmental Design [LEED], ENERGY STAR, Building Research Establishment Environmental Assessment Method [BREEAM]) achieved by making specific retrofits. Some models also take into account the interaction between energy systems such as how a change in one system (e.g., lighting) might impact another system (e.g., heating, ventilating, and air-conditioning [HVAC]).

As in the case of deficiency-based condition assessments,[30] manual energy audits to determine retrofit opportunities are time consuming and expensive. Such audits are used for critical (i.e., mission dependent) buildings or if mandated by federal and state regulatory requirements.

Most BAS vendors support a variety of sensors that provide real-time input that can be read by computerized maintenance management systems (CMMSs) to trigger alerts, alarms, or PM work orders. At the same time, many existing computer-aided facility management (CAFM)/integrated workplace management systems (IWMSs) as well as emerging BIMs include asset information and real-time inputs from sensors to facilitate the analysis required by energy models. Using BAS and asset data, facility managers can identify and locate problems and react to problem situations in a timely manner.

Figure 10.4 shows a variable air volume terminal unit (VAV box), selected and highlighted while the rest of the model is semitransparent for easier identification of the object within the facility. On the right side are the component properties

---

[28] R. Paradis, "Energy Analysis Tools," National Institute of Building Scientists, Washington, DC, last updated June 10, 2010.

[29] J. McGee, E. Teicholz, and S. Slaughter, "U.S. Government Policy Impacts and Opportunities for Facility Management," IFMA Foundation *How-to Sustainability Guide*, 2011.

[30] See Chapter 9.

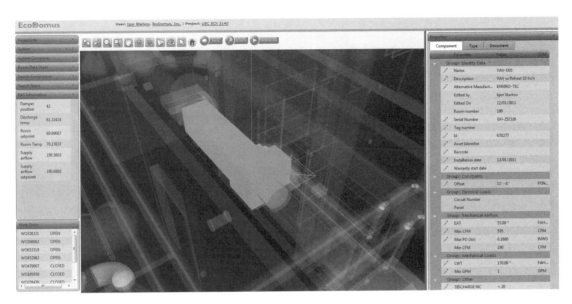

FIGURE 10.4 BIM model and problem asset location and specification.
Reproduced with permission of EcoDomus, Inc.

(attributes of that specific box), type properties (not visible) that contain attributes common for all components of the same type and document tab that contains all documentation for this box. The left panel allows navigating viewpoints (saved camera positions), system, and system components (to navigate building systems), room data sheets (for when a space is selected) to show items belonging to the selected room/space, search component and space tabs, BAS Information (shows real-time [and historical] values from the BAS for that specific component), and work order tab (shows work orders for the selected component [imported from the CMMS]). Such data often is required for energy analysis.

Such data might reside in the BIM itself or within an integrated CAFM/IWMS or CMMS system. Energy models using BIM linked to such systems are just beginning to emerge but represent a promising development platform for such models because of the integrity of the geometry in BIM and the access to potential information about its system components that often reside in a CAFM system.

It should be noted that one of the biggest advantages of BIM for energy modeling is that it offers the potential for early and rapid evaluation of energy use (during early design stages). An early estimate is often sufficiently accurate to allow evaluation of design alternatives. This is also true of estimated construction cost. Thus, a facility manager or owner can make better informed energy-efficient choices before a design progresses too far to allow for such flexibility.

Energy models make inferences for unknown energy-related data based on available data. The more data initially supplied (age, location, use, occupancy, fuel usage, etc.), the better the results obtained from the model. Often, the model will output estimated accuracy statistics based on the amount of input data provided.

Figure 10.5a depicts a "Monthly Usage and Cost" table that shows the monthly energy consumption and cost predicted by the energy model based on the information provided about building systems. The user can toggle between the fuel types present in the building to see the monthly consumption and cost of each. The actual tab will show the actual energy consumption and cost based on historical utility bills provided by the user. This can be compared to the model "Predicted" consumption and cost to gauge the accuracy of the model.

The "Energy Consumption and Weather" chart (Figure 10.5b) displays the monthly energy consumption for each fuel present in the building against the heating and cooling degree days.

The "Consumption Profiles" chart (Figure 10.5c) displays the monthly average daily and hourly consumption profiles for each fuel present in the building.

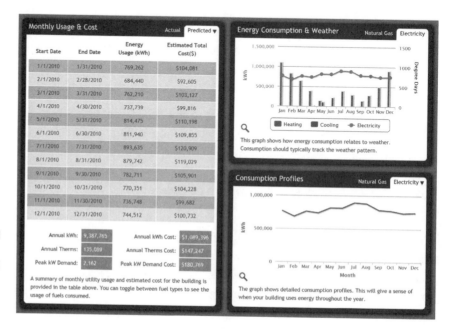

FIGURE 10.5 Modeling energy usage and costs by month: (a) monthly usage and cost; (b) energy consumption and weather; (c) consumption profiles.

Reproduced by permission of Retroficiency, Inc.

Taking into account the initial assumptions, energy models can examine the potential ECMs for the various energy systems.

The "Package Comparison" table in Figure 10.6a shows the total annual savings, installed cost, simple payback period, percent CO_2 equivalent reduction, and percent annual energy savings for three different packages of ECMs. These ECMs are detailed in the "Package ECMs & Performance Summary" table.

The "Package ECMs & Performance Summary" table (Figure 10.6b) outlines the ECMs that comprise the selected package and summarizes the total carbon, energy, and cost implications of the package. Clicking the magnifying glass will open a new window with individual carbon, energy, and cost metrics for each of the ECMs.

The "Performance Metrics" graphs (Figure 10.6c) show the annual carbon emissions, ENERGY STAR rating, energy cost per square foot, and energy use intensity of the "Current" building as well as the "Proposed" building after implementation of the ECMs in the selected package.

The "Consumption by System" graphs (Figure 10.6d) show the end-use energy consumption as a percentage of total energy (measured in MBtu) as well as by units of energy for each fuel present in the building.

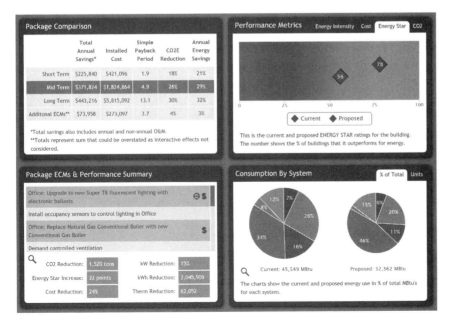

FIGURE 10.6 Proposed ECMs, ROIs, resulting benchmarks, and system consumption data: (a) package comparison; (b) package ECMs and performace summary; (c) performace metrics; (d) consumption by system.

Reproduced by permission of Retroficiency, Inc.

CONCLUSION

In general, computer models and simulations are powerful tools for evaluating many facility management processes. The use of such models can save considerable time and money as well as assist facility managers in identifying optimal or near optimal solutions. Computer modeling and simulation of FM processes increasingly are being used to show how alternative conditions can be used to determine courses of action associated with design/3D modeling, space planning and management, asset management, and energy management. A variety of techniques can be employed to test assumptions and results. The effectiveness of any model will depend on the integrity and currency of the input data, inclusion of significant characteristics and system behaviors associated with the facility management process being modeled, and the depth and validity of the model outcomes.

ADDITIONAL RESOURCE

Adjacency analysis: http://mathworld.wolfram.com/AdjacencyMatrix.html.

Technology and the Workplace*

11

Erik Jaspers and Eric Teicholz

INTRODUCTION

Technology innovation is applicable to multiple aspects of the facility management (FM) profession. Technologies are developing, enabling professionals to manage the physical infrastructure of offices and services in new ways for the workforce. Many of these developments align with developing new and innovative office-like workplaces. Other technology innovations are changing the set of tools that knowledge workers can (and will) use, enabling them to work in new and fundamentally different ways. Each profession will use different tools, which can be shared between them. With the increasing **mobility** of the workforce that results from this, this virtual workplace will nevertheless stay connected to them. People will travel between locations and buildings, but they will always carry their virtual workplace with them. To summarize, the definition of workplace may fundamentally change over the coming years, requiring FM professionals to accommodate these changes.

*This chapter is an edited and expanded version of a work that originally appeared in "Work on the Move," published by the IFMA Foundation (Houston, TX, 2011).

FIGURE 11.1 Workplace typologies.

This implies that FM professionals will have to grasp the essence of the techno-logical developments that take place and position themselves for the changes they will invoke. Further, the facility profession will need to understand how best to implement the new technologies with traditional legacy systems and the potential impact of this integration on the workplace. One can expect that senior facility and information technology (IT) management will work together to define how the organization will support and manage the workplace, both in the physical and in the virtual world. Both worlds interact and mutually influence each other.

DEFINITION OF WORKPLACE

What is the definition of *workplace*? For FM professionals, the built workplace[1] is both the key to and the prime focus of their activities. Obviously, we see some fundamental changes occurring in the built environment. Flexibility and support-ing the mobility of the workforce are significant elements of workplace change.

Specifically for knowledge workers, the definition of workplace is implicitly chang-ing and will continue to do so. A new type of workplace is being added to the built environment: the virtual workplace (Figure 11.1). New software applications and information are emerging.

One could state that the virtual workplace is independent to the people using it. Within this workplace, there are three aspects of IT technology emerging:

[1] Mostly in the form of offices.

- **Devices**. New generations of personal devices are becoming available. Simplicity, ease of use, and high-level user experience are key elements. Devices are expected to be further personalized.[2]
- **Network connectivity**. Being connected to the network/Internet is a factor of increasing importance. Networking technologies are diversifying to meet different connectivity needs.[3] Network connectivity is not only moving toward a ubiquitous service, the increase in bandwidth (the ability to transport large volumes of data) is also enabling new types of applications.[4]
- **Applications and information**. Corporate business applications are gradually allowing people to work independently of a location by use of the Internet.[5] Additionally, there are new types of applications emerging that shape the virtual workplace for it users. Think of social networking tools,[6] as well as tools to enable the sharing and exchanging of information and collaboration, the emergence of services to store data on the Internet[7] and applications for specific Internet-based functions.[8] The way applications can be acquired and installed is simplified through cloud computing, discussed later in this chapter, further lowering thresholds to using them.

IT technology is going through a process of commoditization: tools are becoming easier to use and acquire. This in turn is leading to faster and widespread adoption. This adoption is often done autonomously by people. That is, they use certain tools outside the office and expect their employers to provide access to them as well. In many organizations, IT management is moving away from a prescribed set of tools to support a policy of adaption to change. "BYOC" or "BYOD" (bring your own computer, bring your own device) is a good example of this, where employees are enabled to select devices of their preference[9] and have them connected to the company IT infrastructure.

The key to the virtual workplace is that it enables and enhances the mobility of people. Today's workers are offered the opportunity to work at times and in

---

[2] Wearable devices, surface/flexible displays, and so on.

[3] Examples: 3G and 4G networks, wi-fi and mesh networking.

[4] Think of high-quality videoconferencing and real-time collaboration in engineering and research.

[5] For example, the trend toward Web-based application user interfaces, as opposed to software installation on specific devices.

[6] Facebook, Twitter, LinkedIn, etc.

[7] For example, Dropbox, Box.net, and iCloud.

[8] For example, Google Apps, Microsoft Online, Salesforce.com, Wikis, Asana, BIM (discussed later in this chapter), application stores for smartphone apps, etc.

[9] Laptops, tablet PCs, smart phones, e-readers, etc.

places of their own choosing. Their perception of the workplace that employers offer them is not only created by just the physical environment. This development enables IT, FM, and human resource (HR) management to relate to each other holistically in terms of the workplace.

Active and early involvement of senior IT and information management in workplace innovation projects is a desirable practice, increasing the probability of success. At a 2011 German conference on workplace innovation, 3 out of 14 presenters had chief information officer (CIO) titles.

WIRELESS NETWORKING

In IT, a network is defined as a series of points or nodes interconnected by communication paths. Networks can interconnect with other networks and contain subnetworks.[10] The communication paths in a network can be either hardwired (such as exists in many offices of today), or they can be implemented wirelessly by the use of transmitters sending data and receivers providing the data to equipment and applications.

Wireless networking is an enabler of many new types of workplace innovation applications. Its key contribution lies in the opportunity to connect all kinds of devices with software applications. In the built environment, this creates the flexibility to attach such devices in various locations. Previously, it would not be feasible to connect them to a network, either because it was practically not achievable or just too expensive or disruptive to realize.

There are many wireless technologies currently available and under development. Around the workplace, we see some dominant technologies being used and some others emerging: wi-fi and mesh networks based on ZigBee standards next to the well-known local area network (LAN) and 3G network technologies that normally run on our smartphones and PC devices.

Wireless networking enables ubiquitous connectivity to people and therefore enhances employee mobility. This is an important reason why we see a steep growth of the use of wireless technologies around the workplace. We also see wi-fi adoption in information-sensitive environments (e.g., the financial industry), indicating that concerns about information security on wireless networks are subsiding because of their increased security.

---

[10] For more detailed information, see www.ieee.org.

CURRENT WORKPLACE ISSUES

Various facility management disciplines around the workplace face different challenges for which technology can provide assistance. Table 11.1 summarizes such challenges in terms of strategic, tactical, and operational issues.

The efficient use of facilities in terms of "appropriate for purpose" and matching demand with adequate supply, for example, will impact all concerned. Research has shown significant underoccupancy of desks, not only leading to unnecessary housing costs, but also wasting natural resources. Most research conducted thus far relates to fixed-desk areas. Furthermore, facility managers need relevant knowledge to assess how to plan and size new workspaces, including new and innovative ones.

Now that flexible (hot desk) facilities have emerged and the desk-to-employee ratio will probably fall well below 1:1, defining effective space utilization is further complicated because people also tend to work outside of the office. Furthermore, the principle of part-time work is either existent or emerging in a number of countries.[11] The consequence of this is that space management professionals are being confronted with fundamental changes (variability) in the demand for workplaces. This variability emerges from various causes:

TABLE 11.1 Overview of typical facility management concerns for workplace innovation.

	Footprint (SF, m²)	Appropriate for Purpose	Technical Management	Sustainability and Energy Management
Strategic	Insight in total occupancy building(s), portfolio (fit) analysis	Appropriate building design, comfort, binding of talented staff	Capital and maintenance budget planning	Improvement program identification; certification (LEED, BREEAM)
Tactical	Saving footprint based on occupancy	Demand/supply matching on workspace types	Maintenance on demand (just-in-time)	Saving (costs on) energy and other natural resources
Operational	Insight into use patterns and occupancy of workspaces	Efficient environment, health and safety, user satisfaction	Understanding status of systems and inventory	Sustainable conduct, sustainable user processes

---

[11] In Europe, part-time work is common in a number of countries. It can mount up to workweeks of effectively two to three days, but workweeks of four days are quite common.

- ■ **Changing daily work patterns**. People tend to work at home in the morning, avoiding traffic, and thereby come to work later in the day, leaving early to avoid traffic, and working in the evenings at home.
- ■ **Changing weekly work patterns**. People with part-time jobs tend to take Wednesday and/or Friday off.[12]
- ■ **Changing monthly patterns**. People leave work on holidays, preferably during children's holidays from school. An impact of this is that, during vacation periods, significant percentages of the workforce are absent.
- ■ **Changing multiyear patterns**. Organizations tend to reorganize and may relocate operational units across various properties.
- ■ **Changing hiring patterns**. Many organizations hire personnel for a shorter time frame and hire temporary personnel—often for specialty jobs or projects. In many cases, this leads to a situation whereby facility management professionals, and sometimes HR professionals, do not really know how large the current workforce actually is.
- ■ **The rise of project-based work**, requiring cross-functional team members to cooperate in a timely manner.

Another concern is the effectiveness of the use of specific facilities. In modern flexible office environments, various workspace types are offered to the workforce and fitted out to support different types of activities, such as meetings, teaming, and private activities.[13] Facility professionals (specifically in space management) are confronted with the question of whether the *mix* of workspace types really fits actual demand, and if demand is *changing* over time.

This is not only a concern in the flexible office. It also is relevant in fixed-desk environments where space management professionals have difficulty in (re)defining effective space needs for the operating units.

The *efficiency* of space utilization is a matter of concern as well. This is best explained by the problem of "no-shows"—specifically around scarce and expensive facilities such as (video) conference rooms and team rooms, even when reservation systems are in place. Once a facility is reserved, these systems effectively prevent others from using it at the same time. However, the reality is that people either do not often show up or they use the facility for a much shorter period than indicated. This not only leads to inefficient use of space but often incurs the indignation of colleagues who are forced to find alternative space.

---

[12] Worldwide the number of holidays differs greatly. In a number of European countries it is not uncommon that people have a total volume of 30 free days to spend yearly, apart from official holidays.

[13] Concentration of space, private space, meeting space, teamwork space, desks in open areas, etc.

Another element that impacts use efficiency is how well people "like" a space for the work assigned them. Specifically, in new and innovative office environments, experimentation has been done in an effort to define attractive spaces for people to work. This can result in workers feeling that the new environment is either successful, temporarily successful, or having a negative impact on productivity.

Use efficiency can also be negatively influenced by breakage (defects). In flex offices, in particular, there is an interesting phenomenon occurring called *lack of ownership*. Where people in the fixed workplace environment will naturally report a malfunction, in a flexible environment, they often will not do so. Rather, they prefer to move to a more satisfactory space. In these kinds of environments, broken workspaces can go unnoticed for long periods of time while, at the time, resulting in space underutilization.

A facility information manager of a company in financial services with a multiyear experience in flexing, for example, once expressed the desire to "temporarily shut down" parts of the facility. Closing complete floors of flexible offices on days when there is no demand for them saves heating costs (and resources), as well as cleaning costs (and materials). The challenge is to really understand the use pattern of the facilities.

INVOLVEMENT OF FACILITY MANAGERS

The role of the FM professional is concerned with providing the environment for people to work effectively and with pleasure. The workplace is not just defined by the physical environment in which work is performed. Workplace services are a key concern of facility managers as well, and form an integral part of the work-place experience of the workforce. Three primary workplace services the facility manager must focus on are:

- Space management
- Service management
- Maintenance management

Space management has been very much impacted by the technologies described in this chapter. Space management is concerned with allocating space to the operational units of an organization based on existing and forecasted require-ments and the desired adjacency needs of the organizational units (Figure 11.2).

Space management is fundamentally changing. With the emergence of new work styles and office concepts to support them, new types of space are created, which in turn facilitate new patterns of collaboration and teamwork. Most existing space

FIGURE 11.2 Key aspects of CRE and space management.

planning software for stacking and blocking needs to be reevaluated in the context of a shifting paradigm away from "one person, one desk." In some cases, even the issue of explicit adjacency planning is abandoned and replaced by the policy that people will decide for themselves with whom to sit. In these cases, a goal of space layout might be to foster "accidental encounters" between members of the staff.

The term *soft services* refers to those activities primarily related to individuals of the workforce. Examples of soft services include catering, meeting services, and help desks, as well as the issuance or collecting of work-related goods associated with on- or off-boarding.[14]

Some organizations regard facility management soft services to be of prime importance. In the global competitive marketplace, an increasing number of organizations see the need to provide such services for their knowledge workers. Service definition, contracting/supply chain management and performance monitoring are key components of this field (Figure 11.3).

Maintenance management relates to keeping assets in their required acceptable condition (Figure 11.4). This results in:

- Protection of asset value.
- Provision of a safe environment for workers.
- Minimization of operational disruptions.
- Support of regulatory compliance.

[14] Enabling new employees to feel comfortable in their new surroundings or in assisting employees when they leave an organization.

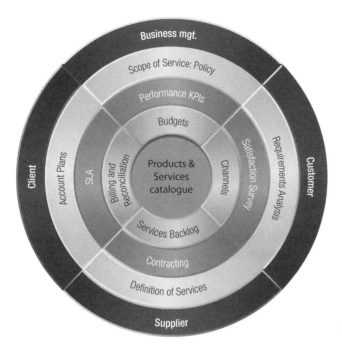

FIGURE 11.3 Key aspects of FM services management.

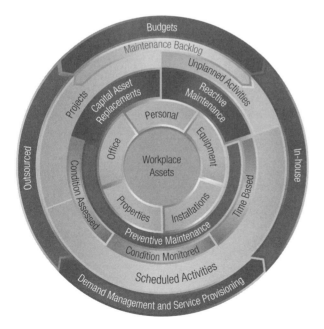

FIGURE 11.4 Key aspects of maintenance management.

Maintenance management staff is interested in the optimal expenditure of maintenance investments, providing desired results in terms of health, safety, and asset quality within the boundaries of regulatory compliance. Budget deficits are a common issue for many organizations. Tight budgets result in maintenance managers looking for "lean" approaches in the planning and execution of work, in deferring maintenance, in identifying work priorities, and in trying to avoid waste in work execution.

TECHNOLOGY LANDSCAPE

The balance of this chapter addresses two primary questions:

1. What does the current facility management technology landscape look like?
2. For what purpose can different technologies be used by facility managers?

CAFM/IWMS/CMMS Systems

Computer-aided facility management (CAFM), integrated workplace management systems[15] (IWMSs), and computer-aided maintenance management systems (CMMSs)[16] are a facility manager's administration/information management systems. These types of systems may have different labels, but they are commonly referred to as comprehensive CAFM/IWMS systems (which often incorporate CMMS functionality). They provide support for all the FM disciplines and add support for project management and sustainability (Table 11.2). In project management, not only construction projects are managed but systems now have the ability to financially manage projects, enabling the planning of expenses and budget control. This is often labeled as *capital project management* and *capital planning*.

Building Information Modeling

Building information modeling (BIM) systems[17] provide a powerful collaborative, virtual modeling environment for the design, construction, and engineering of buildings (see Table 11.3).

Such systems allow users to create three-dimensional digital representations of physical and functional characteristics of a facility (Figure 11.5). A BIM integrated 3D model can access all pertinent graphic and nongraphic data about a facility as an integrated model.

[15] See also Chapters 1 and 10.
[16] By Gartner (www.gartner.com).
[17] See also Chapter 2.

TABLE 11.2 Overview of typical CAFM/IWMS services.

Corporate Real Estate	Space Management	Maintenance Management	Soft Services
Strategic planning	Accommodation planning (all work-space types)	Health and safety management	Service desk
Portfolio management	Move management	Asset (quality) man-agement	Hospitality management (meetings, reservations, visitors, catering)
Transaction management	Financial chargeback	Condition assessments	Personal supplies
Rentable unit man-agement		Maintenance planning: reactive, preventive (time-based, condition monitored)	Access (card) management
Lease administration		Capital replacement planning	
(Employee) Self-service			
Sustainability			
Financials, budgeting			
Contracting and service-level management			
Supply chain, workflow, and (capital) project management			

TABLE 11.3 Overview of potential contribution of BIM.

	Footprint (SqFt, m²)	Fit-for-Purpose	Technical Management	Sustainability & Energy Management
Strategic	Insight in total occupancy building(s), portfolio (fit) analysis	Fitting building design, comfort, binding talented staff	Capital- and maintenance budget planning	Improvement program identifi-cation, certifi-cation (LEED, BREEAM)
Tactical	Saving footprint based on oc-cupancy	Demand/supply matching on workspace types	Maintenance on demand (just-in-time)	Saving (costs on) energy and other natural resources
Operational	Insight into use patterns and oc-cupancy of work-spaces	Efficient environment, health and safety, user satisfaction	Understanding status of systems and inventory	Sustainable conduct, sustainable user processes

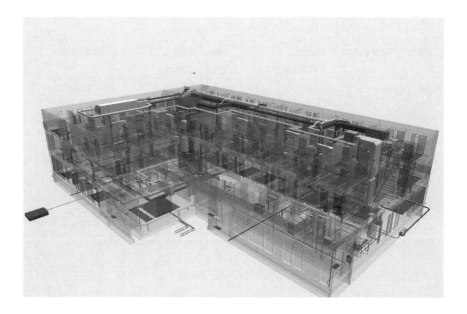

FIGURE 11.5 A 3D BIM model of a building, highlighting specific assets.
Reproduced by permission of Veccins 3D

BIM contains information not only about the 2D and 3D geometry of the building's elements but the types of topological relationships that exist between elements. Thus, if a user makes a change in one view, it is automatically reflected in all views.

The key strength of BIM lies in its capability to allow different participants in the development of the building to collaborate in almost real time.

When buildings are to be constructed or renovated, various disciplines involved can each enter asset information specific to the data required by that discipline. Thus, an asset might incorporate data associated with stakeholders that "touch" the asset throughout its life cycle. These disciplines include:

- Architecture—involved in function, fit, design, and esthetics.
- Engineering—calculating and dimensioning the technical elements of the building (floors, walls) and the sizing of all mechanical, electrical, and plumbing objects in the building.
- Contractors—building the structure according to plan.

In typical construction projects, each participant would independently design their part of the process. In practice, this leads to much communication overhead and erroneous designs that might not integrate easily. On average, each drawing is redrawn seven times over the duration of the project, and many errors are identified late in the process, leading to change orders and high costs.

Conceptually, a BIM is a collaboration tool between stakeholders and, as such, overcomes many of the problems described above, as highlighted below:

■ BIM is repository for drawing information, including document version management.
■ BIM tools exist to manipulate (drawing) models in 3D, including solid modeling.

(a)

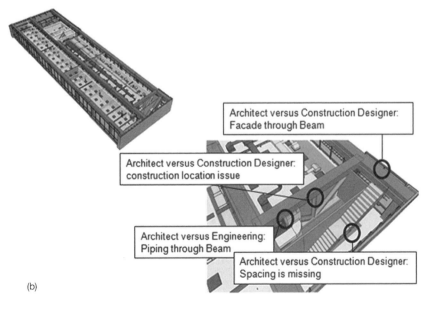

(b)

Architect versus Construction Designer:
Facade through Beam

Architect versus Construction Designer:
construction location issue

Architect versus Engineering:
Piping through Beam

Architect versus Construction Designer:
Spacing is missing

Figure 11.6a and 11.6b
Examples of clash detection. Shows a clash situation in piping, calling for revised elevation of a pipe. Shows various clash situations between construction and design, emerging from different sub-models being put together.
Reproducted by permission of Veccins 3D

- BIM associates nongeometric data parametrically with the models.
- BIM can perform model-checking functions that analyze all design models and run them against predefined rules to which the design has to comply. There is a wide variety of such rules that can be applied. For instance, a set of rules can be implemented ensuring that the designs will remain within the boundaries that have been set by the government organizations involved issuing the required permits. Model checkers enable identification of design clashes as well (Figures 11.6a, 11.6b). "Design clashes" are basically inconsistencies between different designs of different elements of the building. A simple example of this is a pipe that might penetrate a column.
- BIM contains simulation features enabling visualization of model characteristics, such as heat profiles and structural tension (stress) patterns.
- BIM incorporates viewer technology to inspect design results. The strong 3D representation properties of BIM platforms enable fast identification of undesirable construction and design. Both analytic and visual feedback is provided to owners.

BIM systems provide the means for design and construction projects to become agile. Because all stakeholder disciplines add and share their information to the model, the model becomes increasingly rich and enables early detection of errors (Figure 11.7). Research on quality costs has already shown that early detection of errors has a significant contribution to reducing the total cost of projects.

By the richness of the model, BIM systems enable companies to easily extract a complete bill of materials required to build the structure, saving time on project preparation and minimizing errors associated with material calculations. BIM

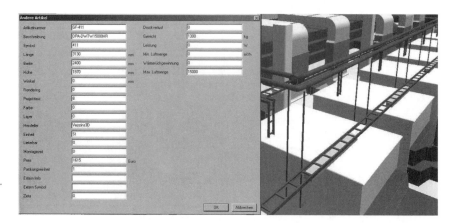

FIGURE 11.7 BIM model depicting construction and associated data in one model.
Reproduced by permission of Veccins 3D

systems provide the features to define the timeline for the construction planning (called the fourth dimension). It can depict the construction stages the project will go through. This allows for planners to better anticipate staffing and materials over time. The ability to "view" the projected sequence of construction allows the checking of potential logistical issues and problems, enabling the planner to solve such problems before they emerge in practice.

BIM projects have already shown dramatic cost reductions for architects, engineers, and contractors. It is only a matter of time before this technology impacts facility management to the same degree.

Building Automation Systems

A key component of building infrastructure is building automation systems (BASs).[18] BASs are concerned with controlling the building's systems for climate control (heating, cooling, air-conditioning, or HVAC), lighting and safety (fire alarms). BASs are primarily involved in energy management and control assets. When they first appeared over 30 years ago, they used proprietary software that made integration of assets impossible.

Over the years, it became possible to connect and control devices from multiple vendors, and BAS devices became interoperable by the use of open protocols (open standards by which devices communicate). Thus, the **BACnet**[19] and LonTalk[20] protocols were developed. BASs have greatly improved over the years. The introduction of Internet protocol (IP) networking in this realm enables direct access to, and interoperability with, components of the BAS infrastructure. An important aspect of this integration enables IWMS/CMMS systems to interact with new generations of BASs to not only identify upcoming potential failures (reactive maintenance), but also make use of sensor readings to schedule upcoming maintenance activities based on actual asset performance (just-in-time, rather than time-based, preventive maintenance).

The new generation of BASs contributes to the productivity of the enterprise by conserving energy and optimizing the efficiency of both the equipment throughout facilities and the people who are responsible for operating and maintaining them. They provide a foundation for sustainable programs and projects by providing the accurate and secure data that is required for decision making and verification.

---

[18] See also Chapter 3.

[19] www.bacnet.org.

[20] www.echelon.com/communities/energycontrol/developers/lonworks.

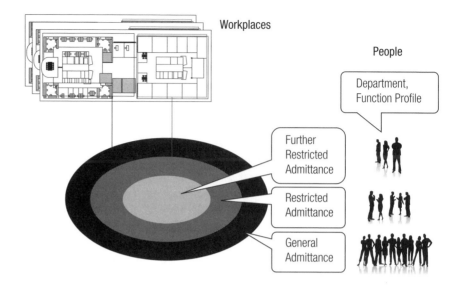

FIGURE 11.8 Typical design of security zones for a building.

For facility management professionals, there is often the problem that, in the average building portfolio, different systems of different ages and versions exist. This fact alone complicates the development of a standardized integration policy involving BAS systems. For each building, specific integration patterns will have to be resolved. New insights derived from sustainable condition-based maintenance indicate that replacing older infrastructures with new ones is financially viable. The benefits achieved in energy savings and improved sustainability of the building over the total life cycle also makes these solutions viable.

There are products emerging that target middleware[21] solutions for managing diverse BMS systems, using one interface and API.[22] This facilitates interfacing diverse BAS systems with a single energy management system or central control (monitoring) system.

Access and Security Management Systems

The core business problem that these systems solve in the context of buildings is the regulated and managed admittance of people to specific areas. Many organizations model their floor spaces to security levels (or security rings) (Figure 11.8). People will have access to specific areas when they are cleared to do so. Access management systems bring tools for managing access profiles and the use of personal tokens (e.g., smart cards) for this purpose. For implementing easy access to

---

[21] Often referred to as the "glue" between diverse software components.
[22] Application programming interface.

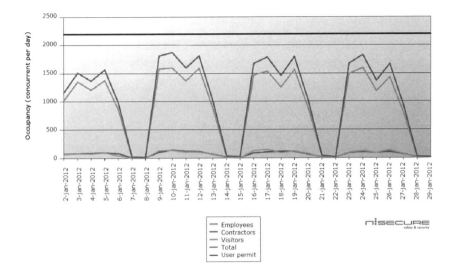

FIGURE 11.9 Real-time building occupancy overview.
Reproduced by permission of NSECURE

space, these systems provide a wide array of sensors (cameras, detectors) and actuators (automated gates, doors), all linked to system networks.

By their nature, access management systems carry information at any time regarding where individuals are located. In buildings where a granular security design has been implemented, this information can well be used by facility and space management staff to evaluate occupancy rates for different areas (Figure 11.9).

By linking access data[23] to the space and workplace management systems that provide workplace capacity data and geographic analysis, meaningful insights can be derived to the use-efficiency of those office areas.

Geographic Information Systems

A geographic information system (GIS)[24] is a system of hardware and software used for storage, retrieval, mapping, and analysis of *geographic* data[25] (Table 11.4). Spatial features are stored in a coordinate system (latitude/longitude, state plane, UTM, etc.), which references a unique location on the earth. Descriptive attributes in tabular form are associated with spatial features. Spatial data and associated attributes in the same coordinate system can then be layered together for mapping and spatial analysis. GIS differs from CAD and other graphical computer applications in that all spatial data is geographically referenced to a map projection in an Earth coordinate system. For the most part, spatial data can be "reprojected"

---

[23] In many cases depersonalized to protect privacy of individuals.
[24] See also Chapter 4.
[25] See www.nwgis.com.

TABLE 11.4 Overview of potential contribution of GIS.

	Footprint (SqFt, m²)	Fit-for-Purpose	Technical Management	Sustainability & Energy Management
Strategic	Insight in total occupancy building(s), portfolio (fit) analysis	Fitting building design, comfort, binding talented staff	Capital- and maintenance budget planning	Improvement program identification, certification (LEED, BREEAM)
Tactical	Saving footprint based on occupancy	Demand/supply matching on workspace types	Maintenance on demand (just-in-time)	Saving (costs on) energy and other natural resources
Operational	Insight into use patterns and occupancy of workspaces	Efficient environment, health and safety, user satisfaction	Understanding status of systems and inventory	Sustainable conduct, sustainable user processes

from one coordinate system into another; thus, data from various sources can be brought together into a common database using GIS software. GIS tools have been successfully applied in fields such as environmental and demographic analysis, utility management, and landscape planning. These powerful tools integrate and analyze data from various sources and relate those to geospatial information. The powerful visual representation and its ability to process and visualize complex relationships make it a valuable asset for FM professionals to use.

Recent research shows that 22 percent of corporate real estate (CRE) organizations use GIS tools. Although this is a relatively high percentage, it still leaves 78 percent of CRE organizations that do not. In March 2011, the applicability of GIS for FM was underscored by a press release from both the Open Standards Consortium for Real Estate (OSCRE)[26] and the Open Geospatial Consortium (OGC)[27] stipulating that "there's a tremendous need for better information exchange among companies and government administrative bodies that buy, sell, own, occupy, insure, inspect, appraise, manage, design, build, and protect real estate. Leveraging this information in a location and time context is critically important for decision making."[28]

---

[26] See www.oscre.org.

[27] See www.opengeospatial.org/.

[28] "OGC and OSCRE Collaborate to Advance Real Estate Standards Across the Globe," March 31, 2011, www.oscre.org/node/409.

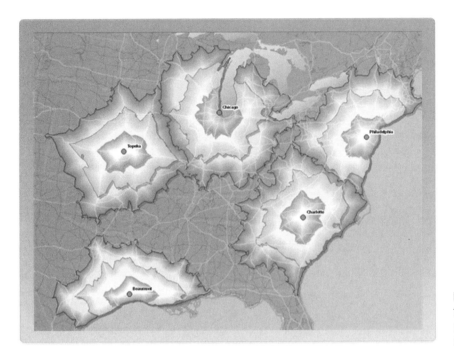

FIGURE 11.10 Average travel time to locations.
Reproduced by permission of ESRI, Inc.

GIS is beginning to play a significant role in real estate and portfolio management, maintenance management, and environmental and sustainability management.

GISs create a holistic view of buildings and the landscape properties where they are situated. A major contribution of GIS is site selection. When evaluating different property propositions, transaction managers will have to take into account numerous functional as well as nonfunctional requirements (Figure 11.10). For example, the accessibility of the workplace by the workforce in terms of distance as well as means of travel (including sustainable means for traveling) is taken into account in LEED classification.

With GIS, it is not only possible to visualize such complex relationships but the technology also allows for the 3D evaluation of the different site proposals. Other environmental properties, such as air-condition temperatures, rain profiles, and the risks involved with the geo position itself (earthquake history, risks of flooding and such), can be analyzed using GIS. These types of data can be associated with the costs of various site options to help in site selection. In retail site selection, GIS is extensively used for analyzing the location and movement of target customer groups and locating the optimum locations for retail shops.

FIGURE 11.11 Using GIS spatial data, locations of underground network service points are shown in the field.

Reproduced by permission of Tensing

In maintenance, analysis of different networks (e.g., water, transportation, natural gas, oil electricity, etc.) that need to be maintained involves geospatial analysis to answer questions such as: "When valve x is closed, which facilities will be affected?" Network analyses play an important role in the planning and preparation of infrastructural maintenance.

We are currently witnessing the emergence of augmented reality applications,[29] often employing mobile technology, using GIS technology to show assets (e.g., pipe joints) that are underground (Figure 11.11). This saves not only time in locating where to work, it avoids the risk of damaging underground infrastructure.

Another important use of geospatial analysis in maintenance is work planning and scheduling. Maintenance activities are typically geographically dispersed and can

---

[29] Applications that associate data with real images as taken at the current location of the user, showing the real-world image, combined with relevant data. These applications are in general "location aware"—that is, they know where the user is located at the time of use.

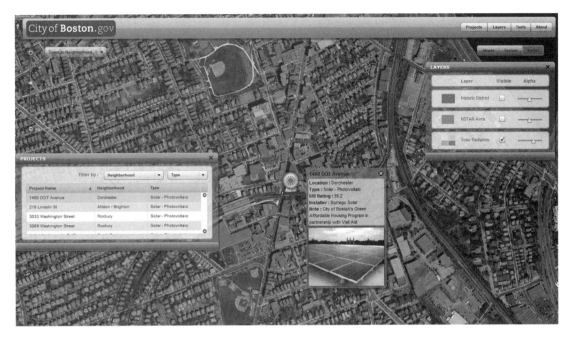

FIGURE 11.12 Example of the application of GIS, depicting the potentials for the use of solar energy, combined with actual project information.
Reproduced by permission of ESRI, Inc.

only be accomplished by professionals (individuals or teams) who are certified to do the work. When setting up work schedules, GIS analysis will provide the information on what staff to deploy, based on the analysis of the current location of the individual and the routing involved to arrive at a specific location.

Sustainability will increasingly become more important. Organizations are looking for ways to reduce the use of energy in their buildings. GIS technology is playing a role in energy data collection and analysis (Figure 11.12). For example, there is GIS software for the analysis of the potential to use solar cells for electricity generation that takes into account sunlight analysis and the optimal orientation of solar collectors for maximum output.

Although GIS technology holds great potential, its adoption is often complex and expensive for organizations that do not use this technology as part of their core non-FM activities. The problem such organizations face is the degree of expertise and sophisticated infrastructure needed to support this technology.

Several recent developments are facilitating the deployment of GIS technology, including:

- **Cloud services for running GIS infrastructures**. GIS systems can be installed and operated using virtual (cloud) computer infrastructures. This alleviates users from the burden of system management by permitting direct access to GIS services.
- **Standardization**. Widely accepted GIS standards already allow cross-platform access to geospatial information. Emerging standardization of GIS in OSCRE may lead to the creation of facility management related GIS services.
- **Business-to-consumer developments**. GIS vendors realize the potential of growth in the facility management sector. Development of open systems and public availability of GIS tools (e.g., viewers) provide a wide variety of mapping data and other geospatial information.

The wide use and adoption of true GIS intelligence for facility management could very well be fueled by the emergence of dedicated applications, providing high-quality spatial analysis and distributed to users as cloud services. Such applications would provide specialized GIS analyses for the benefit of organizations without having to invest in the acquisition of an internal GIS infrastructure. This in turn should substantially lower the cost entry point for using GIS technology.

Digital Signage

Specifically in shared (flexible) office environments, there is a need to support employees and visitors in locating workspaces. Since there is a trend that reduces private ownership of workspaces, people need effective tools to help them find their way around the workplace. Digital signage applications help people in identifying where workspaces are available. By integrating digital signage with space management and workplace reservation systems, people can check for availability on-site as well as remotely and reserve facilities, thereby ensuring their availability.

It has been found, however, that mandating workspace reservations often fails since workers tend to only reserve workspaces in times of scarcity. A pragmatic approach to this problem involves the principle of *optional reservations*. That is, reserving workspaces is not required, but when someone has reserved a space, that person will have precedence in using it. This practical approach provides value to the ones who do make reservations.

There is a risk involved in the use of reservations for individual workspaces when there is a "no-show" or "short-stay" situation. People tend to reserve a space but due to a variety of circumstances, often do not use the space at all or use the space for only part of the time. The risk is that it blurs the meaning of effective

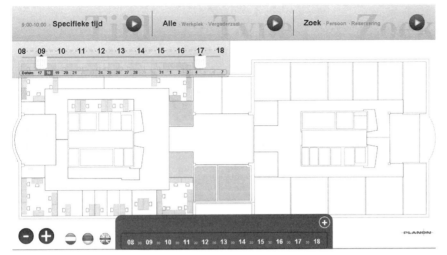

FIGURE 11.13 An example of touch-screen-based interactive digital signage. Reservations can be made in real time.
Reproduced by permission of Planon.

workplace availability.[30] This in fact reflects the need for an automated "check-out" solution not requiring any action on the part of the worker. There is technology to accomplish this as illustrated in Figure 11.13.

Sustainability and Energy Management at the Workplace

Sustainability has recently become of significant importance to facility management professionals. The historic and dreadful consequences of the Japan earthquake and ensuing tsunami in 2011 had a dramatic impact on energy supply, distribution via the energy grid,[31] and supply chain management. In facility management, sustainability certification systems, such as LEED, BREEAM, and ENERGY STAR, are aimed at benchmarking the environmental performance of buildings as they are used by organizations. Sustainability reaches out to all disciplines of facility management.

One clear and understandable approach to sustainability is illustrated by the TriasEnergetica concept,[32] an energy-saving process developed in the Netherlands that is dedicated to three goals (Figure 11.14):

1. The reduction of *the demand for energy by avoiding waste and implementing energy-saving measures.*
2. The use of *sustainable sources of energy, such as wind, solar power, and water.*
3. The use of *fossil fuel energy as efficiently as possible and only if sustainable sources of energy are unavailable.*

---

[30] A well-known phenomenon for meeting rooms.
[31] The energy network, its topology, and the way power is generated to provide a stable supply of energy.
[32] www.triasenergetica.com.

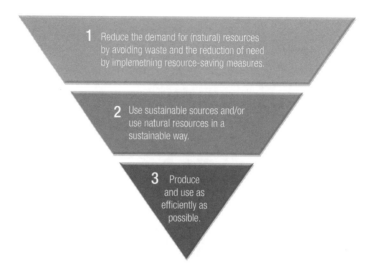

FIGURE 11.14 Trias Energetica concept.

Computer-based energy modeling of buildings and building systems and the determination of cost-effective energy conservation measures (ECMs) is currently receiving a great deal of attention (Table 11.5). This is not surprising since buildings are responsible for almost 40 percent of global energy use[33] and account for

TABLE 11.5   Overview of potential contribution of computer-based energy modeling.

	Footprint (SqFt, m²)	Fit-for-Purpose	Technical Management	Sustainability & Energy Management
Strategic	Insight in total occupancy building(s), portfolio (fit) analysis	Fitting building design, comfort, binding talented staff	Capital- and maintenance budget planning	Improvement program identification, certification (LEED, BREEAM)
Tactical	Saving footprint based on occupancy	Demand/supply matching on workspace types	Maintenance on demand (just-in-time)	Saving (costs on) energy and other natural resources
Operational	Insight into use patterns and occupancy of workspaces	Efficient environment, health and safety, user satisfaction	Understanding status of systems and inventory	Sustainable conduct, sustainable user processes

[33] NEED Project, "Energy Consumption," Manassas, VA, 2011, p. 6, www.NEED.org.

FIGURE 11.15 Modeling energy usage and costs by month.
Reproduced by permission of Retroficiency.

close to 50 percent of the United States' landfill waste[34]; buildings (mostly HVAC systems) consume almost 75 percent of our electricity;[35] and they account for almost 40 percent of the United States' carbon emissions.[36]

Models exist that take into account location, building type, occupancy patterns, available energy rebates, and electrical and lighting loads to optimize retrofits. Energy models also have been developed showing the result of ECM on return on investment (ROI) and benchmarking calculations (e.g., LEED, ENERGY STAR). Some models also take into account the interaction between energy systems, such as how a change in one system (e.g., lighting) might impact another system (e.g., HVAC).

---

[34] Richard Paradis, Director, "Construction Waste Management," *Whole Building Design Guide*, National Institute of Building Sciences, 2011.

[35] USGBC. *Green Building and LEED Core Concepts Guide*, 2d ed. (Upper Saddle River, NJ: Prentice Hall, 2011).

[36] Ibid.

Energy models need to make inferences for unknown data. The starting point for these models is either whatever input data the user knows about the building (e.g., age, location, use, occupancy, etc.) or energy data automatically pulled from other systems (e.g., utilities, BAS systems, etc.). Based on analyzing this initial data, the software infers other energy-related data and, based on the amount of input data, calibrates the degree to which the model feels its analysis is accurate (Figure 11.15).

The emergence of a new generation of intelligent meters are specifically equipped to be retrofitted at any desired location in buildings and have wireless communication capabilities to transfer their readings to applications such as IWMS energy management and BAS systems. For energy management purposes, they enable the modeling of buildings into "energy consumption segments," registering actual consumption of those segments.

Energy management modeling can allow for modeling the consumption profile of a building not only by the use of physical meters/counters. It can also allow for the introduction of virtual meters and counters. Virtual meters are software components used in the computer model only. They can be "located" at any place in the meter network (Figure 11.16) and the function they provide is adding the readings from a number of physical submeters/counters. The advantage of a virtual meter/counter is that it can be defined for any building location. For example, it can be used to calculate the total energy consumption for a rentable unit when there are submeters already installed on all related spaces but not at the rentable unit level itself.

These types of applications can not only be used for energy management (identification and correction of energy waste), they can also be used to calculate energy surcharges in a precise manner, providing the flexibility for the sensors to be relocated when the occupants change their footprint in the building.

Interesting options are now emerging for wireless energy management "at the wall outlet level" as well.[37] These consist of (ZigBee) networked devices that are plugged on the wall outlets and perform the following functions:

- Measure consumption
- Switch power (wireless)

This type of technology provides the means to schedule asset energy consumption based on the availability of green energy. Some assets (e.g., washing machines) can be scheduled to be switched on, based on the expectation when

---

[37] See, for example, www.plugwise.com.

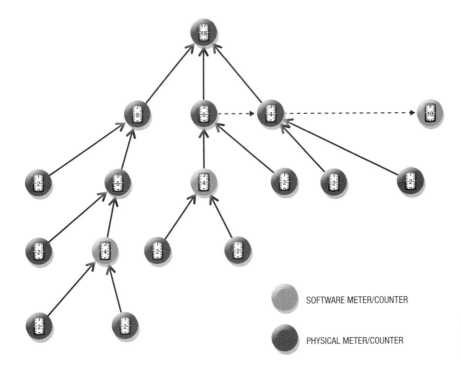

SOFTWARE METER/COUNTER

PHYSICAL METER/COUNTER

FIGURE 11.16 A principle of in-building wireless energy management.

green energy is to be produced by linking up to weather forecasts. These types of applications are based on the implementation of "smart grids."

At a building level, there are normally assets that serve no purpose being switched on during nonworking hours. By measuring and analyzing consumption profiles and switching assets on/off at optimal times, energy savings can be achieved independently of the building management systems.[38] These types of applications are neither complex nor disruptive to install and use.

EMERGING TECHNOLOGIES

Smart Infrastructures

New and emerging applications related to intelligent or **smart infrastructures** include wireless networks consisting of sensors, intelligent meters, and/or switches (Table 11.6). Such networks enable space and real estate professionals to register events around the workplace, analyze them, and act on the information they provide. The advantage that these solutions provide is that they are inexpensive to install (retrofit) since they do not impact existing walls, floors, and ceilings.

[38] Coffee machines, printers, and such (see www.plugwise.com).

TABLE 11.6 Overview of potential contribution of smart infrastructure.

	Footprint (SqFt, m²)	Fit-for-Purpose	Technical Management	Sustainability & Energy Management
Strategic	Insight in total occupancy building(s), portfolio (fit) analysis	Fitting building design, comfort, binding talented staff	Capital- and maintenance budget planning	Improvement program identification, certification (LEED, BREEAM)
Tactical	Saving footprint based on occupancy	Demand/supply matching on workspace types	Maintenance on demand (just-in-time)	Saving (costs on) energy and other natural resources
Operational	Insight into use patterns and occupancy of workspaces	Efficient environment, health and safety, user satisfaction	Understanding status of systems and inventory	Sustainable conduct, sustainable user processes

Sensors/actuator networks can be applied for a range of purposes, including energy savings, access control, monitoring and analyzing workspace use, health and safety monitoring, and no-show management.

Specifically for dense wireless-networked environments like the typical modern office, technology is being developed that will enable capturing the position of people in the building by means of the smartphone they carry. This localization technology is expected to be accurate to the level of 1 meter (40 inches). The ability to rapidly and accurately locate colleagues has many uses, such as disaster recovery and space utilization patterns.

Linking occupancy information to digital signage solutions will result in the indication of real-time workspace availability which in turn will support users in quickly locating appropriate locations to work.

Applications of Sensor Networking around the Workplace

Various devices are currently available that, apart from performing their function, also operate as a node in a mesh network. Among those devices are:

- A variety of sensors, ranging from simple infrared (IR) sensors to complex ones; such sensors have the ability to sense light (cameras), sound, temperature, presence of gases like CO_2 and other environmental data.

■ Intelligent meters, which have the ability to record consumption readings related to the date and time of the reading and transmitting this data to applications, such as BMS and CAFM/IWMS systems, for subsequent processing.

■ Actuators, such as power-switching devices that can be remotely controlled by software applications.

Specific examples of where sensor networks add value in the workplace include:

■ Managing no-shows.
■ Managing supply for demand: parking.
■ Managing workplace demand: space management.

Perhaps the simplest use of sensor networking is to be found in no-show applications. In facilities that have reserved spaces (e.g., meeting rooms), a simple IR sensor is either hung or an existing one is connected with the room booking system. There exist various suppliers of platforms that manage this hardware, such as security system platforms or specific vendors who specialize in the management of AV equipment for meeting rooms.

Apart from the "technical" advantage of increasing the availability of expensive spaces, no-show detection can be used to change people's behavior in a noninvasive way. Reservation systems in general provide the means to notify people in advance that a meeting with room reservations is due. The objective here is that people will cancel the meeting when it is not being held, which will avoid simply not showing up. With no-show detection technology, one can personalize this message in such a way that only people who have a track record of no-shows will be notified.

Room-booking systems can simply interrogate the room by checking the sensor status to see whether people are present or not. If no one is present, the reservation system can automatically cancel the meeting (including room services), freeing the facility for use by others, notify the organizer about the event, and charge costs if incurred.

Automated no-show detection also will provide space management staff with an accurate overview of the effective use of the facilities. People will often take a voluntary action only if there is value created for them in return (i.e., "when I reserve a room, I am sure that I shall have access to it"). As a consequence, people will be motivated to use the reservation system but will rarely manually check out when leaving. This is because the action of checking out does not bring value to them apart from perhaps thinking this is the responsible thing to do.

In summary, the availability of even simple sensors in meeting rooms can be used for automated check-in and check-out. This is convenient for users, keeps the availability of meeting rooms at its maximum capacity, and produces reliable use data for space management professionals to analyze.

Parking places share many commonalities with meeting rooms: they are expensive, scarce, and in high demand. Reservations systems enable spaces to be reserved for parts of the day, particularly important for visitor spaces. As with meeting rooms, parking no-show situations occur that result in the spaces going unused.

The use of sensor networks in parking areas is becoming fairly common (Figure 11.17). Wireless sensor technologies allow sensors to be installed without the need to wire them, resulting in inexpensive and easy retrofitting. Sensors also allow for **measurement** of actual occupation. Linking this information to the reservations system enables effective management of no-show spaces that in turn allows for better use of available resources using the simple formula:

Space Capacity Available = (Currently Nonoccupied Places) – (Number of Reservations Open)

This equation enables facility managers to have more accurate data that in turn results in higher use efficiency. Used with digital signage, users entering a garage

FIGURE 11.17 Parking garage in Frankfurt, Germany. Sensors above each space allow for accurate estimation of available capacity.

can be told where free parking spaces are available. The use of such systems has resulted in increased employee satisfaction since they are not turned away from a parking lot where they observe free spaces.

This technology is capable of managing high volumes of assets. In the Netherlands, for example, many people go to the railway station to travel to work using bicycles. A major railway company is currently equipping its bicycle parking lots in a number of train stations with 90,000 sensors, each identifying if a bike location is occupied. When bicycles are not picked up for a long time, they are tagged and removed. This practice eliminates the need to expand bicycle parking capacity. Sensor battery life is well above 10 years.

A second example of this technology is a hospital that had a requirement that, at all times, a minimum number of ambulances had to be ready to respond to emergency calls. By equipping ambulance parking spaces with sensors, the system monitors this requirement and alerts staff when the requirement is not met. What can be done in parking lots can, in principle, be applied to the workplace.

With the increased flexibility of organizational workforces, both in dedicated as well as shared workplace environments, real estate and space managers need to adapt faster to changes in workplace demand. Space management is becoming more of a real-time dynamic process. Apart from traditional space planning approaches, the ability to "inspect and adapt" to change in demand, as it is occurring, will become a standard practice.

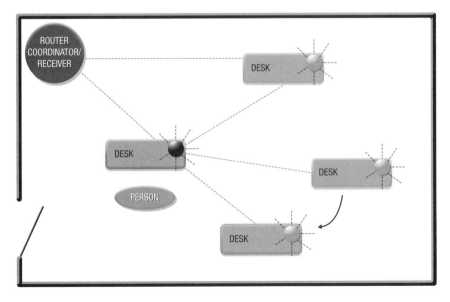

FIGURE 11.18 Sensor technology indicating the status of workspaces.

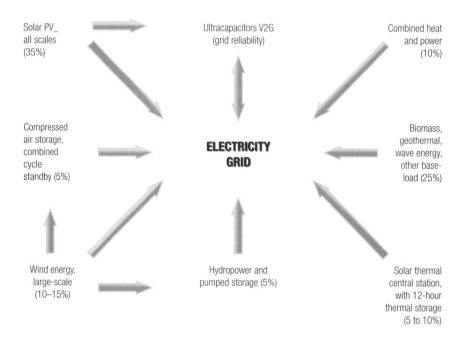

FIGURE 11.19 Smart grid principles.

There is an increasing need to adapt space and to know what is happening within a space. Technology is emerging where sensor technology is attached/located at workspaces, identifying their status: occupied or available (Figure 11.18).

Not only are sensors with wireless networking capabilities explicitly suitable for this, but also other networked sensors, such as cameras and radio frequency identification (RFID) technology, can be used for this purpose. There are a number of possible implementations emerging in applying sensor technology around the workplace.

Energy Management: Smart Grids

Technological developments are designed to lessen the demand of electricity and other natural resources (tier 1).[39] Notable developments take place in tier 2 as well.[40] "Smart grid" technology is gradually finding its way into the workplace (Figure 11.19). Although a standardized definition of smart grids has not yet been established, a definition was described by the European Union as follows: "an electricity network that can intelligently integrate the actions of all users

---

[39] Also called scope 1 emissions. Embodies emissions directly generated by a sector or building.

[40] Tier 2 (scope 2) emissions are those emissions used by a sector or building.

connected to it—generators, consumers and those that do both—in order to efficiently deliver sustainable, economic and secure electricity supplies."[41]

The major benefit of smart grids is their ability to link natural energy sources[42] to the energy network of facilities and manage assets in such a way that they preferably consume energy at the times when sustainable energy is expected to be generated. In real estate, the goal of smart grids is that modern buildings should be able to produce electrical power themselves instead of just consuming it. This way, modern buildings become a node in the energy grid.

Improved performance of buildings in terms of their use of electricity is not only a matter of corporate responsibility, but also results in societal and financial benefits. The ongoing rising demand of electricity will increase energy prices significantly.

Cloud Computing

Cloud computing, software-as-a-service (SaaS), and on-demand computing are labels to denote all types of IT services that are necessary to run applications. The unique property of cloud-based services is that they run on multiple servers on the network (or the Internet) in such a way that it seems as if it were just one powerful computer that serves the vast amount of users connected to the services. In many cases, these types of computing models consist of multiple interconnected virtual servers and storage media. This redundancy in processing infrastructure renders high reliability and uptime: "the computer virtually never fails."

The users do not have any notion of where the cloud services run and how they are managed. The users just use the services rendered to them, for which the sole requirement is network/Internet connectivity. Within the concept of cloud computing, different *services* are offered for customers to use. Where cloud computing denotes the computing concept, the services rendered by service providers running such infrastructures are often denoted by an "as-a-service" label (Figure 11.20).

Cloud-based services are attractive for their ease of use, lack of any installation, high availability and absence of any requirement to manage them (no systems management). Furthermore, the services are in general rendered on a pay-for-use basis, which makes adoption easy and in many cases affordable.

Currently, some concerns about their use do exist. Among the most discussed ones are:

[41] See www.smartgrids.eu/web/node/56#12 ("What Is SmartGrids") and www.oe.energy.gov.
[42] For example, solar energy, wind energy.

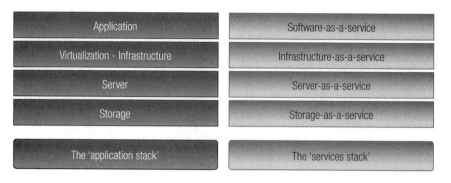

FIGURE 11.20 Virtual computing, cloud services. *Note that there are more divisions than represented in this figure. The authors deliberately limited this overview to clarify the main principles.*

- **Data and information privacy**. Does the user have guarantees that information uploaded to or generated in the cloud is not disclosed to third parties to whom the user does not want it to be disclosed? To what terms does the provider of the services commit and how can compliance be monitored?
- **Data security**. How well is the data safeguarded against malicious acts of third parties to obtain information unrightfully?
- **Level of availability (uptime guarantees)**. How robust is the processing infrastructure? Is it able to recover from hardware, software, and network failure without affecting the rendering of service?

To address these kinds of issues, providers deliver different cloud services options, among which are:

- **Open (Internet) cloud services**. No specific conditions are prearranged, but general conditions are published by the vendor.
- **Trusted cloud services**. Cloud services that are used by a limited group of users, sharing conditions between them.
- **Private cloud services**. Cloud services that are rendered based on a service-level agreement (SLA) with the customer. In this SLA, various agreements can be negotiated.

Cloud and on-demand computing services are expected to considerably impact the IT landscape over the near term. They encourage employee mobility by their ease of adoption and generally low price levels.

Radio Frequency Identification

Radio Frequency Identification (RFID)[43] technologies can be used for real-time location of people and assets (Figure 11.21). They can also be used in conjunction with sensors. Sensors using RFID technology might detect air flow for energy analysis.

[43] See also Chapter 5.

FIGURE 11.21 Active and passive RFID technologies are depicted.

In the health care industry, for example, such technology might be used to detect radiation or hazardous materials.

RFID technology employs two components:

1. A radio tag containing a microchip for storing data about an object and an antenna for transmitting such data.
2. A reader that provides power for the tag and then reads and processes such data.

Although the International Organization for Standardization (ISO) holds some RFID standards, this technology is less well standardized and vendor-specific proprietary solutions are the rule. In general, smart cards, as used by security systems, are based on RFID technology.

The location of people or goods is established when the tag is present in the range of the scanner. RFID tracking is therefore *personalized*. The tag identifies the person or asset concerned. RFID infrastructures are in general regarded as expensive to install when compared to simple barcodes. At present, it is estimated that barcodes cost half a cent (U.S. dollars) each, while passive RFID tags cost more than 5 cents (U.S. dollars) each.[44] However, when you start to look at other variables, such as the speed of collecting data or the cost of RFID scanners versus barcode interrogators and the number of times you need to perform the asset inventory, the cost delta is impacted and the costs become somewhat more equal.[45] Note that RFID technology may be already present by means of the access control system installed in the facilities.

[44] G. Shih, "Game Changer in Retailing, Bar Code Is 35," *New York Times*, June 25, 2009.
[45] M. Roberti, "Bar-Code Technology Is Not Cheaper than RFID," *RFID Journal*, June 2009.

Perhaps the most dominant application of RFID technology around the workplace is found in smart cards, used to identify people and granting them access to facilities. For assets, RFID technology is increasingly used for asset condition in BAS systems and for energy control software input.

Mobility

The rapid deployment rate at which mobile technologies are being adopted today is unparalleled. This rate of adoption is fueled predominantly within "**consumerization**" markets. People are embracing mobile devices and integrating them into their everyday lives. As a consequence, the adoption of mobile technologies is no longer a mere issue of operating efficiency but it is also becoming a tool for employee satisfaction and retention.

Facilities managers are perfectly positioned to take advantage of the rapid evolution of today's powerful phones and tablet computers. Many FM field services are well suited to be supported by mobile technologies. More significantly, FM managers can address a new audience using mobile technologies: the total workforce of the organization. By providing smart applications, the added FM value can be clearly communicated throughout the organization.

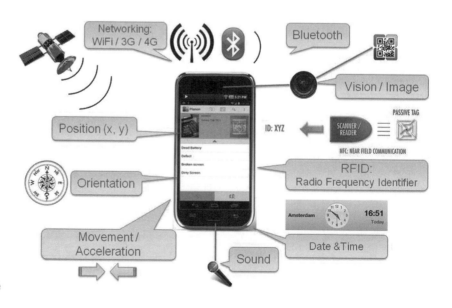

FIGURE 11.22 Active and passive RFID technologies are depicted.

Mobile devices are not merely miniaturized PCs or laptops. These devices are fundamentally new types of information devices equipped with capabilities that are not to be found in today's PCs and laptops (Figure 11.22).

Some applications (or apps as they are called) will be Web-based applications running locally on the mobile device using its browser. Additionally, however, applications will actively involve the use of the device's sensors. For example, the interaction with RFID tags will allow for efficient collecting and transmitting of information and replace a multitude of manual functions, thereby creating greater user efficiency. For example, for assets tagged with RFID or **quick response code tags**, a service engineer can place the mobile device near the tag to retrieve relevant maintenance or warranty information automatically without requiring manual input. Location awareness, which can be derived from the mobile device's sensors, can be used to provide users with relevant contextual information.

For employee services, mobile technologies are expected to play a role in digital signage, making for personalized signage information. Other applications will be developed that will enable facility occupants to effectively communicate with their environment. This will result in a vastly improved user experience of the facility itself.

In summary, there are few accepted mobile technology standards because of the rapid evolution of this technology. The implications for FMs will be significant as locational and contextual information is collected, communicated, and analyzed by remote computers and results either sent to the mobile user or directly controlling various devices. For the "early adopters" of such technology, it is important for the FM to get the involvement of internal IT resources.

CONCLUSION

This chapter summarizes how technology is evolving as it relates to managing and using the physical workplace. It depicts how technology impacts both how and where we work. Drivers that impact how these technologies are implemented are financial, social, legal, and environmental. Like technology itself, these drivers are evolving rapidly and dramatically impact the workplace.

These factors in turn influence the facility manager and the role of facility management in organizations. The knowledge base required of the facility manager includes not only the technology but how such technology can affect how and where work is performed. This in turn will increase the importance of the facility manager in assisting senior management in making strategic decisions that impact the workplace. Given the dynamic nature of technology and the continuously evolving drivers that impact the workplace, facility management professionals will need to determine what technologies are available to support the strategic objectives of their organizations and how facility-related operations and services support such objectives.

ADDITIONAL RESOURCES

S. Rich and K. Davis, "Geographic Information Systems (GIS) for Facility Management," IFMA Foundation, www.ifmafoundation.org, Houston, TX, 2010.

Eric Teicholz, ed., "Facility Management Technology Update," IFMA Foundation, www .ifmafoundation.org.

The Role of People and Process in Technology

12

Angela Lewis

INTRODUCTION

IFMA defines facility management as "a profession that encompasses multiple disciplines to ensure functionality of the built environment by integrating people, process and technology."[1] This chapter discusses the importance and interactions between people, process, and technology.[2] Although the concepts discussed can apply to many facility management technologies, the chapter uses energy and maintenance management software to frame the discussion.[3]

The chapter first discusses some fundamental concepts and definitions, and then provides an overview of the challenges that result when technology, people, and process are not balanced during a technology planning and implementation project. The discussion of current needs is followed by a discussion of what is needed to support emerging technologies. The chapter closes with two case studies. The first case study provides an overview of how to use a building automation

[1] IFMA, "What Is FM? Definition of Facility Management," www.ifma.org/resources/what-is-fm.htm (accessed April 12, 2011).

[2] This chapter was written from the findings of the PhD thesis, "A Framework for Improving Building Operating Decisions for Energy Efficiency."

[3] The author wishes to thank Louis Coughenour, PE, Energy Management Specialist of Schneider Electric, for providing the screen shot of the energy benchmarking score card within the chapter.

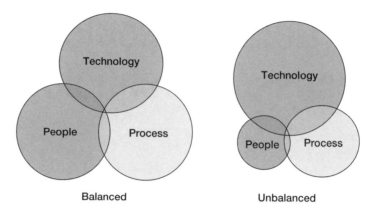

FIGURE 12.1 Balanced and unbalanced facility management technology implementation projects.

system (BAS) to benchmark and improve energy efficiency within a lab building. The second case study summarizes the importance of people and organizational roles within a software enterprise system integration project, with an emphasis on lessons learned.

Successful facility management balances people, process, and technology. However, many technology implementation projects are unbalanced (Figure 12.1). The technology receives the most attention, while people and process aspects receive minimal attention. The goal of this chapter is to help identify why the imbalance occurs and provide insight through lessons learned of how to better balance these three factors.

Within Figure 12.1, technology is defined as the system, tool, or software the facility management team is evaluating or implementing. Most of the chapters within this book provide detailed examples of technology. Process includes the details about how to plan and implement a specific business-related task, practice, or activity. Best practices are actions, tasks, and processes that allow an organization to produce superior results using a systematic process.[4] The use of best practices can help organizations to be recognized as a leader within their respective market.[5] Within this context, the term *people* is used to describe the culture of the organization, training, education, skills, and competencies of facility management team members.

Energy and Maintenance Management Technologies

Energy and maintenance management are used to frame the discussion within this chapter. In concept, energy and maintenance management are interrelated.

---

[4] BPC, "The Best Practice Club, Corporate Presentation," from www.bpclub.com/content/home.asp (accessed December 30, 2010).

[5] T. Wireman, *Benchmarking Best Practices in Maintenance Management* (New York: Industrial Press, 2004).

A building can be designed and constructed to include the most energy-efficient systems. However, over time, without proper maintenance, even the most energy-efficient equipment becomes less efficient because belts wear, sensors drift out of calibration, and operational needs can change. From a process perspective, energy and maintenance management practices are often not well coordinated in facility management organizations. Individuals responsible for maintenance are different from the individuals responsible for energy efficiency. In some cases, the two departments may be completely separate and rarely communicate with each other. As a result, the technologies and data used for decision making are generally in separate databases and may not be shared across the organization.

Although it is possible using current technology to integrate and exchange data between such software systems, it is not standard practice. Therefore, the challenge of integration is not the capabilities of the technology, but the development of processes to support what should be integrated, who has access to what data, as well as service providers and in-house facility management teams having the skills necessary to support the planning, implementation, and use of integrated software solutions.

CURRENT NEEDS

The two largest needs to support successful technology deployment are (1) further development of standard processes, and (2) people-focused efforts. More specifically, process needs include clearly defined project goals and moving beyond benchmarking. People-focused needs include training and education and overcoming the resistance to change.

Process Needs

Within this chapter, a process is defined as a group of related and structured actions, changes, functions, and/or tasks to produce a result.[6] A well-developed process will be developed as the result of a project or business goal. Thus, processes can be further defined as project or business processes. A project process is used to manage a task with a clearly defined beginning and end. Project processes typically have five steps: initiate, plan, execute, control, and close.[7] A business process is broader in scope than a project process, as it seeks to serve the goals of a specific organization in response to a need either internal or

---

[6] B. Dickenson, *Strategic Business Engineering* (Brisbane CA: LCI Press, 1992).

[7] Ibid.

Are energy performance goals set during design?

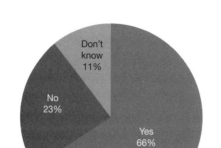

Do you know if energy performance goals set during design were met during the 1st year of operation?

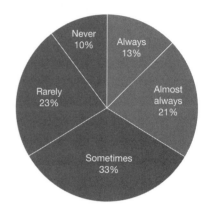

FIGURE 12.2 Survey results contrasting if energy goals are set and team member awareness of goal achievement.

external to the organization. One or more project processes can be completed to support business processes. Multiple project processes may be necessary to develop a successful business process. Thus, within this chapter, both project and business processes are discussed.

Establishing Project Goals

Goals define the objectives and scope of a project. Goals are the foundation of a successful project. A key finding of a survey conducted in 2009[8] was the magnitude of the difference between the frequency goals were set and the frequency of team members knowing if goals were met one year after the project was complete. As shown in Figure 12.2, goals were set 66 percent of the time for energy management projects. However, it was found that only 13 percent of respondents always knew and 21 percent almost always knew if project goals were met during the first year of operation. A similar finding was found for maintenance management projects. Goals were found to be set 56 percent of the time, while it was known if goals were always met during the first year of operation by 5 percent of respondents and almost always by 17 percent (Figure 12.3). (It should be noted that with many surveys, an optimism bias can result. From review of the data described in Figures 12.2 and 12.3 an optimism bias is likely. An optimism bias

[8] A. Lewis, D. Riley, and A. Elmualim. "Development of a Framework for Improving Building Operating Decisions: Findings from the Questionnaire." Proceedings of the 6th International Conference on Innovation in AEC 2010. State College, PA, June, 2010; A. Lewis, "Designing for Energy-Efficient Operations and Maintenance," *Engineered Systems*, August 2010. www.esmagazine.com/Articles/Feature_Article/BNP_GUID_9-5-2006_A_19781118382837873588.

Are maintenance goals and/or requirements determined during design?

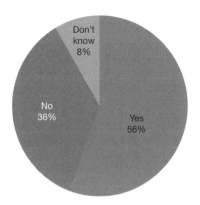

How often do you know if maintenance goals were met during the 1st year of operation?

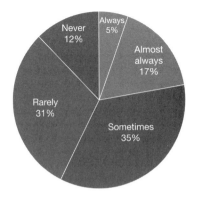

FIGURE 12.3 Survey results contrasting if maintenance goals are set and team member awareness of goal achievement.

means that the percentages of "yes" and "always/almost always" responses are likely smaller than reported by the survey results because people have a tendency to report actions or conditions as better than their actual state.)

As energy efficiency seems to be generally understood across facility management teams, and maintenance is often not seen as an opportunity to add value to an organization, it is not surprising that the percentages for energy management (Figure 12.2) of yes and always or almost always responses are greater compared to maintenance. The core finding revealed that energy and maintenance management goal setting is not a standard facility management practice. Additionally, when goals are set, the business process to ensure the goal is met is not well established. The findings may also reveal that the goal was not understood across the facility management or broader project team, or there was insufficient buy-in of the goal.

This challenge may occur because of how facility management is positioned within the buildings industry. The buildings industry includes design, construction, operations and maintenance, and demolition professionals. Any new project starts with design, followed by construction. Each sector typically has clearly defined deliverables, roles, and responsibilities. Given traditional design and construction practices,[9] the designer hands over the design, once complete, to the contractor. The contractor then constructs the building and turns it over to

[9] The author acknowledges that the use of integrated design and design-build processes are increasing. However, these practices are not standard industry practice.

the operations and facility management team. This traditional approach allows each team to have separate, often disconnected goals. The goal of the designer is to complete the design documents. The goal of the construction contractor is to build the building. The goal of the operations and facility management team is to operate and manage the building to meet the needs of the building occupants. However, when goals to operate and manage the building are not understood by the design and construction team, it is possible that details important to the facility management team were not sufficiently addressed. Thus, it may be difficult for the facility management team to meet their goals. To support goal alignment across the design, construction, facility management, and operations practices, facility managers and building operators should be involved during design and construction.

Successful technology implementation requires acknowledging the importance of goal setting. The current lack of focus on goal setting demonstrates a lack of focus on both business and project processes and people in technology planning and implementation. If people and processes were a core focus of technology implementation, then goals would be a foundational part of more projects.

To move from reactive to proactive use of energy efficiency and maintenance management technologies requires the standardization and use of best practices. Some best practices to consider include:

- Documentation of work completed and the time it took to complete the work.
- Use of data for decision making.
- Recalibration of meters and sensors before they drift out of calibration.
- Use of report generators to translate data and information into actionable recommendations.

To improve energy efficiency benchmarks, an energy audit or commissioning project process can be completed for the building(s). Either of these efforts can help to identify specific systems or equipment that is operating inefficiently. To improve maintenance benchmarks, there are several different approaches, depending on the practices already in use. If maintenance is entirely reactive, the goal should be to move toward proactive maintenance. To do this, developing a maintenance plan is a good first step. If a maintenance plan is already in place, evaluating what systems and equipment could cost effectively use condition-based (predictive) maintenance, opposed to time-based maintenance (preventive) is a good first step. For either scenario, the goal is to have control over operating conditions and to manage the process proactively.

When a project starts with a quantifiable goal, proactive, data-driven decisions can be made. Additionally, the success of the planning and implementation of both business and project processes can be tracked. Over time, in-house benchmarks can be established as part of a continuous improvement program.

BEYOND BENCHMARKING: A NEED FOR DATA-DRIVEN DECISION MAKING

Benchmarking helps a facility management team to determine a quantitative starting point to measure performance of their facility against their own facilities or other facilities with similar characteristics and to measure improvement.

When benchmarking metrics are selected, it is important to balance the type of data collected. Data about building performance and also team member performance can be collected. Building performance data should include building, system, and equipment level data. If only building level data, such as utility billing data is collected, it will be difficult to identify specific systems or equipment that are not operating in an energy efficient manner. Data about team member performance can include percent craft utilization, craft service quality, schedule compliance, and percent of work orders complete.[10] When selecting team member performance metrics, be sure that the team understands why the data is being collected. Without explaining why, data may be recorded inaccurately or some members of the team may not be supportive of the data collection efforts, negatively impacting success of the effort. See the case study section for further discussion of metric selection.

After the metrics are selected, it is important that the data or information from the metrics be presented in a clear, actionable format. Raw data or long documents of tables of information can be difficult to interpret to support efficient decision making. Ideally, a report generator should be used to automatically transform raw data into actionable recommendations. However, currently, it is often necessary to analyze data and information using spreadsheets, word processors, and other tools that require hours of labor.

Although it is a very valuable practice, benchmarking is not a decision-making business or project process and does not necessarily provide guidance on what to do with the benchmarking results. After completing a benchmarking process, the next step should be to determine what to do as a result of the benchmarking, especially for facilities with performance below desired levels. Low benchmarking results may also indicate that sustainability goals are not currently being met.

---

[10] R. W. Peters, *Maintenance Benchmarking and Best Practices* (New York: McGraw Hill, 2006).

Benchmarking data, especially when the data are available over a several-year period, can be valuable to:

- Justify system and equipment upgrades and controls optimization projects.
- Demonstrate the existence of proactive maintenance programs.
- Justify staffing needs or demonstrate the need to hire more staff or staff with a specific skill set.
- Recognize the value of the facility management organization to the building owner.

To improve benchmarking levels, four steps should be followed:

1. Determine the level of improvement necessary.
2. Determine what must be done in order for the necessary level of improvement to be achieved.
3. Implement the performance improvements.
4. Implement a plan to ensure the performance improvements are maintained.

People and Technology Needs

The people-related needs include training and education and overcoming resistance to change.

Overcoming Resistance to Change

The success of the implementation of a new technology requires a proactive change management approach. As new technologies are implemented; the amount of available data increases. However, just because the data is available does not mean people will use it. To understand the impact of this statement, consider the use of current technologies, such as computerized maintenance management systems (CMMSs) or building automation systems (BASs). Both of these systems have the ability to collect and process large amounts of data. However, these systems are underutilized in many organizations. Additionally, although these systems can store large amounts of data, this functionality is often not effectively used. For example, trend data collected by a BAS is often only stored for a few days before being overridden with new data. CMMSs are mainly used for work order management, when they are also capable of being used to manage proactive maintenance and inventory control.

Change is often seen as a threat, as it can require people to think, act, or communicate differently. It is not uncommon for individuals within an organization to have a strong culture of "we've always done it this way." When this type of culture exists, change is seen as a threat, especially if roles and necessary skill sets may change as a result of the new technology. However, if people and business and project processes are ignored during the technology change, the technology will likely not be fully implemented, causing the project to not meet initial goals. Facility managers committed to successful technology implementation must not ignore that the implementation of a new technology may cause required skill sets and roles to change. Although change can be challenging and wrought with organizational politics, if the implementation team is not willing to face these realities, it may be worth asking the question, "Is it really worth implementing this new technology?" The unwillingness to address organizational change can result in ineffective use of limited funds. Thus, perhaps it may be more effective to use the funds elsewhere where the opportunity for true success is greater. The second case study in this chapter provides some practical insight for addressing change within large organizations.

Training and Education

Within the facility management profession, as well as many other professions, the role of the knowledge worker is increasing in importance. As technology becomes more data driven, knowledge workers must have the skills necessary to manipulate, analyze, and review data for decision making. Thus, the importance of training and education within facility management organizations is increasing in importance. Education is especially important because it provides the reasons why something is true or should be done a certain way. When team members understand why they are doing something, they are more likely to buy in to new ideas and support organizational change. Training is the process and actions necessary to gain a new set of skills—but does not necessarily explain why. Training and education must be understood as a fundamental need within facility management organizations. Unfortunately, within many facility management organizations today, training (and maintenance budgets) is often cut first when operation costs need to be reduced. To overcome this challenge, organizational cultures need to shift—people and their knowledge are assets to organizations, not just technology. Facility management teams need to be educated about how to use technology for proactive decision making. This means knowing how to analyze data, generate reports, and communicate the significance of the data to stakeholders, among other topics.

PROCESSES AND PEOPLE NEED TO SUPPORT EMERGING TECHNOLOGIES

Two key areas of development within energy and maintenance management technologies that will be impacted by people and both business and project processes include building information modeling and high-performance, green, and smart buildings. Both of these future visions require further development and acceptance of business and project processes to support utilization of BIM, high-performance, green, and smart technologies.

Impacts of Process on Building Information Modeling

The core benefit of building information modeling (BIM)[11] to facility management teams is the information in the model. Although the geometry can provide information to help locate items within the building, the information from the model often will be most valuable to the facility management team. The vision is that information within the BIM can include anything from maintenance manuals and warranty information to real-time linking to sources of building performance information, such as energy data.

BIM has been successful in the construction industry for clash detection and other applications. At this time the use of BIM in facility management is still in its infancy. In order for BIM to be used successfully within facility management, business and project processes of how to collect, verify the accuracy of, and clean data is critical. If the data are not accurate, they cannot be used reliably for decision making, making the purpose of the BIM inadequate. See Chapters 2 and 10 for further discussion about BIM.

High-Performance, Green, and Smart Buildings Require Data-Driven Processes

The concepts of high-performance, green, and smart buildings are interrelated. Green is one component of a high-performance building, and high performance is one characteristic of a smart building (see Glossary for definitions).

Reaching building performance goals, whether federally mandated or internal to the organization, requires effective use of technologies. The design, selection, and installation of the technology is important; however, the operations and maintenance of the technology is equally important. Unfortunately, the core focus of the building industry and research efforts within the building industry has historically been design, selection, and installation technologies. Less focus has been placed on processes. Project processes have received more attention than processes to support proactive operations and maintenance.

---

[11] The author acknowledges that BIM is more than a technology. See Chapter 2 for further discussion of BIM.

In order to meet building performance goals, the importance of business and project processes cannot be neglected. When processes are neglected, the benefits of technology cannot be fully realized. For example, for many years building automation systems have had the capability to collect data from equipment-level sensors and submeters and to store data on servers. In many cases the data collected from sensors and submeters (when installed) is used only for real-time monitoring and to alert building operators of an undesirable condition through an alarm. Although not currently common practice, it is possible to store the sensor and submeter data on servers and use this data to track performance and support benchmarking and troubleshooting efforts.

As project budgets will always be limited, decisions need to be made about how to best utilize limited funds. At times, budgets are set with a core focus on the purchase of the technology. However, this may not necessarily include adequate funding to implement the technology; this is especially true for facility management software. Unfortunately, in some cases, the money to populate the software with asset records or setup reports to support effective decision making is never allocated. Thus, some of the benefits of the technology demonstrated during the procurement project process are never realized.

As more high-performance buildings are built and more existing buildings are renovated to be high performance, it is important that facility management teams acknowledge that purchasing high-performance technologies is just the starting point—without well-established business and project processes, as well as proper training of facility managers and building operators, high-performance buildings will fall short of project goals.

CASE STUDIES

Two case studies describe the role of people and both project and business processes in technology deployment. The first case study, a lab building on a college campus, focuses on the process used to more fully utilize the existing building automation system. The second case study, a large community college district, focuses on the impact of team interaction and communication during a software integration project.

A Focus on Processes: Use of a Building Automation System to Benchmark Energy Consumption

A facility management team at a university set a goal to develop a quarterly benchmarking score card using data from their building automation system. To meet this goal, a pilot project was completed for one lab building. The building was a five-story, 176,000 square foot (1,635 square meter) steel frame building that houses H-8 occupancy laboratories, offices, and an animal vivarium constructed in 2003.

The goal of the facility management team was to identify metrics to benchmark building energy performance for a lab building at the building, system, and equipment level. After identifying the metrics, a business process to generate quarterly benchmarking score card reports using the existing building automation system (BAS) was developed. To complete this process, the facility manager selected a team to assist a facility management consultant with the decision-making process of what metrics to use. The complete project process consisted of five steps:[12]

1. Develop a comprehensive list of potential metrics, measurements, and benchmarks
2. Select appropriate metrics, measurements, and benchmarks
3. Determine data collection methods and evaluate building automation system functionality
4. Determine the analysis logic
5. Program building automation system and configure report generator

A screen shot of the score card developed is shown in Figure 12.4. The main section of the figure visually depicts both historic and current energy consumption.

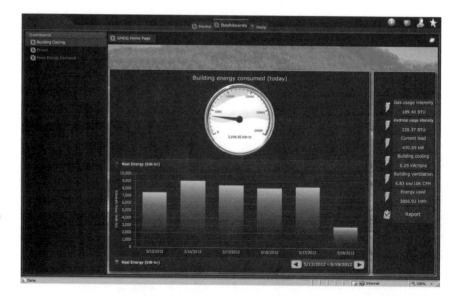

FIGURE 12.4 Screen shot of energy benchmarking score card.

Reproduced by permission of Schneider Electric

[12] Further discussion of the steps can be found in A. Lewis, "How to Quantify Building Energy Performance," *FMJ*, September/October 2010.

The bars from May 13 to 17 depict historic energy data, while the bar for May 18 depicts the energy consumption of the building at the given time the screen shot was taken. The graphic of the dial also depicts current energy consumption at a much higher level of accuracy than the bar graph. The right side of the screen shot summarizes other metrics that are monitored by the building automation system, including gas usage intensity, electrical usage intensity, current load, building cooling load, building ventilation load, and energy used. Further details, similar to those shown for energy consumption, are available to the dashboard users for the other metrics.

Several lessons were learned during the scorecard development:

- Data needed by the building operators may be different than the data needed to quantify energy consumption.
- Trend data from the BAS will nearly always require some analysis to support effective decision making.
- Management and interpretation of large amounts of data generated from sub-meters and sensors can be challenging. Therefore, graphical representations of the data can be very useful.

The largest difference in the data needed by the building operators, compared to the data needed to quantify energy performance, is the manner in which the data were collected. The building operators generally preferred change in value (COV) data. In contrast, data collected at a common time interval, such as every hour or every 15 minutes, is easier to normalize to quantify energy performance. After the data are collected, it is sometimes necessary to convert units, normalize the data, or perform other mathematical calculations to transform the data into a format that is easy to understand and can support effective decision-making business processes.

A Focus on People: Software Integration

As facility management becomes more data driven, there is a need to integrate data sources. This is often completed as part of an enterprise system planning and implementation project. The second case study discussed is a software integration planning project for a large community college district. The main focus of the planning effort was to define the needs of a computerized maintenance management system (CMMS) and to determine how the CMMS could be integrated with other facility management software and business processes, including building automation systems (BAS), geographical information systems (GIS), an enterprise resource planning (ERP) system, and building information modeling (BIM). The solution of how to integrate and exchange data between systems is shown in Figure 12.5.

Although understanding how different software solutions interact to exchange data and where the data will be housed is an important part of a project, understanding, and possibly negotiating, who has the rights to modify, view, and generate reports with the data is equally important. Since facility management teams can be large and include many roles, making decisions about the accessibility of data can be complex. Within project processes supporting data exchange and software interactions, the format and organization of the data and naming conventions are critical because they have large impacts on future business processes.

Lessons learned from the software integration project include:

■ Within large organizations, multiple and often significantly different naming conventions may exist that need to be coordinated.
■ Acceptance of organizational change is necessary for software integration to be successful.
■ Educate facility management and information technology (IT) team members about what an integrated system does and why it adds value.

Resolving naming conventions can be challenging because each user group values assets differently and reasons for using existing naming conventions can be deep rooted within business processes. It may also be valuable to determine

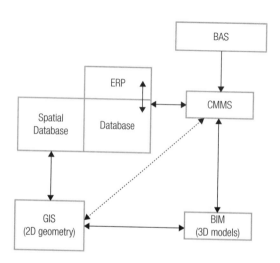

FIGURE 12.5 Information flow for an integrated software solution for a large community college district.

if standards, such as the **OmniClass** Construction Classification System tables, to support the use of open standards should be used.

Acceptance of organizational change requires buy-in. Buy-in from team members is gained slowly through understanding the current needs and challenges of the users of the different types of data. For this project, to gain buy-in, the facility management consultant first worked closely with the executive facility management team to understand the project goals. Then, the consultant met individually with each of the facility managers and IT managers across the district to understand any concerns with the vision of the executive team and help to address concerns and find answers to questions. As the consultant met with each manager, she shared what was learned with the other managers during conversations. Periodically, the consultant would also update the executive team and the full team during meetings.

When educating the team about what an integrated system does and why it adds value, it is important that a consistent and clearly communicated message is delivered. As system integration is a complex task; clear communication is needed to help deliver a consistent message about why the integration effort will support the overall objectives of the organization. To help deliver a consistent message, select a person to champion this effort. The person serving as the champion can be an in-house team member or a consultant. For this project the champion was a consultant. Since the consultant was external to the organization, there was an opportunity for information to be gathered as an objective third party seeking to align the goals of the executive team and the facility and IT managers.

If the person selected to champion the project was from the existing in-house team, it is possible that the person selected may have been perceived to have a bias for the campus he/she formally worked at, putting the goals and objectives of that campus above the others. When selecting a project champion, it is important that the person selected is knowledgeable about project goals and the technology being implemented. He/she must also be willing to listen to team member concerns and be able to find answers to concerns.

CONCLUSION

The scope of any technology implementation project cannot just be about the technology. A well-developed plan that balances people and both business and project process requirements must be a key part of a technology implementation process. As stated through example within the two case studies, the processes and the people aspects of a technology project are essential for success.

ADDITIONAL RESOURCES

A. Lewis, "How to Quantify Building Energy Performance," *FMJ*, September/October 2010.

A. Lewis, D. Riley, J. Elmualim, *"Defining High Performance for Operations and Maintenance,"* International Journal of Facility Management (IFJM), 1(2), 2010, www.ijfm.net/index.php/ijfm/article/view/26.

P. Mathew, *Laboratories for the 21st Century: Best Practice Guide—Metrics and Benchmarks for Energy Efficiency in Laboratories* (Golden, CO: National Renewable Energy Laboratory, 2007).

Social Media

13

Dean Stanberry

INTRODUCTION

With the first known uses of the term occurring around 2004, Webster's dictionary defines **social media** as "forms of electronic communication (as web sites for social networking and microblogging) through which users create online communities to share information, ideas, personal messages and other content (as videos)." A few short years later, social media permeates the breadth of commercial enterprise and personal lives on a global scale.

This chapter is organized into three primary components. First, we explore the convergence of technologies that culminate in the rise of social media; second, we examine facility management (FM)-centric social media applications; and we conclude with a discussion of how facility professionals can leverage social media in their daily work and to enhance career opportunities.

Social Media: Revolution or Evolution?

To better understand social media's impact, let's look at other technological innovations that fundamentally changed the way we work and communicate. The 1920s witnessed the first large-scale commercial availability of telephone service, which forever changed the way companies connected and transacted business.

With the advent of transatlantic service in the mid-1920s, the world took another baby step toward globalization. It would be a few decades before the next technological sea change in communication would occur.

In the late 1970s, the first uses of commercial voicemail systems occurred. Initially marketed to large corporate clients, the emergence of voicemail again changed the way companies communicated and transacted business. Where the telephone enabled real-time communication across vast distances, voicemail began to supplant the need for real-time conversation. The sender could contact the receiver any time, day or night, leaving a brief message with their questions or instructions. The receiver was able to retrieve the messages at their convenience, responding or taking action as appropriate. Though an unintended consequence, this seemingly innocuous technological advancement was a catalyst for the "always on" global workplace. The concept of "business hours" began to evolve from 8–5 Monday through Friday to 24/7/365.

From this point, the pace of technological change expanded at an exponential rate. The year 1982 marked the first appearance of the personal computer (Figure 13.1), as well as the first automated teller machine (ATM). No longer constrained to esoteric groups, technology had infiltrated the general public's daily lives.

The next milestone on the social media path was e-mail. E-mail predates the inception of the Internet and reaches back to the early **ARPANET**.[1] Commercial

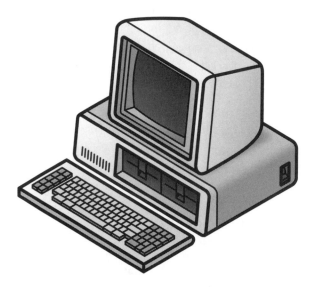

Figure 13.1 First IBM PC—circa 1982.
Source: iStock.

---

[1] The Advanced Research Projects Agency Network (ARPANET) was the world's first operational packet switching network and the core network of a set that came to compose the global Internet.

applications of e-mail arrived in the early 1980s with systems such as IBM's PROFS and Digital Equipment Corporation's ALL-in-1. These early implementations were proprietary in nature and initially did communicate from one company to another. As e-mail began to reach more corporate users, the need to exchange e-mail between companies created the demand for a common protocol. First published in 1984, Message Handling Systems (MHS), more commonly known as e-mail, formally was defined by the X.400 suite of ITU[2] recommendations that define standards for data communication networks.

Getting Connected

Early personal computers essentially were stand-alone devices with no inherent mechanisms to exchange digital information in real time. This would change with the commercial availability of **modems**[3] allowing anyone with a computer to connect to another computer, transmitting and receiving information. Modems utilized the existing analog telephone network to make point-to-point connections with other computers. At the pinnacle of their performance, modems (Figure 13.2) were capable of data transfer speeds up to 56 Kbps (kilobits per second).

While this would be considered incredibly slow by present-day standards, information exchange at the time predominantly was text-based files or small executable programs (applications). Nonetheless, modems gave the public access to e-mail and bulletin board systems (BBSs)—social media in its infancy. The glory days

Figure 13.2 USRobotics 56 Kbps modem—circa 2000.

Reproduced by permission of USRobotics

---

2 The ITU Telecommunication Standardization Sector (ITU-T) is one of the three sectors (divisions or units) of the International Telecommunication Union (ITU); it coordinates standards for telecommunications. The standardization work of ITU dates back to 1865, with the birth of the International Telegraph Union.

3 A modem (modulator-demodulator) is a device that modulates an analog carrier signal to encode digital information, and also demodulates such a carrier signal to decode the transmitted information.

of the BBS were the mid-1980s to mid-1990s. The popularity of BBS platforms began to wane with the appearance of more full-featured information services.

Broadband Internet access experienced double-digit growth between 2000 and 2003, when the Federal Communications Commission (FCC) estimated that about 39 percent of U.S. households enjoyed broadband Internet service. Broadband's dramatic speed improvement over dial-up modems enabled entirely new categories of information and entertainment services available to the consumer market. Downloading a 100-Mb file with a 56-Kbps modem would take about 4.5 hours, whereas the average broadband speed of 15 Mbs would take just over one minute. At the current industry-leading speed of 30 Mbps, the same 100-Mb file is downloaded in approximately 30 seconds.

INFORMATION SERVICES RISE UP

No discussion of early information service providers would be complete without highlighting CompuServe Inc., the first major U.S. commercial online service. As early as 1989, CompuServe was the first online service to offer Internet connectivity when it linked its e-mail service to allow incoming and outgoing messages from other Internet-based e-mail addresses. With thousands of hugely popular moderated forums, the service attracted hundreds of thousands of users. Many of these forums were operated by hardware and software companies to provide product support to their customers. This signaled the first departure from printed manuals toward digital media and online technical support. Around 1992, CompuServe offered the first known "what you see is what you get" (WYSIWYG) interface for its e-mail content and forum services.

In the 1990s, CompuServe began to lose market share as other information services sprang up and companies abandoned CompuServe's online forums in favor of creating their own Internet presence. Acquired by America Online Inc. (AOL) in 1998, CompuServe continued to operate as a division of AOL. In April 2009, CompuServe announced that CompuServe Classic would cease to operate effective June 30, 2009. The newer version of CompuServe 2000 was unaffected by this announcement and continues to operate.

BIRTH OF THE WORLD WIDE WEB

While services like CompuServe and AOL provided access to the Internet, they were built upon proprietary software platforms. The Internet held great promise as a communications medium for the masses, but accessing the Internet needed to be independent of information service providers and computing platforms in order to gain widespread acceptance. This was accomplished with the introduction of the Web browser as hardware and services providing independent means to "surf the Web." This period also introduced new terms into our lexicon such as **URL**[4] and **HTTP**.[5]

Sir Tim Berners-Lee created the first Web browser initially called World Wide Web, and later renamed Nexus. His efforts soon were followed by a number of commercial alternatives vying for the prestigious rank of dominant Web browser platform, based on total number of users. Illustrated in Figure 13.3, the first graphical browser, NCSA's Mosaic, was introduced in 1993 and was soon followed by Netscape's Navigator in 1994. Competition heated up in 1995 with Microsoft introducing Internet Explorer, which came bundled with the Windows operating system. Opera Software soon followed with its Opera browser in 1996, but never achieved widespread adoption. In an attempt to leverage the open source software model, Netscape launched the Mozilla Foundation in 1998, which evolved into the Firefox browser. Apple first released its Safari browser in 2003 and continues to dominate browser usage on the Apple hardware platforms. Although the most recent player, Google's 2008 release of its Chrome Web browser has enjoyed rapid growth and overtook Internet Explorer as the most widely used Web browser in 2011.

While the Web browser is simply a vehicle to retrieve and display Internet-based content, its rapid technological advancement in the 2000s helped fuel the explosion of digital media accessible to anyone with an Internet connection. University

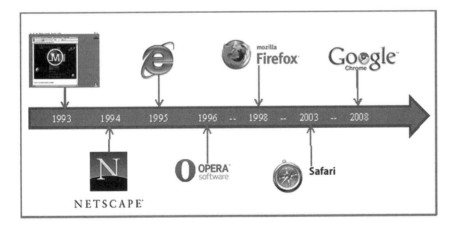

Figure 13.3 Evolution of the Web browser

[4] A uniform resource locator or universal resource locator (URL) is a specific character string that constitutes a reference to an Internet resource.

[5] The Hypertext Transfer Protocol (HTTP) is an application protocol for distributed, collaborative, hypermedia information systems. HTTP is the foundation of data communication for the World Wide Web.

of Southern California scientists calculate humankind has stored 295 exabytes of information (that's a number with 20 zeros in it!). Their report, released in February 2011, indicates the majority of our technological memory has been in digital format since the early 2000s, with 94 percent of data stored in that format by 2007.

WEB 1.0 → WEB 2.0

So what do we do with all this information? In their initial incarnation, now often referred to as Web 1.0, Web browsers fundamentally retrieved and displayed "static text." In other words, users were limited to passive viewing of content created for them. Although it first surfaced in 1999,[6] the term **Web 2.0** rose in popularity with the 2003 O'Reilly Media conference. In their opening remarks, John Battelle and Tim O'Reilly outlined their definition of the "Web as Platform," where software applications are built on the Web as opposed to on the desktop. The unique aspect of this migration, they argued, is that "customers are building your business for you." They argued that the activities of users generating content (in the form of ideas, text, videos, or pictures) could be "harnessed" to create value.

Today, the term *Web 2.0* is associated with Web applications that facilitate participatory information sharing, interoperability, user-centered design and collaboration on the Web. A Web 2.0 site allows users to interact and collaborate with each other in a social media dialogue as creators of user-generated content in a virtual community. Examples of Web 2.0 include social networking sites, **blogs**, wikis, video sharing sites, hosted services, Web applications, and mashups.

So this brings us back to the question in the title of this section: is social media the product of revolution or evolution? This brief historical summary, illustrated in Figure 13.4, would indicate social media is the evolutionary product of converging technological advancements, which are occurring at an increasingly exponential rate. Recall that several decades passed between the first commercial uses of the telephone and the appearance of voicemail systems, changing the way we work and communicate. Fast-forward to present day and dramatic advancements with the potential to alter the fabric of society are measured in weeks and months, not years.

Generally speaking, humankind is better at analyzing technological change in hindsight rather than foreseeing its future impact. To date, the social media wave has profoundly reshaped the path of commerce and become the medium of choice for an entire generation. Such far-reaching influences are difficult to fully

---

[6] The term "Web 2.0" was first used in January 1999 by Darcy DiNucci, a consultant on electronic information design (information architecture), in her article "Fragmented Future."

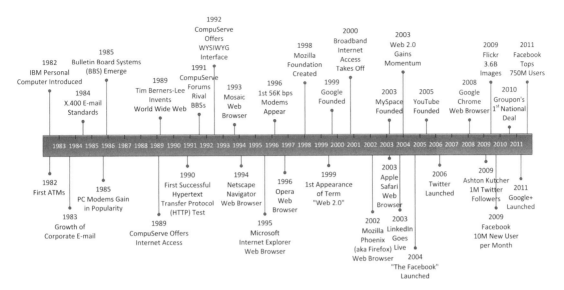

Figure 13.4 Building blocks of social media.

grasp, but the timeline shown in Figure 13.4 depicts 30 years of technological building blocks that bring us to today. To bring this dialogue back to the home front, in the next section we will focus our attention on the influence of social media within the FM profession.

FM-Focused Social Media

Social media takes on many forms including magazines, Internet forums, weblogs, social blogs, micro blogging, wikis, podcasts, photographs or pictures, video, rating, and social bookmarking. Within each of these forms, you will find a diverse genre of topics and quality of content. Accordingly, one of the drawbacks of consumer-generated content is a general lack of authentication. However, consumer-driven scrutiny of published content tends to expel purveyors of questionable material and elevates the stature of those who offer credible, quality information. The phrase "trust, but verify"[7] comes to mind, as it is always a good idea to find alternate, authoritative sources that corroborate information found on the public Internet.

As we examine examples of the aforementioned media forms, keep in mind this will represent but a small sampling of the Web-based content available. Readers are encouraged to conduct their own explorations of media sources to find the desired niche among the spectrum of facility management topics.

[7] "Trust, but verify" was a signature phrase adopted and made famous by former U.S. President Ronald Reagan.

Print Media Goes Digital

For generations, print media in the form of newspapers, magazines, newsletters, and reports served as the primary source of information on current events and professional matters. With the advent of digital publishing, most major media sources are moving away from print to digital, online formats. While there is still a market for print material, it cannot match the speed and multimedia capabilities of digital publishing. Many publishing houses currently offer both print and digital versions of their products, but digital forms are beginning to overtake print in terms of circulation. It is just a matter of time before print media is no longer a financially viable delivery method, like the horse and buggy giving way to the automobile.

Anyone with a computer and a Web browser already owns an "e-reader" capable of displaying a considerable amount of digital content. Table 13.1, taken from *Wikipedia*,[8] compares e-publishing formats with a sampling of available e-reader devices. As you can see, the only universally adopted format among the represented devices is "Plain Text."

As a consumer of digital media, how do you choose? In this crowded market, the best strategy is to identify the types and sources of media you most likely will consume, and pick an e-reader platform that most likely will satisfy your known range of needs.

Let's look at a few digital magazine titles focused on facility management:

■ *Today's Facility Manager*

This free online magazine offers a facilities blog, articles by discipline, features, columns, FM resources, advertisements, and "knowledge channels" to educate readers on specific FM topics. It also offers a newsletter subscription, online (interactive) forums, webinars, and FM whitepapers. (www .todaysfacilitymanager.com)

■ *FMJ Online*

Published by the International Facility Management Association (IFMA), the *Facility Management Journal* (FMJ) is available to IFMA members in both print and digital format via paid subscription. The online version offers an FMJ blog, "extended" content available only via the online version and FMJ Unscripted—a **podcast** available via **RSS**[9] or iTunes. (www.fmjonline.org)

---

[8] Comparison of E-Book Formats, http://en.wikipedia.org/wiki/Comparison_of_e-book_formats#eReader (retrieved January 22, 2012, from *Wikipedia*).

[9] RSS (Really Simple Syndication) is a family of Web feed formats used to publish frequently updated works—such as blog entries, news headlines, audio, and video—in a standardized format.

TABLE 13.1 Comparison of e-reader devices and publication formats.

Reader	Plain text	PDF	ePub	HTML	Mobi-Pocket	Fiction-Book (Fb2)	Djvu	Broadband eBook (BBeB)	eReader	Kindle	WOLF	Tome Raider	Open eBook
Amazon Kindle 1	Yes	No	No	No	Yes	No	No	No	No	Yes	No	No	No
Amazon Kindle 2, DX	Yes	Yes	No	Yes	Yes	No	No	No	No	Yes	No	v	No
Amazon Kindle 3	Yes	Yes	No	Yes	Yes	No	No	No	No	Yes	No	No	No
Amazon Kindle Fire	Yes	Yes	Yes	Yes	Yes	No	Yes	No	Yes	Yes	No	Yes	Yes
Android Devices	Yes	Yes	Yes	Yes	Yes	Yes	Yes	No	Yes	Yes	No	Yes	Yes
Apple iOS Devices	Yes	Yes	Yes	Yes	Yes	Yes	No	No	Yes	Yes	No	Yes	Yes
AzbookaWISEreader	Yes	No	Yes	Yes	Yes	Yes	No	No	No	No	No	No	No
Barnes & Noble Nook	Yes	Yes	Yes	Yes	No	No	No	No	Yes	No	No	No	No
Barnes & Noble Nook Color	Yes	Yes	Yes	Yes	No	No	No	No	No	No	No	No	No
Bookeen Cybook Gen3, Opus	Yes	Yes	Yes	Yes	Yes	Yes	No	No	No	No	No	No	Yes
COOL-ER Classic	Yes	Yes	Yes	Yes	Yes	Yes	No	No	No	No	No	No	No
Foxit eSlick	Yes	Yes	Yes	No	No	No	No	No	Yes	No	No	No	No
Hanlin e-Reader V3	Yes	Yes	Yes	Yes	Yes	Yes	Yes	No	No	No	Yes	No	No
Hanvon WISEreader	Yes	Yes	Yes	Yes	No	No	No	No	No	No	No	No	No
iRex iLiad	Yes	Yes	Yes	No	Yes	No	Yes	No	No	No	No	No	v
Iriver Story	Yes	Yes	Yes	No	No	No	Yes	No		No	No	No	No
Kobo eReader	Yes	Yes	Yes	Yes	No	No	No	No	No	No	No	No	No
Nokia N900	Yes	Yes	Yes	Yes	No	No	Yes	No	No	No	No	No	Yes
NUUTbook 2	Yes	Yes	Yes	No	No	No	No	No	No	No	No	No	No
OLPC XO, Sugar	Yes	Yes	Yes	Yes	No	No	Yes	No	No	v	No	No	No
Onyx Book 60	Yes	Yes	Yes	Yes	Yes	Yes	Yes	No	No	No	No	No	No
Mac OS X	Yes	Yes	Yes	Yes	Yes	Yes	Yes	?	Yes	Yes	?	?	Yes
Windows	Yes	Yes	Yes	Yes	Yes	?	Yes	?	Yes	Yes	?	?	Yes
Pocketbook 301 Plus, 302, 360°	Yes	Yes	Yes	Yes	No	Yes	Yes	No	No	No	No	No	No
Sony Reader	Yes	Yes	Yes	No	No	No	No	Yes	No	No	No	No	No
Viewsonic VEB612	Yes	Yes	Yes	Yes	Yes	No	No	No	No	No	No	No	No
Windows Phone 7	Yes	Yes	Yes	Yes	No	No	No	No	No	Yes	No	No	No

Source: Wikipedia

253

- *Premise & Facilities Management (pfm) Magazine Online*

  pfm is a free British-based online magazine offering featured articles, an FM Report, a Guide to FM; it hosts an annual pfm Awards and an industry-specific search engine titled SiteFind. (www.pfmonthe net.org)

- facilitiesnet

  This site is home to both *Building Operating Management* and *Maintenance Solutions* online magazines. Subscriptions are free with online registration, and both publications offer media-rich audio and video content covering timely FM topics. (www.facilitiesnet.com)

- *Sustainable FM*

  Another British-based online magazine, *Sustainable FM* is available to facility managers, energy managers, building managers, LA21 officers, environmental managers, and purchasing managers throughout the public sector and multinational private-sector companies. (www.abbeypublishing.co.uk/sustainable/page1.html)

- *The McMorrow Report*

  Backed by 22 years of industry publishing experience, Eileen McMorrow produces the *Corporate Facilities Management Report, Sustainable Facilities Management Report, Healthcare Facilities Management Report*, and *Government Facilities Management Report*. Reports are available online and are free to registered subscribers. (www.mcmorrowreport.com)

These and other digital magazines are available online, many simply for the asking. A simple query with your favorite Web search engine should result in a multitude of options for your review.

Internet Forums

Where digital magazines offer publications for reader consumption, Internet (online) forums present the opportunity to engage in interactive discussion on a variety of FM topics. Forums represent perhaps the oldest form of social media, originating with the bulletin board systems (BBSs) of the 1980s and evolving into the CompuServe online forums popular in the 1990s. While the concept of forums has evolved into items such as Twitter followers, LinkedIn groups, and Facebook groups, classic forums still exist. Many are associated with professional associations, publications, or companies—but still offer the opportunity to learn or have a spirited discussion with like-minded individuals. Following are a few FM-focused forums:

■ FM Forum

Sponsored by industry news source FMLink, FM Forum offers three topic areas: discussion items and opinions, questions by users and other participants, and FM tips and best practices. (www.fmforum.org)

■ IFMA Online Community

Members of the International Facility Management Association (IFMA) have access to the IFMA Online Community site. This site has sections for IFMA chapters, councils, communities of practice, special interest groups, and other groups. More than a discussion forum, IFMA community (see Figure 13.5) offers the ability to post blogs, upload files, and create wikis. IFMA may also be found on LinkedIn's Groups. There are 120+ groups aligned with IFMA. Just search the Groups section using the term *IFMA* and browse the results for specific groups of interest. (https://ifmacommunity.org)

■ Autodesk Users Group International (AUGI): Facilities Management in Practice

Sponsored by software company Autodesk, publisher of AutoCAD software, this forum discusses general facility management concerns and questions. The AUGI also offers a number of other topic areas including collaboration, data management, CAD, architecture, engineering and construction (AEC), general design, civil engineering, geospatial, manufacturing, design visualization (BIM/3D) and programming. (http://forums.augi.com/forumdisplay. php?f=519)

■ LinkedIn: Facilities Management and CMMS Forum

This LinkedIn group lists its purpose as a "Forum to discuss topics, share best practices, and network with like-minded professionals in the areas of preventive maintenance, facilities management, asset management and

Figure 13.5 Forum locating example: IFMA web site—Communities menu.

CMMS solutions." If you are a LinkedIn user, you can simply search in the Groups section for the above name to join the group. (http://www.linkedin.com/groups/Facilities-Management-CMMS-Forum-4109429/about)

■ British Institute of Facilities Management (BIFM) Forums

BIFM is a British-based professional association. BIFM membership is required to participate in their forums. Existing BIFM members must register to access the forum's site. (www.bifm.org.uk)

The list could go on, but chances are you will find discussion forums on many of your favorite online information sources. As illustrated in Figure 13.5, browse the menus on the Web site home page to locate available forums or online community sections.

Blogs

The term *blog* is a contraction of the original title of Web log. A form of online diary, blogs have evolved to a unique status on the Internet. Supported by authoring tools such as Google's Blogger, WordPress, and Joomla, blogging is available to virtually anyone with access to a computer and an Internet connection. There are many different types of blogs, differing not only in the type of content, but also in the way that content is delivered or written. Types include:

■ Personal blog: an ongoing diary or commentary by an individual.
■ Corporate or organizational blog: typically business blogs designed to enhance communication with employees or consumers.
■ By genre: focused on a particular subject such as politics or travel.
■ By media type: specialized blogs focusing on media such as video, sketches, or photos.
■ By device: blogs defined by the device used to compose it, such as a mobile/smartphone.
■ Reverse blog: blogs composed by its users as opposed to an individual.[10]

Blogs are generally a good source of targeted information. If the blogger doesn't know the answer to your question, chances are one of their readers will. Let's take a look at a few:

■ Strategic Advisor

Consultant and award-winning author Michel Theriault hosts a business web site, offering a wealth of free information, and a blog site. Visit both sites;

[10] "Blogs," http://en.wikipedia.org/wiki/Blog (retrieved January 22, 2012, from Wikipedia).

you will likely come away with something useful. (www.strategicadvisor.ca; http://thebuiltenvironment.ca)

■ *IWMS News*

More than a simple blog focused on integrated workplace management systems (IWMS), president/owner Steve Hanks covers industry news, solution areas, business challenges, implementation, research, and technology. The main site also offers a forum (IWMS). Hanks recently conducted a poll to identify the top 20 IWMS, computerized maintenance management systems (CMMS), and computer-aided facility management (CAFM) sites to watch in 2012, and has consented to present the list here:

■ *Ask Ebiz*

This is the blog for e-business strategies, and the blog is updated weekly with leadership topics on corporate real estate and workplace management. (http://askebiz.com/blog)

■ PeopleCube's *Scheduling Chronicles*

For the third consecutive year, PeopleCube's Scheduling Chronicles has been included in the IWMS News list. The real estate management, energy management, and resource management blog of PeopleCube is updated almost weekly with very interesting articles on a variety of topics. (www .peoplecube.com/blog/)

■ *The BRG Blog*

BRG provides workplace management solutions. BRG specializes in business advisory services, technology deployment, and staff augmentation in support of corporate real estate and facility management organizations. On the BRG blog, you'll find team insights about industry trends, emerging technologies' and innovative, fresh takes on facility management. (http:// brg.com/Blog)

■ *FacilityBlog*

One of the most widely read blogs about facility management is FacilityBlog. FacilityBlog began in May 2005 and has been revamped in 2011. This great resource on facility management is a must-read for IWMS, CAFM, and CMMS professionals. (www.todaysfacilitymanager.com/facilityblog/)

■ *IBM Asset Management Blog*

The purpose of this blog is to inform readers about current activities and offers for the asset management solution, as well as to provoke conversation about areas of interest in the market. It is also the new location of the former *Tririga Insights* blog. (http://ibm.com/blogs/assetmanagement/)

- *FM & Beyond*

  FM & Beyond, Thoughts on the Practice of Facility Management, is the blog of Ken Burhalter, a seasoned FM and project management professional with more than 30 years' experience with a wide range of organizations. As deputy director of facilities services at The RAND Corp., Burkhalter is primarily responsible for capital project planning and implementation. (www.fmandbeyond.blogspot.com)

- Manhattan Software IWMS blog

  Nancy Sanquist of Manhattan Software frequently is posting thoughts and opinions on Manhattan Software and the industry. This is a very interesting blog from one of the industry's leading IWMS vendors. (www.manhattan software.us/blog)

- *The Agile Workplace*

  The Agile Workplace is the blog of AgilQuest. AgilQuest provides managers and employees tools to adapt and thrive in today's workplace. Main topics of the blog include mobility, hoteling, space usage, sustainability, and business intelligence. (http://theagileworkplace.wordpress.com)

- FM:Systems blog

  FM:Systems provides IWMS, CAFM, business information modeling (BIM), and sustainability solutions to help FMs and real estate professionals deliver better customer service, reduce costs, and improve productivity. Connecting people, places, and processes is the blog of FM:Systems with news and thoughtful insights. (http://fmsystems.tumblr.com)

- Mintek blog

  Stuart Smith is Mintek's InBound marketing specialist. He works hard at creating compelling content to keep Mintek's customers and prospects informed with relevant information. (www.mintek.com/blog/category/eam-cmms)

- *The Built Environment*

  For the second consecutive year, Michel Theriault's *The Built Environment* blog has made it to the author's list. Last year, Theriault launched the book *Managing Facilities & Real Estate* and has cohosted a Planon webinar, Information-Based Decisions. The blog is an extension of Theriault's thorough knowledge of the industry. Yes, Theriault appeared at the beginning of this segment, but he also was voted on to this list in a poll conducted by IWMS News. His other sites offer more information than that found solely on his blog. (www.thebuiltenvironment.ca)

■ Esri blogs

Geographic information system (GIS) technology leverages this geographic insight to address social, economic, business, and environmental concerns at local, regional, national, and global scales. What's more it is becoming increasingly important in our industry. Therefore, the author has included Esri in the 20 blogs to watch in 2012. (www.esri.com/news/blogs/index.html)

■ CFI blog

CFI is an all-encompassing consulting and systems integration firm working exclusively in real estate and facility management. CFI has redesigned their web site in 2011 and they now frequently post on all kinds of IWMS-related topics. (www.gocfi.com/news/)

■ *The Future of Work*

The Future of Work helps senior executives understand the changing nature of work, the workforce, and the workplace so they can design and build more effective organizations. (http://thefutureofwork.net)

■ Qube Global Software blog

For the second year on the IWMS News list is Global View, the Qube Global Software blog. Main categories of the blog include news archives, property management software, and Qube Global Software. (www.qubeglobal.co.uk/blog/)

■ *PM Tips*

The authors of PM Tips have many years of experience in IT consulting, project management, and IWMS. They discuss project management from different perspectives such as the project manager, the consultant, the customer, and others. If you want to have more information about IT project management, PM Tips is a resource we would recommend. (http://pmtips.net)

■ *IWMS News* blog

Of course, IWMS needed to include their own *IWMS News* blog in the list. Thanks to their followers, they have been expanding their web site constantly. They hope you will keep coming back to their blog for more information about IWMS, CAFM, and other topics. (www.iwmsnews.com)

■ CoreNet Global blogs

CoreNet Global Workplace community is a new list item. CoreNet's knowledge function within the community is actively seeking participation and contributions in a number of areas. What's more, many blog posts and interesting articles are available already, and more are on the way. (http://network.corenetglobal.org/Workplace/Blogs/ViewBlogs/)

- Lucernex IWMS blog

  For the third consecutive year, *IWMS News* has included the Lucernex IWMS blog as a blog to watch in 2012. Although the Lucernex team hasn't posted as many articles as in previous years, still Lucernex is a good IWMS read. (www.lucernex.com/files/index.php/category/blog)

- *Lease Accounting* blog

  The *Lease Accounting* blog of Kelvin Smith, vice president of Financial Computer Systems Inc., and chief developer of the EZ13 lease accounting software. He also frequently publishes on the expected lease accounting changes. This resource is extremely valuable for anticipating the impact of the lease accounting changes. (http://financialcomputer .blogspot.com)

Whew! That's quite a batch of blogs. If you've wondered whether there was anything worth reading in the blogosphere, now you know. As you can see, there is a bit of something for just about everyone. I'm sure there are even more industry or specialty-focused blogs out there—it's all there for you to consume once you know where to find it.

WIKIS

A wiki is a web site whose users can add, modify, or delete its content via a Web browser using a simplified markup language or a rich-text editor. Wikis typically are powered by wiki software and often are created collaboratively by multiple users. Examples include community web sites, corporate intranets, knowledge management systems, and note taking. The most famous, *Wikipedia*, is billed as "The Free Encyclopedia." Much has been written about Wikipedia and its crowd-sourced content; mostly citing the questionable authenticity of the information it contains. While I am not advocating you take information found on *Wikipedia* at face value (remember "trust, but verify"), it is unquestionably one of the largest consolidated collections of information on just about any topic you can imagine.

So what about FM-focused wikis? Yes, they do exist. Many are hosted and curated by educational institutions (Penn Wiki, http://bim.wikispaces.com/ Facility+Asset+Management). Others represent the FM knowledge repository for an organization. The power inherent in a wiki is its ability to organize, link, and cross-reference information. A savvy wiki administrator can create an invaluable knowledge repository for their organization—easing the fear that organizational memory only exists in the form of tribal knowledge.

PODCASTS, VIDEO, PICTURES, RATING, AND SOCIAL BOOKMARKING

Podcasts[11] have become a familiar delivery vehicle for audio content, typically associated with an ongoing series of informational or instructional material. IFMA's own FMJ Online publishes a regular podcast called FMJ Unscripted (www.fmjon line.org). The American Institute of Architects (AIA) is a prolific producer of podcast material, with 239 episodes at the time of this writing (www.aia.org/podcasts/). Podcasts are great for catching up on topics of interest while commuting or during lengthier travel stretches.

With the advent of inexpensive digital HD video recorders and powerful video editing software, video is an increasingly popular delivery medium for social media content. From instructional material to advertising to general commentary—you can find video media embedded within many Web-based content delivery vehicles. Google's YouTube is one of the more well known, and popular, video archiving sites. A simple search for the term *YouTube Facility Management* will yield a number of hits. (www.youtube.com/watch?v=9h_P6dl6Tqc)

Photo-sharing sites provide a niche service within the social media world. Popular sites include Flickr, Google's Picasa, Snapfish, and Shutterfly. Many offer free subscriptions and some amount of storage for your account. Some, like Snapfish or Shutterfly, offer photo finishing services for books, albums, coffee mugs, calendars, and more. These services tend to be oriented toward sharing family photos rather than business images. Nonetheless, you can find some facility management content. The Atlanta Chapter of IFMA maintains a Facebook page where they post images from chapter events.[12]

Rounding out this section are rating and social bookmarking services. As the name implies, rating sites generally are focused on providing a vehicle for the general public to rate establishments, services, or people. The well-known Yelp service provides customer ratings for restaurants and other food and beverage institutions. If you're on the fence about trying the new restaurant down the street, check its rating on Yelp before stepping through the door. Unfortunately, many of the rating sites lean toward the politically incorrect—such as the "Hot or Not" site for rating the looks of people whose pictures appear on their site. Clearly, some people have more time on their hands than I do. . . .

---

[11] A podcast is a type of digital media consisting of an episodic series of files subscribed to and downloaded through web syndication. The word is a neologism derived from "broadcast" and "pod" from the success of the iPod, as podcasts are often listened to on portable media players.

[12] *IFMA Atlanta*, www.facebook.com/pages/Atlanta-Chapter-of-International-Facility-Management-Association-IFMA/ 55545331362?sk=app_159237157423118#!/pages/Atlanta-Chapter-of-International-Facility-Management-Association-IFMA/55545331362?fbhref=flickr.php%3Fpage%3D3&a (retrieved January 26, 2012).

On a related note, social bookmarking sites offer a means to record (bookmark) Web sites you happen across and want to return to later. These sites generally provide a means to categorize and organize your discoveries, and also share them with others. One such site is Delicious.com, which publishes categories of bookmarks collected by Delicious users. The categories range from interesting to (potentially) offensive. The service remains popular and serves a segment of the social media population. It's a matter of personal choice whether you will find such services useful in the context of your profession.

SECTION NOTES

I was not able to locate any authoritative data on the number of web sites currently in existence, but the estimates run into the hundreds of millions. With such rich sources of content, expanding one's base of knowledge is easier than ever. Hopefully, this segment will help guide your exploration of available facilities management information sources.

Making Social Media Work for You

Why Does It Matter?

The social media revolution isn't as revolutionary as some people would have you believe, writes Glenn Croston. Businesses always have thrived by building relationships and using them to generate sales, Croston argues, and social media marketing is simply another tool to facilitate that process. "Reach out to people, and they'll reach out to you. And the business will flow from there," he writes.[13]

By accounts from a number of sources, people use social media to connect with brands and products, learn about new products and services from social networking sites, and use social media to recommend products or services to friends. Over half of small-business owners have reported using social media to gather information about companies, products, and prospects before buying or doing business with them. Businesses with an active presence on Twitter, Facebook, or Company Blog report acquiring customers through those channels.

Here is where the lines begin to blur as to whether social media is more oriented toward the personal or to the professional. For the youngest generation in the workforce, many indicate that there is no distinction between their work and personal lives. No matter how you approach social media, it is, in effect, your

[13] G. Croston, *FastCo*, August 10, 2010, www.fastcompany.com/1679825/how-facebook-and-twitter-are-chang ing-the-business-world-and-how-they-aren-t (retrieved January 27, 2012, from FastCompany Expert blog).

digital calling card—your personal brand. Your brand is your image, and it is how the rest of the world perceives you. It is something to be cultivated and cared for.

Social media changes the dynamic of communication. E-mail, for example, is typically one-to-one communication; you must direct (address) communication to one or more people. But with networks of hundreds, if not thousands, of individuals, how do you maintain an effective connection with so many? Social media offers a simpler means of ambient communication. You put some information out there, and those who have chosen to listen to what you have to say will see it (i.e., Twitter, Facebook, or LinkedIn). Conversely, you choose the topics and people you wish to follow. If one of your well-meaning friends likes to share pictures of his kids or kittens on a daily basis, it is typically within your control to ignore those updates without having to "unfriend" them.

Much has been written about the forces driving these societal and cultural changes, but a few of my personal favorites include:

- *Grown Up Digital* by Don Tapscott

  Through observation of his own children and their peers through adolescence to young adulthood, the author offers pointed insights into what it means to grow up in a completely digital generation.[14]

- "Free Agent Nation" by Daniel Pink

  First published as an article in *Fast Company* magazine,[15] the author intimates a movement where a significant percentage of workers effectively become "free agents." Later in book form, the author expands on the ideas first proposed in the 1997 article citing additional research.[16]

- *Drive* by Daniel Pink

  Building on his earlier works, the author delivers, in his own words, "the surprising truth about what motivates us."[17]

- Me 2.0 by Dan Schwabel

  The author describes the steps to achieving career success through the power of a well-crafted personal brand.[18]

---

[14] D. Tapscott, *Grown Up Digital* (New York: McGraw-Hill, 2008).

[15] D. Pink, "Free Agent Nation," December 31, 1997, www.fastcompany.com/magazine/12/freeagent.html (retrieved January 27, 2012, from *Fast Company*).

[16] D. Pink, *Free Agent Nation* (New York: Warner Books, 2002).

[17] D. Pink, *Drive* (New York: Riverhead Trade, 2011).

[18] D. Schwabel, *Me 2.0: 4 Steps to Building Your Future*, rev. ed. (New York: Kaplan Publishing, 2010).

In the next section, the focus is on available social media outlets, the basics of developing a social media strategy, building your social network, and curating your online presence.

Which Ones Are for Me?

Have you ever searched online for your own name? Were you surprised at what you did or did not find? The Internet has a long memory; with increasingly sophisticated search mechanisms, information may be retrieved from long-forgotten digital crevasses.

What more reason do you need to proactively manage your online presence? I'm reminded of a quote from former General Electric CEO Jack Welch: "Control your own destiny, or someone else will." With the explosion of social media services, the choices may appear daunting. However, with a bit of investigation and planning, your personal online presence strategy will emerge.

If you are unfamiliar with the social media landscape, an investigation of the dominant services is in order. Figure 13.6 lists the current major players in the social media arena. Take a look at what they do and how they do it. Search each candidate service to see how many of your existing friends, family, or colleagues are current users. What features does the service offer that will enhance your personal or professional life?

There is no right or wrong as to the number of services where you might have a presence. Just remember that each online presence should be kept current and could grow to require a considerable investment of time to maintain them all.

What If I Don't Want to Be Found?

While this chapter is focused on those who would want to leverage social media, we also must acknowledge that some people will prefer to maintain their relative

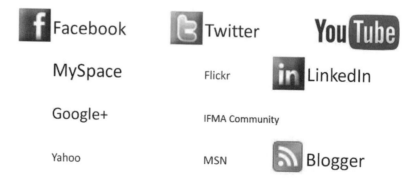

Figure 13.6 A sampling of social media services.

anonymity. If you count yourself among this group, you might want to review the *PC Magazine* article, "How to Stay Anonymous Online" by Eric Griffith.[19] The article offers a number of tips for safe surfing, anonymous e-mail, instant messaging protection, and securing social media sites.

Have a Networking Strategy

Different people will have different strategies driving their approach to social media. If you are involved in business development, your strategy might involve using social media to understand your customers' product and service needs. If you are a job seeker, your strategy might be to leverage your network in order to gain an advantage with a specific job opportunity. The main message here is that you should develop a networking–social media strategy to suit your needs, and then stick to it.

For the typical facility manager, you might have a two-pronged strategy. First might be to seek out connections and groups that serve as resources for your daily responsibilities. For example, if your employer is looking to reduce operating costs through energy efficiency initiatives, look for connections who already have achieved results in this area or groups that offer ideas, insights, or assistance. Seeking additional education or certifications is certainly an option, but there is no substitute for practical experience and proven results. The second prong of your strategy should be to expand your network of connections well beyond your current geography and scope of responsibilities. If we've learned anything from the last two recessions, it's that no success lasts forever. Your rock-solid company and position therein may evaporate overnight. It takes a year or more to build a meaningful (read "useful") network that might assist you in a time of need—such as a job search. Trust me when I advise that the time to start building your network is not the day after you become unemployed.

Your strategy may evolve over time, and that's okay. It is a good idea to reevaluate your strategy on a periodic basis to ensure it still meets your needs. Expect that the people you connect with are doing the same thing. Keep in mind that social media is as much about giving as getting. When one of your connections reaches out to you for assistance, it is strongly recommended you do your best to help him out. The point being is you may find the tables turned and in need of assistance in the future. People are more inclined to help those who have helped them in the past. Ideally, there should be no expectation of reciprocity. Be a resource

[19] E. Griffith, "How to Stay Anonymous Online," *PC Magazine*, May 2, 2010, *www.pcmag.com/article2/0,2817, 2363302,00.asp* (retrieved January 2012, from *PC Magazine*).

because you can, not because of an expected payoff down the road. That is the essence of what it means to be a model citizen of the social media metropolis.

Get LinkedIn and Like It ...

Moving on to specifics—let's explore LinkedIn's services. LinkedIn went live as a service in 2003. Where Facebook is clearly the dominant service for personal connections, LinkedIn has enjoyed steady growth as the premier social media service for professionals. As of this writing, LinkedIn has more than 135 million users, 1.18 million groups, and 2.38 million listed companies globally. LinkedIn tracks your connections by "degrees of separation." So the people you are directly connected with are your first-degree connections. The people connected to them are your second-degree connections, and then the people connected to them are your third-degree connections. By way of example, I currently have 642 first-degree connections, which then extend to 267,000+ second-degree connections, and then out to 9,932,200+ third-degree connections, for a total of 10,199,900 + total connections in my network. Your first- and second-degree connections are going to be of greatest value to you. But in my case, that still equates globally to 267,000 people! What does this really mean? Well, there are very few companies, industries, countries, or professions that I cannot find within my network.

So if you are not a LinkedIn member yet, you should be. The basic service is free, and completely within the user's control as to how much information he or she shares, or not, within LinkedIn and his network. To join, simply go to www.linkedin.com and sign up (as shown in Figure 13.7).

However, before you begin you will want to gather some information to complete your LinkedIn profile. Following is a list of the information you should consider including:

- **History**. This would include your work history and related professional activities, such as professional associations or charitable works. This generally includes titles, dates, and a description of responsibilities or accomplishments. It is your choice as to how much or how little information you include.
- **Summary**. This can be a brief bio or aspirations. What is it you would want most people to know about you, what interests you, and/or where you are headed on your career path?
- **Photo**. It is your choice whether to include a photo with your profile, but it is a good idea. If you're concerned about exposing too much personal information, search the LinkedIn help for "settings." For example, you can limit visibility of your photo to just your network connections and not to the general user population. There is considerable flexibility available via your profile settings.

Figure 13.7 LinkedIn main page.

Do check out the options and make your own choices as to what the public sees or does not see.

- **Education**. Optional, but potentially useful. It is recommended to include undergraduate and above educational achievements.
- **Skills and certifications**. LinkedIn provides an extensive list of skills that you can associate with your profile. There is no harm in including all possible skills. Any professional certifications you hold should be listed. These items most often are searched by recruiters seeking candidates for positions they are looking to fill. This is true for much of the information in your profile, so it is a good idea to be complete and accurate. Just keep in mind that embellishments may come back to haunt you later.
- **Recommendations**. LinkedIn provides a means to secure recommendations from colleagues, former superiors, customers, peers, etc. These do not need to be extensive, but if you have people willing to sing your praises, don't be shy about adding it to your profile. LinkedIn does not consider your profile complete until you have at least three recommendations.
- **Other details**. LinkedIn provides a number of other available information fields associated with your profile. Items include publications (i.e., any published

works), your Twitter user ID, geographic location (city, state), general profession (i.e., facilities services), and any personal or professional web sites (i.e., your company web site or personal blog).

If you are unsure about what to include in your profile or how to phrase it, review the profiles of colleagues or individuals you admire for inspiration. In fact, it would be a good idea to browse a few profiles before creating your own. Keep in mind that LinkedIn offers extensive online help, or an Internet search for the phrase *LinkedIn tips and tricks* will yield a wealth of other information sources.

Once you have created your account and completed your profile, you are ready to start connecting. This is where the true power and value of LinkedIn comes into play.

Building Your Network

This segment assumes you already have an account on LinkedIn, or just created one. LinkedIn specializes in networking professionals worldwide. To get a sense of its scope, following are a few facts taken directly from LinkedIn's About page:

LinkedIn facts

- As of November 3, 2011, LinkedIn operates the world's largest professional network on the Internet, with more than 135 million members in more than 200 countries and territories.
- Fifty-nine percent of LinkedIn members currently are located outside of the United States.
- There were nearly 2 billion people searches on LinkedIn in 2010. Based on third-quarter 2011 metrics, LinkedIn members are on pace to do more than 4 billion searches on the LinkedIn platform in 2011.
- Headquartered in Mountain View, California, LinkedIn also has U.S. offices in Chicago, New York, Omaha, and San Francisco. International LinkedIn offices are located in Amsterdam, Bangalore, Delhi, Dublin, London, Melbourne, Milan, Mumbai, Munich, Paris, São Paulo, Singapore, Stockholm, Sydney, Tokyo, and Toronto.
- The company's management team is comprised of seasoned executives from companies like Yahoo!, Google, Microsoft, TiVo, PayPal, and Electronic Arts. LinkedIn's CEO is Jeff Weiner. (http://press.linkedin.com/about)
- LinkedIn is currently available in 16 languages: English, Czech, Dutch, French, German, Indonesian, Italian, Japanese, Korean, Malay, Portuguese, Romanian, Russian, Spanish, Swedish, and Turkish.

■ As of September 30, 2011 (the end of the third quarter), LinkedIn has 1,797 full-time employees located all around the globe. LinkedIn started off 2011 with about 1,000 full-time employees, up from around 500 at the beginning of 2010.

So how do you tap into this global network? In short—start with who you already know. Most professionals have an e-mail account with an address book. Chances are, a significant percentage of the contacts in that address book also have an account on LinkedIn. Fortunately, LinkedIn provides means to import your existing contacts, giving you a quick start to building your professional network. As Figure 13.8 indicates, you can import contact data directly from Microsoft Outlook, or by exporting your contact list from other services into a commonly accepted file type.

Once imported, LinkedIn provides options to selectively invite contacts to connect with you on LinkedIn. Search for "sending invitations to connect" in LinkedIn's Help Center if you need additional coaching. Whether extending an invitation to connect to an individual or a group, you should craft a personal message to accompany the invitation. Figure 13.9 displays the default invitation text accompanying a typical LinkedIn connection invite.

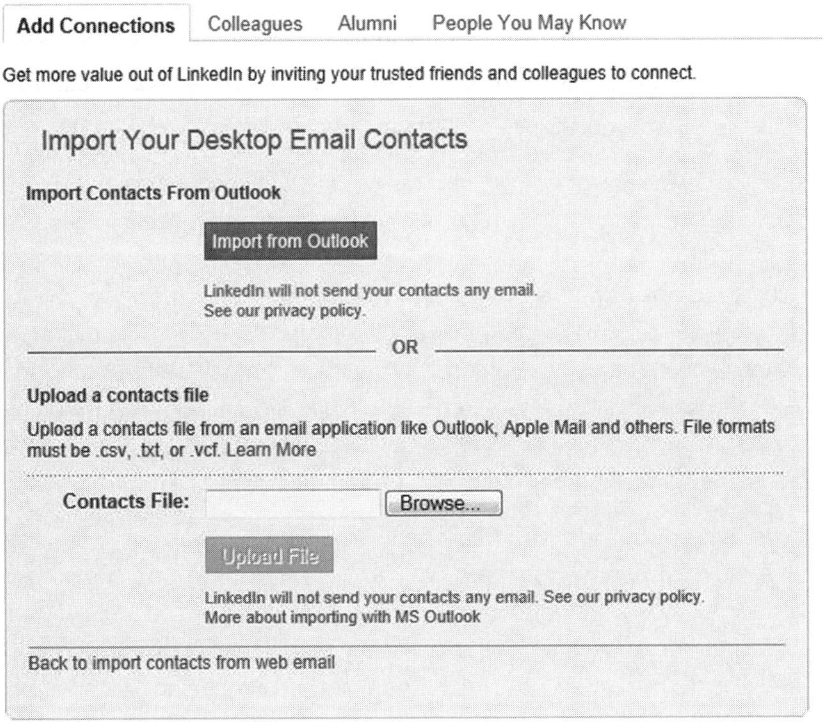

| **Add Connections** | Colleagues | Alumni | People You May Know |

Get more value out of LinkedIn by inviting your trusted friends and colleagues to connect.

Import Your Desktop Email Contacts

Import Contacts From Outlook

Import from Outlook

LinkedIn will not send your contacts any email.
See our privacy policy.

———————————————————— OR ————————————————————

Upload a contacts file

Upload a contacts file from an email application like Outlook, Apple Mail and others. File formats must be .csv, .txt, or .vcf. Learn More

Contacts File: [＿＿＿＿＿] Browse...

Upload File

LinkedIn will not send your contacts any email. See our privacy policy.
More about importing with MS Outlook

Back to import contacts from web email

Figure 13.8 LinkedIn connection import page.

Figure 13.9 LinkedIn connection invitation (default text).

Every LinkedIn user has seen this message before. So here's the thought process: if you are not willing to take the time to write a brief personal message, why should I bother to accept your invitation? It's about the "social" in social media.

Once you have established connections with the people you already know, you can work on expanding your network. Within LinkedIn's Contacts pages, there are options to connect with colleagues—people who you may have worked with or share membership in a professional association—or with People You May Know—people who may share some other common connection. No matter how or where you come across someone you wish to connect with, simply create the connection invitation and send it out. In most cases, if you have created a thoughtful invitation outlining the reasons you would like to connect with the person, they probably will accept.

Conversely, you will receive invitations to connect from other LinkedIn users. Some you may know, and some you won't. While LinkedIn takes steps to ensure that their members are not harassed or spammed by users with questionable motives, the decision to accept an invitation is within your control. Remember the earlier discussion on establishing your networking strategy. Connect with individuals who meet your strategy criteria and "ignore" invitations from those who don't. You are under no obligation to accept an invitation just because someone sent it.

One of the purposes of services like LinkedIn is to share information, thoughts, opinions, and knowledge. This is accomplished most often within your network. Things you choose to share are seen by your network, and things they choose to share are seen by you. This is the essence of social media.

TIPS FOR JOB SEEKERS

As this chapter is written, unemployment remains high across the United States. Most job search authorities will attest that a new job typically is secured through an individual's network of contacts, and not by blindly posting résumés to job ads. Here again, LinkedIn provides a wealth of resources for the job seeker. Search for *Job Seeker Tips* in LinkedIn's Help Center for topics of interest to the job seeker. Figure 13.10 highlights a number of LinkedIn features directly benefiting the job seeker.

In addition to the jobs features, LinkedIn also highlights companies. You can search for companies, follow companies and discover connections you may have within a company. For job seekers, this can provide valuable insights into a company and the movement of personnel within. Most job offers are decided not by wide margins in skills and qualifications, but in small details. The well-prepared job seeker sometimes can gain the advantage through those small details.

As a parting reminder for this segment, you want to have a strong network in place to support you in good times as well as bad. Building your network on the first day of unemployment is not a good place to start.

Figure 13.10 LinkedIn job search options excerpt.

CLOSING THOUGHTS

Hopefully, this discussion has provided some insights into the social media phenomenon. While social media has evolved through successive technological advancements, it is equally fueled by widespread cultural adoption. It is a delightfully surprising progression in the way humanity communicates and stays connected. Although some focus was given to the LinkedIn professional networking service, there are a plethora of alternatives available to meet most any appetite. Social media is not a spectator sport, but one that demands participation from its constituents. If you've not done so already, it's time to stop observing from the sidelines and get in the game.

ADDITIONAL RESOURCES

Current Situations and Trends in Building and Facility Operations, Research Supporting Educating Technicians for Building Automation and Sustainability, www.laney.edu/wp/environmental_control_tech/building_operations_report.

"Designing for Energy-Efficient Operations and Maintenance," *Engineered Systems*, August 2010, www.esmagazine.com/Articles/Feature_Article/BNP_GUID_9-5-2006_A_197811 18382837873588.

Glossary

Active RFID tag
A tag that has an on-board battery that periodically transmits its ID signal.

AEC
Architecture, engineering, and construction. Relates to the entire spectrum of design, engineering and construction industries.

Adjacency matrix
A matrix whereby the number of rows and columns reflect the size of the data set. The scores contained in the cells of the matrix record information about the desired adjacency between each pair of elements.

Animation
A collection of tracks that define the dynamic property changes to associated objects.

ANSI/TIA/EIA Standard 569
A United States industry standard published jointly by ANSI (American National Standards Institute) and the EIA/TIA (Electronic Industry Alliance/Telecommunications Industry Alliance) specifying a generic structured cabling system for commercial buildings.

API
Application programming interface. A particular set of rules and specifications that software programs follow to communicate with each other.

APPA
Originally APPA was the Association of Physical Plant Administrators of Universities and Colleges. Now, APPA is the Association of Higher Education Facilities Officers.

ARPANET
The Advanced Research Projects Agency Network (ARPANET) was the world's first operational packet switching network and the core network of a set that came to compose the global Internet.

Assignments
The designation of a resource to a process step to perform an action.

Attribute data
Tabular or textual data describing the geographic characteristics of features.

BACnet
A data communications protocol for building automation and control networks.

Barcode
An optical machine-readable representation of data, which shows data about the object to which it attaches.

BAS
Building automation system—control system of a building consisting of a computerized, intelligent network of electronic devices, designed to monitor and control the mechanical and lighting systems in a building.

Benchmark
"A particular value of a metric that denotes a level of performance" (from P. Mathew, "Laboratories for the 21st Century: Best Practice Guide—Metrics and Benchmarks for Energy Efficiency in Laboratories," National Renewable Energy Laboratory). An example of a benchmark is 1.3W/SF (watts per square foot).

BI
Business intelligence, as it relates to facility management, refers to the use of computer techniques for extracting and analyzing facility business data for making business decisions.

BIM
Building information modeling or building information model—software application or process of generating and managing building information during its life cycle.

Blog
The term *blog* is a contraction of the original title of Web log. A form of online diary, blogs have evolved to a unique status on the Internet. Supported by authoring tools such as Google's Blogger, WordPress, and Joomla; blogging is available to virtually anyone with access to a computer and an Internet connection.

bSa
buildingSMART alliance. The bSa creates BIM tools and standards that enable electronic projects to be built before they are built physically.

Buffer
A polygon enclosing a point, line, or polygon at a specified distance.

Building asset management
The systematic collection of key data, the application of analytical tools, and the creation of business intelligence (BI), which managers can use to make sound investment decisions about their organization's buildings.

Building condition
The collective state of health of a building's systems and their components.

Building Condition Index (BCI) series
A family of predictive (leading) physical state-based condition indexes that are computed at the component section level by the Engineered Method and rolled up to determine the physical state for a system, facility, portfolio subset, and/or entire portfolio.

Business intelligence

Refers to the use of computer techniques for making business decisions by extracting and analyzing facility business data.

Business process management (BPM)

Business Process Management is a management approach to align all aspects of the business under an optimized model, delivering efficient processes across all business lines and operations for increased communication and performance.

CAD

Computer-aided design (software application). A software package used to design physical characteristics of an object.

CAFM

Computer-aided facility management—software designed to assist in the on-going maintenance and management of buildings.

Change detection

A process that measures how the attributes of a particular area have changed between two or more time periods

Cloud computing

Software that runs on multiple servers on a network (e.g., the Internet) in such a way that it seems as if it were just one powerful computer that serves users connected to the services.

CMMS

Computerized Maintenance and Management System (software application)—software to support the facilities operations and maintenance needs of an organization, such as work orders, preventative maintenance, safety, among others.

Coaxial cable

An electrical cable consisting of an inner conductor surrounded by an insulating spacer, surrounded by an outer cylindrical conductor.

Condition

The state of health of a facility, a facility system, or a component of a facility system.

Consumerization

The adoption of mobile technologies taking place in the consumer markets, impacting employee expectations towards their employers in the provision of services.

Current replacement value

The total expenditure in current dollars required to replace any facility, inclusive of construction costs, design costs, project management costs and project administrative costs. Construction costs are calculated as replacement in function versus in-kind.

dBase

A relational database management system first marketed by Ashton-Tate Corporation in the early 1980s. The data formatting conventions utilized by dBase quickly became industry standards that are still in use today.

Decision points

Points within a process where a decision or an attribute affects the activity. Common actions based on control points include termination, progressing forward in the process flow, looping back to a previous point in the process flow, taking an alternative path in the process flow.

De-marc

Also called minimum point of entry (MPOE), the location where a telecommunications provider's wiring crosses or enters a building.

Defect

A visual clue (e.g., corrosion) that a building component (e.g., gutter) is deteriorating or even is in potential or actual failure mode.

Deferred maintenance & repair (DM&R)

Maintenance and repairs that were not performed when they should have been or were scheduled to be and which are put off or delayed for a future period.

Deficiency

The written statement of scope and estimated cost to correct a defect or set of defects.

Deficiency-based technique

One of three techniques of the Monetary Method of building condition assessment. This technique draws on scope and dollar estimates of needed work obtained from engineers' or architects' detailed visual inspections.

Density

A function that distributes the quantity or magnitude of point or line observations over a unit of area to create a continuous raster—for example, population per square kilometer.

Distress

A record of a particular defect's attributes including: component identity, distress type, severity, and density or quantity.

Drop

Also called a jack, a socket that accepts a plug at one end and attaches to electric circuitry at the other.

EAM

Enterprise asset management software provides a holistic enterprise management of assets. Evolving from computerized maintenance management software, EAM applications encompass the entire lifecycle from design through retirement to integrate operational and financial management functions to optimize operational efficiency and document total cost of ownership.

ECM

Energy conservation measures relate to the installation, modification or remodeling of an existing building that results in the reduction of energy use and associated operating costs.

Electronic paper

Electronic media that mimics paper. Also known as e-paper.

Engineered Method

One of two major categories of building condition assessment methods. The engineered method uses inspector-collected distress data to compute the building condition index (BCI series) as well as the two, monetary-based metrics called "backlog" and "facility condition index (FCI)"

Enterprise resource planning (ERP)

Enterprise resource planning (ERP) systems integrate internal and external management information across an entire organization, embracing finance/accounting, manufacturing, sales and service, customer relationship management, etc. The purpose of ERP is to facilitate the flow of information between all business functions inside the boundaries of the organization and manage the connections to outside stakeholders.[1] 1. Bidgoli, Hossein, (2004). *The Internet Encyclopedia*, vol. 1, New York: John Wiley & Sons, p. 707, as quoted in "Internet Resource Planning," *Wikipedia*, http://en.wikipedia.org/wiki/Enterprise_resource_planning.

Entrance facility

The various types of telecommunications network cables that enter the building and continue to the wiring closet.

Escalation

Attribute associated with a process activity that monitors time limits of process steps. Once the process step exceeds the minimum or maximum limit threshold defined, this attribute triggers an event or messaging appropriate to the requirement.

EVA

Economic value added (EVA) reflects the estimated economic profit of a company. It is calculated by subtracting the cost of financing capital from the profit earned by the company.

Facility assets

Fixed physical assets including buildings (such as hospitals, barracks, schools, and offices), other types of structures (such as parking, storage, and industrial), and infrastructure (such as power plants, water and sewer systems, railroads, roads, and bridges.

Facility asset management

A systematic process of cost effectively maintaining, upgrading, and operating physical assets. It combines engineering principles with sound business practices and economic theory, and provides tools to facilitate a more organized, logical approach to decision making. A facilities asset management approach allows for both program or network-level management and project-level management, and thereby supports both executive-level and field-level decision making.

FCI

Alternately, facility condition index or financial condition index; a lagging (after the fact) metric produced by the monetary method of building condition assessment.

Flow

Describes the sequence of activity for a workflow process.

FM

Facility management. IFMA defines facility management as "a profession that encompasses multiple disciplines to ensure functionality of the built environment by integrating people, place, process and technology."(www.ifma.org/resources/what-is-fm/default.htm)

FM automation

Any computer or technology based tools that facilitate FM processes.

Geocoding

A code representing the location of an object, such as an address, a census tract, or a postal code.

Geographic information system (GIS)

An integrated collection of computer software and data used to view and manage information about geographic places, analyze spatial relationships, and model spatial processes.

Geospatial

A set of technological approaches for acquiring and manipulating geographic data.

GHG

Greenhouse gas—gases that trap heat in the atmosphere. Primarily water vapor, carbon dioxide, methane, nitrous oxide, and ozone.

GIS

Geographic (or geospatial) information system—computer application that that captures, stores, analyzes, manages, and presents data that are linked to location(s), merging data, analysis and cartography.

Global positioning system (GPS)

A system of radio-emitting and receiving satellites used for determining positions on the earth.

Green building

A building that is designed, constructed and operated to minimize environmental impacts and maximize resource efficiency while also balancing cultural and community sensitivity (from A. Lewis, D. Riley, A. Elmualim, "Defining High Performance for Operations and Maintenance," *International Journal of Facility Management*, 1(2). www.ijfm.net/index.php/ijfm/article/view/26).

GSA

U.S. General Services Administration (www.gsa.gov). A U.S. Federal agency that establishes Federal policy as it relates to Federal procurement, real property management and information resources.

High-performance building

"A building that integrates and optimizes on a lifecycle basis all major high performance attributes, including energy [and water] conservation, environment, safety, security, durability, accessibility, cost-benefit, productivity, sustainability, functionality, and operational considerations" (Energy Independence and Security Act 2007 401 PL 110–140).

Homerun

A type of cabling design in which each jack has its own cable running back to a central distribution device.

HTTP

The Hypertext Transfer Protocol (HTTP) is an application protocol for distributed, collaborative, hypermedia information systems. HTTP is the foundation of data communication for the World Wide Web.

ICT

Information and communications technology, all technologies for the manipulation and communication of information.

IFC

Industry foundation class (data format). The IFC is a neutral and open specification (i.e., not controlled by a single vendor). It was created by buildingSMART (International Alliance for Interoperability, IAI) to facilitate interoperability in the AEC industries using BIM.

IFMA

International Facility Management Association. IFMA is a member-centric association that guides and develops FM products, services and resources for facility managers (www.ifma.org).

Inputs

Entry or changes made which are inserted into a workflow process and which activate and or modify the process and or process step.

IT

Information technology. IT is the technology of the producing, storing and communicating information using computer technology.

ITU-T

The ITU Telecommunication Standardization Sector (ITU-T). One of the three sectors (divisions or units) of the International Telecommunication Union (ITU); it coordinates standards for telecommunications. The standardization work of ITU dates back to 1865, with the birth of the International Telegraph Union.

IWMS

Integrated workplace management systems.

Knowledge-based condition assessment

The primary technique of the Engineered Method of building condition assessment. Uses knowledge (quantifiable information) about a facility's systems, components, and risk potential to select the appropriate inspection type and schedule throughout its life cycle. Inspections are planned and executed on the basis of knowledge, not merely the calendar.

LAN

Local area network. A LAN is a computer network that spans a relatively small area (usually within a single building).

Latitude-longitude

A reference system used to locate positions on the earth's surface. Distances east–west are measured with lines of longitude (also called meridians), which run north–south and converge at the north and south poles. Distances north–south are measured with lines of latitude (also called parallels), which run east–west.

LC

Limited combustible, fire-resistant cable with insulation made of a synthetic material called fluorinated ethylene propylene (FEP). This insulation allows LCC to withstand higher temperatures for longer periods of time than ordinary cable. Another advantage claimed for LCC is that it lasts longer before the insulation begins to contaminate the cable, a process that is an inevitable part of cable aging and that can increase cable loss. In addition, LCC is more tolerant of prolonged high humidity or exposure to corrosive chemicals or pollutants.

LEED

Leadership in Energy & Environmental Design, an internationally recognized green building certification system, providing third-party verification that a building or community was designed and built using strategies promoting sustainability.

Maintenance and repairs

Activities directed toward keeping fixed assets in a target condition. Activities include preventive maintenance; fixing or replacement of parts, systems, or components; and other activities needed to preserve or maintain the asset.

Massachusetts Institute of Technology (MIT)

A private, coeducational research university located in Cambridge, Massachusetts, United States.

Measurement

A value read either manually or automatically from a sensor or meter.

MEP

Mechanical, electrical, and plumbing. Refers to work performed by an engineer in the mechanical, electrical of plumbing industries.

Messaging

A form of communication used within the technology to notify recipients about a specific activity or action required.

Metric

A unit of measure that can be used to assess a facility, system or component (from P. Mathew, "Laboratories for the 21st Century: Best Practice Guide—Metrics and Benchmarks for Energy Efficiency in Laboratories," National Renewable Energy Laboratory.). An example of a metric is watts per square foot (W/SF) to document lighting power density.

MIT campus map

Online map for viewing building information using MIT GIS data.

Mobility

Hardware and software technologies that enable people to access and process information using devices they carry.

Modem

A modem (modulator-demodulator) is a device that modulates an analog carrier signal to encode digital information, and also demodulates such a carrier signal to decode the transmitted information.

Modular

For furniture: units that can be rearranged or stacked in different configurations. For equipment: plug-in units which can be added together to make the system larger, improve the capabilities, or expand its size.

Monetary Method

One of two major categories of building condition assessment methods. The Monetary Method uses inspectors' dollar estimates of needed work to compute two, monetary-based metrics called "backlog" and "facility condition index (FCI)."

Motes

A node in a wireless sensor network. It can perform any of three functions: process data, gathering information from sensors and communicating with other network nodes.

MPOE

Minimum point of entry (aka "de-marc") is the location where a telecommunications service provider's network wiring terminates in a building, demarcating their responsibility from the building owner or occupant. Wiring inside the building past the MPOE is not the responsibility of the telecommunications service provider.

MVA

MVA, or market value added, is defined as the difference between the value of investor capital in an organization and the real market value of that organization.

Nanotechnology

Engineering systems at the molecular level.

NBIMS

National Building Information Model Standard project. A National Institute of Building Sciences Facility Information Council standard to integrate building life-cycle information for the AEC/FM professions.

OmniClass

A classification for the construction industry, useful for many applications from organizing library materials, product literature, and project information, to providing a classification structure for electronic databases.

Oracle

A powerful relational database management system that offers a large feature set. Oracle is widely regarded as one of the most popular full-featured database systems on the market.

Output(s)

Effort or work product(s) that are a result of the work performed during the workflow process and or process step.

Overlay

The addition of a layer without changing existing layers in a multilayer system.

Parametric models

Parametric models are models that have parameters (i.e., attributes) associated with it. Such models also contain the location of the parameters within the model.

Passive RFID tag

Uses the radio energy transmitted by the reader as its energy source. This energy source provides the power needed to transmit its ID signal.

PBX

Private branch exchange, a telephone system owned by a private party that is not part of a public telephone network system owned, managed, and maintained by a telecommunications service provider.

PC

Personal computer. A computer designed for personal use.

PDA

Personal digital assistant. An electronic device that performs specific tasks.

Plant Replacement Value (PRV)

The estimated cost of replacing an existing facility at today's standards.

Plenum

The space that can facilitate air circulation for heating and air conditioning systems. Space between the structural ceiling and the dropped ceiling or under a raised floor is typically considered plenum.

Podcast

A type of digital media consisting of an episodic series of files subscribed to and downloaded through Web syndication. The word is a neologism derived from *broadcast* and *pod* from the success of the iPod, as podcasts are often listened to on portable media players.

PoE

Power over ethernet, a system to transmit electrical power, along with data, to remote devices over standard twisted-pair cable in an ethernet network.

Process

A predefined set of work steps set in sequence and/or parallel order to complete a defined business requirement usually resulting in a specific output or work product.

Process delays

Activity type that defines a lapse of time in the process.

Projected coordinate system

A reference system used to locate x, y, and z positions of point, line, and area features in two or three dimensions. A projected coordinate system is defined by a geographic coordinate system, a map projection, any parameters needed by the map projection, and a linear unit of measure.

Quick Response code tags

QR or Quick Response tags are printed tags that provide direct information about the asset they are attached to, granting the user direct access to its relevant information as printed on the tag itself.

Radio frequency identification (RFID)
Is the use of a wireless noncontact system that uses radio-frequency electromagnetic fields to transfer data from a tag attached to an object, for the purposes of automatic identification and tracking.

Raster data
A spatial data model that defines space as an array of equally sized cells arranged in rows and columns, and composed of single or multiple bands.

RE
Real estate. Property consisting of land, the buildings and the natural resources located on it.

Relational Database Management System (RDBMS)
A type of database in which data is organized across one or more tables. Tables are associated with each other through common fields called keys. In contrast to other database structures, an RDBMS requires few assumptions about how data is related or how it will be extracted from the database

Renewal
Repair by replacement.

Repair
Restore to target condition.

Resource
A participant (user/role) assigned to a process step and/or a piece of equipment (technology/machine/product) assigned or required for a process step to complete the activity.

RFID
Radio frequency identification. RFID is a data collection technology that uses electronic tags for storing data. The tag consists of an RFID chip attached to an antenna which transmits data to a reader.

Riser
Cable that is to be run between floors in nonplenum areas is rated as riser cable.

Risk
A measure of the probability and severity of adverse events.

Roles
A group of participants that have a commonality of purpose. This allows the workflow flexibility for an assignment to a group of users and completion of action within a process step. It also supports a more efficient means of administration by the organization.

RSS
RSS (Really Simple Syndication) is a family of Web feed formats used to publish frequently updated works—such as blog entries, news headlines, audio, and video—in a standardized format.

Semiconductor
A solid material that has electrical conductivity in between a conductor and an insulator; it can vary over that wide range either permanently or dynamically.

Semipassive RFID tags

Has a small battery on board that is activated when in the presence of a RFID reader.

Sequential activity

Process steps that are dependent on one process step to be completed before another process step can start.

Smart (intelligent) building

A building that integrates people, process, and technology in an efficient and sustainable manner through the use of high levels of integrated technology, including but not limited to HVAC, plumbing, electrical, renewable energy systems and sources, information technology, control systems and management software to provide a safe, healthy and productive environment for building occupants that adapts quickly to change at the lowest possible lifecycle cost (from A. Lewis, D. Riley, A. Elmualim, "Defining High Performance for Operations and Maintenance," *International Journal of Facility Management*, 1(2). www.ijfm.net/index.php/ijfm/article/view/26).

Smart infrastructures

Smart (sometimes called intelligent) infrastructures have either attached or built-in components that collect and transmit information about the state of that infrastructure to a central computer. They can, in some instances, receive back instruction from the computer which in turn results in controlling various IT devices.

Social media

With the first known uses of the term occurring around 2004, Webster's dictionary defines social media as "forms of electronic communication (as web sites for social networking and micro-blogging) through which users create online communities to share information, ideas, personal messages, and other content (as videos)."

Spatial analysis

The process of examining the locations, attributes, and relationships of features in spatial data through overlay and other analytical techniques in order to address a question or gain useful knowledge.

State changes

The alteration of the "in-process" work product based on the completion of a process step or control/decision point.

Structured cabling

Building telecommunications cabling infrastructure that consists of a number of standardized smaller elements.

Subprocesses

A grouping of activities/process steps that are either complex enough to create a definable work product necessary in the current process flow or are a set of recurring activities/process steps that are used throughout an organization (repeatable "best practice) in other process workflows and/or a combination of both descriptions. Sub process steps are generally used to make the current workflow process succinct and easy to understand.

Thematic mapping

A mapping technique designed to convey information about a single topic or theme.

TCO

Total cost of ownership. A financial estimate to determine direct and indirect costs of an asset, system, or facility, which provides a cost basis for determining the economic value of an investment.

Telco closet

Telecom closet (TC) or telecom room, the location of the connection between horizontal cabling to the backbone and, frequently, electronic equipment.

Telepresence

A set of technologies that allow a person to feel as if they were present, to give the appearance that they were present, or to have an effect at a location other than their true location.

Thresholds

The limits or boundaries that determine a minimum/maximum requirement for further action.

Uniformat

An organization schema that organizes information by functional elements (e.g., systems and assemblies).

URL

Uniform resource locator or universal resource locator—a specific character string that constitutes a reference to an Internet resource.

USGBC

U.S. Green Building Council—nonprofit trade organization that promotes sustainability in how buildings are designed, built, and operated. Best known for developing and supporting LEED rating systems.

Users

Specific participants directly involved in a process step.

Value engineering

A systematic method to improve the "value" of goods and services by using an examination of function, as opposed to only examining cost.

Vector data

A coordinate-based data model that represents geographic features as points, lines, and polygons.

Web 2.0

The term "Web 2.0" was first used in January 1999 by Darcy DiNucci, a consultant on electronic information design (information architecture), in her article "Fragmented Future."

Wiki

A wiki is a web site whose users can add, modify, or delete its content via a Web browser using a simplified markup language or a rich-text editor. Wikis are typically powered by wiki software and are often created collaboratively by multiple users.

Wireless access point

Also called WAP or AP, a device that allows wireless communication devices to connect to a wireless network. The WAP usually connects to a wired network and can relay data between the wireless devices (such as computers or printers) and wired devices on the network.

Zone boxes

The location to which cables are routed in a zone cabling system before being routed to each work area in that zone.

Index